MANDALEY PERKINS's love of writing evolved out of a fascination for Southeast Asia and its colonial history, and the experiences of her own family. Born in Darwin, she has travelled widely in Asia researching and retracing the events in her books. She was educated in Perth, completing postgraduate studies at the Australian Maritime College in Tasmania. She currently lives in Brisbane with her husband and three children. Mandaley is also the author of *Tropic Tide*.

Also by Mandaley Perkins

Tropic Tide

Hanoi, adieu

A bittersweet memoir of French Indochina

Mandaley Perkins

HARPER PERENNIAL

HarperPerennial
An imprint of HarperCollins*Publishers*, Australia

First published in Australia in 2005
This edition published in 2006
by HarperCollins*Publishers* Pty Limited
ABN 36 009 913 517
A member of the HarperCollins*Publishers* (Australia) Pty Limited Group
www.harpercollins.com.au

HarperCollins*Publishers*
25 Ryde Road, Pymble, Sydney, NSW 2073, Australia
31 View Road, Glenfield, Auckland 10, New Zealand
77–85 Fulham Palace Road, London, W6 8JB, United Kingdom
2 Bloor Street East, 20th floor, Toronto, Ontario M4W 1A8, Canada
10 East 53rd Street, New York NY 10022, USA

National Library of Australia Cataloguing-in-Publication data:

Mandaley Perkins.
Hanoi, adieu : a bittersweet memoir of French Indochina.
ISBN 9780 7322 8197 7.
ISBN 0 7322 8197 0.
1. L'Herpinière, Michel. 2. Vietnam – History – Biography.
I. Title.
959.7

Front cover images: Hanoi street scene and photo of Michel L'Herpinière supplied by author; image of flowers from Lonely Planet Images: 3718-28
Back cover image by Corbis/APL SY001237 (ref CV-54162)
Cover design by Wideopen Media wideopen.net.au
Map by Laurie Whiddon, Map Illustrations
Typeset in Sabon by Helen Beard, ECJ Australia Pty Ltd
Printed and bound in Australia by Griffin Press.

50gsm Bulky News used by HarperCollins*Publishers* is a natural, recyclable product made from wood grown in sustainable plantation forests. The manufacturing processes conform to the environmental regulations in the country of origin, New Zealand.

6 5 4 3 2 07 08 09

To Michel,
and to those on all sides who suffered
through conflict in Vietnam.

Contents

C H I N A
Red
Cao Bang
Lao Kay
Long Son
Lai Chau
T O N K I N
Dien Bien Phu
Yên Bay
Thai Nguyên
Mon Cay
Son La
Bac Ninh
BURMA
HANOI
Hai Phong
Nam Đinh
B. Hotel Sai
Sam Ngua
Mekong
Luang Prabang
Thanh Hoa
Kien Kuang
Gulf of Tonkin
HAINAN
A N N A M
L A O S
Vinh
VIENTIANE
Thakhek
Lakhon
Dông Hôi
B. Dua Makeng
Huê
Savannakhét
Tourane
Chao Phraya
Kemmarat
S I A M
Saravane
Korat
Ubun
Quang Ngai
Paksé
Ayuthia
Kontum
Pleiku
Cu-Ty
BANGKOK
Sông Cau
Stung Trengh
Siem Reap
Barrambang
C A M B O D I A
Ban Methuot
Chanthaburi
Kompong Thom
Kradé
Pursat
Đa Lat
Kompong Chhnang
Kompong Cham
Mekong
PHNOM PENH
Tay-Ninh
Bien-Hoa
Saigon
Kâmpôt
Tân An
Long Xuyên
Go Công
Gulf of Siam
COCHIN CHINA
Tra Vinh
Soc Trang
SCALE
0
200 miles
0
200 kilometers

Preface

These pages contain the recollections of a child of the French Empire, my stepfather, Michel L'Herpinière. They are the story of a boy's turbulent journey into manhood and a sense of place in the world. They are the story of his love for Indochina and its people, and of why Hanoi, the place where he wanted to make his life, could never be his. They are the story of the march of folly that led France into war with the Vietminh, and of how the scene was set for the tragedy of the Vietnam War with the United States. Hanoi is where Michel lived from his teenage years, from 1936, and this is the story of how decisions made far away in Paris, Saigon and Washington affected the lives of the people in this beautiful and provocative city.

Indochina was the name given by the French to its colonial possessions in South East Asia that today make up the nations of Cambodia, Laos and Vietnam. Under the Indochinese Union, proclaimed in 1888, Cambodia and Laos were protectorates of France while Vietnam was divided into three regions. The southern part of Cochinchina, including Saigon and the fertile Mekong Delta, was a colony ruled directly from Paris. Annam, the long, narrow centre of Vietnam, and Tonkin, in the northernmost region, were both French protectorates. In theory they were ruled by the Emperor from the capital, Hue, with French advisors and administrators. In reality, France ruled all three regions of Vietnam. The last emperor, Bao Dai, acceded to the throne at the age of twelve, while still studying in France.

For the Vietnamese people, occupation by a foreign power was not new. For a thousand years, to 938 AD, the Chinese had ruled their country, renaming it An Nam, the Pacified South. (Under French colonial rule the Vietnamese were still referred to as Annamites, or, anglicised, Annamese.) Since then the people of Vietnam had rarely been free of attempts by their northern neighbours to swallow them once more. These centuries of struggle had bred into the Vietnamese a strength, resilience and sense of self-sacrifice alongside their graceful and gentle disposition.

The French occupation of Indochina was to last the relatively short period of seventy years. During this time the French dealt with Vietnamese resistance with a heavy hand and, though nationalist sentiment remained high, since the turn of the century outbreaks of rebellion had been few. The last one before this story begins, an isolated uprising at Yen Bai in 1930, had been brutally repressed.

In Indochina, the following decade was a time of peace and prosperity. In Tonkin the capital, Hanoi, had a population of around 150 000 and life for the Europeans was gracious, elegant and carefree. For the French, these were to be the last of the golden years of Empire.

Of what has been published in English about the period, most has been written by people who were in Hanoi only briefly or who were never there at all. For this reason, Michel wanted his story told. I chose to write it in the genre of a memoir because it is very much a personal account. I have worked with Michel closely in writing this book, and have attempted to recreate some of the most vividly remembered scenes in his life. These are his experiences, his memories, his sentiments. Only the words are mine.

One

The Execution

It was the moment I lost my innocence. My senior officer drew deeply on a Gauloise Bleue and looked at me steadily across his desk through a cloud of exhaled smoke, resolute yet relaxed. Perhaps I had turned pale, for he dropped his eyes and seemed to study his notes as if giving me a moment to regain my composure. Outside on the parade ground, I could hear an Annamese drill sergeant putting a platoon of infantry through its paces. I wished I could take his place.

'You went through the exercise in officer training?' he said. 'You know the procedure for a firing squad?' They were more statements than questions. It was as though he had ordered me to round up my unit for roll call.

My voice was surprisingly steady as I replied, '*Oui, mon capitaine*.'

'It will be an unpleasant task,' he continued, 'but an essential one, and I expect you to carry it out with speed and efficiency.' His voice hardened a little. 'Remember, Lieutenant, these men are Communist spies — enemies of France.' He smiled, that brief military smile that said nothing more than 'good luck'.

I was almost fresh from high school in Hanoi. This was not what I had imagined.

On the outbreak of World War II in Europe the previous year, I had put off my university studies in a moment of patriotism, and raised my age to enlist. My father was a career soldier, France was in crisis and it seemed the right thing to do. But this . . .

It was early September of 1940. This was my first posting since Officer School, at the frontier post of Lang Son in northern Tonkin, Indochina, 20 kilometres from the Chinese border. I'd had twelve months of intensive training in artillery and I had never fired a shot except in practice. Now I was to command an execution of men, sentenced to death for their political beliefs.

Until recently it had been acceptable to be a Communist, not only here in Indochina but in France itself. The war in Europe had brought many changes to French politics, but I had never heard of Communists being executed just for being Communists. Was this to be the first such execution? It was a disturbing idea.

I needed a friend. That night I went to the Mess. Gaston was still not there and I was momentarily annoyed. But then, perhaps it was a good thing. I wasn't sure I wanted to tell even Gaston about this, and he was my closest friend in Lang Son. The notion of what I had to do disgusted me. How would he feel about it? Gaston was Annamese. These prisoners tomorrow would be Annamese. How would it look to him?

Gaston's real name was Nguyen Nga, but we French had difficulty with Annamese names and he never seemed to mind being Gaston. I had missed his tranquil, intelligent company since I returned from leave. Where was he?

There was a new man behind the bar where Gaston usually worked. The fellow shrugged when I asked after Gaston, and spread his hands in a Gallic gesture.

'I do not know, *mon* Lieutenant. I am sorry,' and he turned away to pour me a drink.

I don't know why I got on so well with Gaston. It could have been because he was not much older than myself; because I was a bit of a loner in Lang Son. Most of my fellow officers in the Mess were career soldiers, old-guard French Army or Foreign Legion. They commanded largely Indochinese units, and their interests were the interests of soldiers. These older men had little time for *blanc becs* — white beaks — like me, not yet nineteen and fresh from officer training.

It had been a habit of mine on the weekends to stay on at the Mess well after closing time. Gaston and I would sit on the verandah until 2 a.m., the moon filtering through the tamarind trees, discussing the topic of the day as the cool damp of night crepitated to the call of cicadas. Sometimes we would wander the frontier town of Lang

Son together, through the bustle of the markets where the white *képis* and scarlet epaulettes of the Legionnaires and the black *képis* with the gold anchor ensigns of the colonial troops towered over the neat Annamese figures.

I was young, with an open mind, and curious about the way the local people thought, about their beliefs. I had a real interest in their traditions and felt privileged that Gaston had taken me into his circle. There were many times he and I went together to watch Annamese classical theatre, *hat tuong*. These travelling theatre troupes had been roving the country for centuries and we would sit in the makeshift open-air stalls, cross-legged on the grass, mine the only European face among a sea of Annamese, mesmerised by the colourful, exotic costumes of an ancient culture, the shrieks and drums and great jarring clashes of cymbals.

The words meant nothing to me, but it was clear enough who was who — the white-faced traitors and baddies, with their erect painted eyebrows; the red faces of the courageous characters, their eyebrows painted horizontal to portray loyalty and integrity; the giveaway low-drawn eyebrows of the cowards, and the green faces of the lowlanders. In the rare quiet moments Gaston would lean across and tell me something of the plot, mostly historical, about conflicts going back thousands of years. When it was over he and I would join the cast for a glass of tea, maybe a bowl of *pho*, for Gaston always seemed to know the actors.

Until now my life in Lang Son had been easy. Our unit was attached to a long-range field artillery battery

10 kilometres from town, and there hadn't been a great deal of activity. But across the Chinese frontier, trouble was brewing. Japan had invaded China in 1937 and the fighting continued. Japan was convinced that victory in China depended upon stopping supplies being sent to the Chinese government through Tonkin, and she was now threatening our own borders.

But in my youthful naivety I never really believed we would be attacked by the Japanese. In the past three months I had been unhurried, unconcerned, organising ammunition depots and observation points in the hills around Lang Son. By four or five each afternoon I was back from the field. There seemed no rush.

Now, alone at one end of the bar, I wanted to block from my mind the coming morning. It seemed too unreal, a nightmare from which I would wake at any moment. I took another swig of my drink. Refusing or failing to comply could culminate in a court martial and long prison sentence, perhaps even a firing squad for me. The French Army dealt severely with anyone disobeying an order. There was no escape.

The barman handed me another Pernod. I breathed in the aromatic fumes of the liquid, then tossed it down, hoping it would send me quickly to sleep.

The first glow appeared over the hills to the east as I climbed into the truck, a wispy shroud of mist barely visible in the dim light. It was going to be hot for September. There were few people around that morning as we drove in the near darkness through the wide streets of Lang Son. Just another day for most. Some early starters, men and women in loose brown peasant trousers, were trotting along with baskets on each end of carrying poles, to be first to set up at the marketplace. Here and there, sleepy chickens wandered out into the darkness of the street and then fled, squawking and flapping as our convoy of four trucks shattered the morning routine.

Again and again I thought, 'Why me?' Was it some elaborate scheme to test my reaction under duress? Was it because nobody else wanted to do it, this the worst of jobs, and since I was the most junior, I was chosen? I swore at the unfairness of it all. The post was full of battle-hardened mercenaries, Legionnaires who had seen active service and to whom death was all in a day's work. I had never fired a shot in anger, let alone seen a dead man. Yet today I was to command an execution.

In the back of each of the four vehicles was a firing squad, a group of twelve men, one group for each of the four prisoners to be executed. Ten minutes behind us would be the truck carrying the prisoners. Ten minutes behind again another team would be preparing to leave, their task to collect the bodies and return them for burial.

There had been a further briefing. The drill was simple enough. Bumping over the dirt roads, I went through the procedure in my mind. I would line up the troops and issue each man with a bullet. Eleven would be live, the twelfth blank. The blank looked the same, gave a similar recoil upon being fired, but disintegrated as it left the muzzle. Nobody would know who got the blank. Each soldier could believe, if he wished, that it had been he who received the blank, that he had not killed a man that morning. The prisoners would be brought out and I would offer them blindfolds. With the formalities complete I would give the order to fire. Afterwards the final grim task for me, as the officer in command, was to deliver the *coup de grâce* to the bodies — a shot to the temple of each, just to make sure.

It was a straightforward exercise. I tried to feel detached. These men had been conspiring against the country and had to be eliminated. I was under orders and I had a job to do.

I shifted uneasily in my seat. For the last twelve months I had been concentrating on my studies in the theory of accurate artillery practice. There had been lectures on politics to which I, not being a political animal, had given no more attention than need be. At some time I had heard my father speak of the attempted revolution in 1930, before our time in this country, and of how the dissidents had been put down with severity, but until recently, as far as I was aware, the French authorities had been reasonably tolerant of any shadowy undercurrents of dissent in Indochina. But now things had changed.

The previous day's briefing had covered Hitler's pact with the Russian Communist leader, Joseph Stalin. Since the pact in 1939, French Communists had opposed the war against Hitler. From that moment they had been outlawed. In France the Communists, whether they were party members or sympathisers, had disappeared from the streets. These people, who had once been a legitimate political force in alliance with the Socialists under the banner of the Front Populaire, became hunted men. The same thing, it seemed, was happening in Indochina. The Communists were being forced underground and had suddenly been labelled as spies, traitors, enemies of the country. These were the men to be executed today.

The drive out to the disused limestone quarry north of town was not long. We turned in as the light of dawn began to bathe the pit, and I recognised the flat rock face, the one to serve as a backdrop for the executions. Things began to happen very quickly. As the Annamese troops tumbled out of the trucks, I placed four markers on the ground, about 10 metres apart in front of the rock face. A quick re-briefing, and the men took their positions.

I stood waiting, feeling very uneasy. It was one thing killing a man in battle, quite another shooting a defenceless person in cold blood. I did not look at the troops, but remained in position, staring straight ahead. There seemed a deathly silence over the place. Not even a bird was singing. We were ready.

The sound of the prisoners' truck jarred me out of my trancelike state. It seemed to take an age for the vehicle to enter the quarry and come to a halt. Guards jumped out and began to open the back door. Suddenly someone shouted, one of the prisoners: 'Down with Imperialism! Independence for Vietnam!' Then all four of them began to shout. I looked across as the men were marched to the marks I had set. They turned to face us — and my heart missed a beat. The one at the end threw his fist into the air. '*Vive le Vietminh!*'

It couldn't be. How could it be? I peered at the man, and knew I had been right. It was Gaston.

I was confused, stunned. Gaston! Gaston here, inflamed, indifferent, shouting Communist slogans. Nguyen Nga, a Communist? But he was my friend! I felt physically ill. It was hard, too hard. I needed time to think.

But there was no time. All four of them were yelling Communist slogans now, anti-French slogans, standing at their markers, fired up, angry, unafraid. I stood rooted to the spot, until the tough little Annamese sergeant jolted me out of my stupor. I had to step forward and shout the business about the blindfolds to make myself heard, and it was then that Gaston looked at me for the first time. His face was passionate, not the mild, humorous face I had known. It did not change expression as he saw who I was. There was nothing, no sign of recognition, no word. Mine was no longer the face of a friend, but the face of the executioner, flushed with emotion, then pale, grim, appalled.

The blindfolds were brushed aside and the four stood defiant, still shouting '*Vietnam doc lap!*' — 'Independence for Vietnam!'. I stared straight ahead. Through the fog in my mind I heard my voice, loud and clear, yet within me ethereal and remote. 'Ready . . . Aim . . . Fire!' And at that moment, God forgive me, I looked away. The sound of forty-eight shots reverberated against the rocks. Only when the echoes had died did I raise my eyes, to see the four bodies slumped on the ground. It was done.

Just one more duty, *pour la France*, *le coup de grâce*, the death blow. Hazily I walked up to the nearest in the line, to Gaston. His body had twisted slightly as it fell, bloody and lifeless, and his familiar face lay turned towards me, eyes wide open, already glazing in death. My arm was wooden by my side. I wanted to wipe the sweat from my palm as my fingers curled tight around the handle of the revolver. I felt for the trigger. A wave of nausea swept over me and I choked back a dry retch as I took aim and fired the one shot into his temple. His body kicked a little from the force of the blow, and blood, thick and viscous, welled from his nose and mouth in a slow crimson flow onto the ground.

I had forgotten to breathe and now my lungs filled suddenly as my mind mercifully shut down. I had killed my friend. My friend was dead. Stiffly, mechanically, I walked towards the next body in the line.

Two

Enfant d'Empire

I did not know then how a country that one did not belong to could break a man's spirit. But then, for a long time I couldn't see that I did not belong to Indochina. The French and the Annamese, France and Indochina, Hanoi and me. We were two cultures combined effortlessly on the streets of Hanoi in an enchanting mélange of east and west. At least, that was how I saw it.

But I was living a lie. We were all living a lie.

I had grown up a child of the French Empire. As a boy I did not think much about roots or nationality, about where it was that I could call home. Home was wherever I found myself, be it Madagascar, or France, or Morocco. Then in 1936 we moved to Hanoi and over time the transitory sense of place we carried with us began to evaporate. There was something about Hanoi. Never had I seen my mother and father so happy, so animated. I was older then, just sixteen, in my formative years and imbued with a growing aesthetic and cultural awareness. Perhaps it was youthful hormones that honed my consciousness, but for the first time I began to look ahead to the future and see it clearly. A life in Indochina, a land I came to want desperately to call my own.

The war to end all wars had been over for eight years when Papa joined the French Colonial Army in 1926. His decision came as a surprise to Maman. In the Great War my father had earned a Croix de Guerre and been made an Officer of the Legion of Honour for his services. He had re-entered civilian life with painful memories, vowing never to fight again. But during the 1920s France was depressed, and the French government was looking for men willing to travel to foreign climes. There was never going to be another world war, my father told my mother, and life in the Colonial Army was simply a matter of peace-keeping at worst. It was an opportunity to move around the world a little, see how other people lived.

Morocco was our first posting. For a small boy of seven, Casablanca was an Arabian Nights fairytale, right from the first enthralling ride through the streets of the city in an open carriage to the big, minareted hotel where porters hovered around us, all strangely dressed in nightshirts and fez — and me feeling very small on the vast, white-tiled floor. Later we'd wander the *souks*, the marketplaces, and I would gaze wide-eyed at the throngs of dark men and women in their layers of white robes and head-dresses like tea-towels, at the mysterious snake charmers sitting cross-legged on the pavement, their only tools of trade a curious pipe and a cobra languishing in a round basket. There *ghali-ghali* men could make chickens appear out of my ears, and everywhere brassware gleamed bright and exotic from the market stalls.

Papa bought me a red fez with a black tassel and we sat at sidewalk cafés like the ones in France, where little dishes filled with salted bits and pieces kept appearing on the table. In shops full of handsome rugs Maman and Papa would sip hot mint tea, turning over piles of fine silk and wool carpets. At one shop I ventured out the back to find two young girls working a loom, bright threads moving quickly through their small fingers. They looked up from their work and smiled at me and a dark, unfriendly man with a heavy moustache scolded them harshly as I scuttled back to the shop front.

Our destination then was south to Khenifra, at the base of the mountains of the Middle Atlas, along rough, winding roads, past small villages of flat-roofed mud huts, where donkeys trundled under enormous loads of wood, and young boys, their robes hitched up, shepherded herds of multi-coloured goats. An occasional group of tribesmen, long-muzzled muskets slung high across their shoulders, trotted along on colourfully attired horses, pompoms swinging. I forgot my carsickness in the excitement of stopping alongside a train of camels loaded with great wooden crates of salt, while our driver asked directions from the Arab cameleer.

Khenifra was a small village at the edge of an isolated and dangerous desert. Foreign Legionnaires from the tough, largely fugitive but highly disciplined army patrolled the desert and mountain trouble spots on foot, and we rarely saw them. The village itself was inhabited by no more than a hundred Arabs. There were a few other French children, around eight of them, mostly older than me. Happy, and used to my own company, I found amusement where I could, in adventures collecting turtles from the river, building a pond for them in our walled yard, feeding, polishing, racing them. My little donkey, Bourico, my most constant companion, lived there in the yard too, and trundled me to the tiny school to join the only other child in my class. Afterwards I would potter across to the stables to help out the groom with the beautiful Arab horses on which my father patrolled the eight desert artillery posts under his command.

The horrors of the place: even they provided a small boy with a diversion. Scorpions crept out of the desert at night, stealthily into my bedroom and onto the newspaper our Senegalese batman always laid around my bed. If I heard the sound of their scrabbling I aroused myself from sleep to dispatch them with my specialist scorpion tool. There was the threat of the *chleuh*, the dissident Arabs who roved the desert as armed bandits, attacking the villages and robbing them of their flocks and sometimes their women. And of course the Touaregs, more frightening for a child with their faces painted blue, who had taken the whole army family that we were replacing, the father, the mother, the children. They had strayed over to the forbidden far bank of the river, the Oumer Rebia, where the best turtles could be found, sunning themselves on the rocks.

I was an only child and the one constant in my life was my mother, whom I adored. Later, as I passed from childhood into youth, there were times I felt smothered by her deep love, though the bond between us always made it easy for me to forgive her. For most of my childhood my father was a transitory figure, a man I barely knew, straight-backed, formal, a man in uniform who shook my hand rather than kissed me and who was away a lot. I had great respect for him, but I never felt I knew him well. His relationship with my mother was devoted, a restrained affection after the fashion of the time and quite unlike my mother's demonstrative affection for me.

Maman was a sociable creature when there was any society to be had. There were few other French women in Khenifra — just the wives of the vet and another officer, the school teacher and two or three others — and she tried hard to keep up her old ways. Our house was a place of frequent evening gatherings for the ladies and their husbands, for we had the only gramophone in town. After dinner I was allowed to stay up late and watch the dancing, as long as I kept winding the handle.

I enjoyed the music, the long dresses swishing in time to the foxtrot, the two step, for the ladies dressed for such occasions as they tried to escape for the moment the reality of their lives in this remote and dusty back-block of the French empire.

When I was eleven, we journeyed south to Madagascar, to the island country east of Mozambique that had been a stepping stone for French navigators sailing the routes across the Empire. The small frontier post of Diego Suarez in the north of the island became our home, a place so tranquil that there was little for Papa to do in the military line but maintain a presence. There, for the first time in my life, my father had some time to spend with me.

Sometimes we would hail a square-sailed native outrigger off the rocky beaches, with a large, smiling African at the helm, and skate around the coast on the afternoon breeze to secret, sheltered places to fish, drifting in the sunset. The water, alive with undesirables — caimans, electric eels, electric rays and stonefish — only seemed to add to the thrill.

In the dripping jungle Papa and I would search for butterflies, magnificent butterflies as big as birds with 10-inch wingspans and marvellous colours, all the time watching for the enormous boa constrictors that had been known to take the natives. The country was virgin, virtually untouched by humans, a feature attracting the few French tourists who came there from the southern capital of Tananarive. They would visit the lake near town, to crouch behind bamboo screens on the shore and watch the caimans furtively feeding. Of lighter build than crocodiles, the caimans were up to 8 or 9 feet in length with long, sharp snouts, and they would turn on their tails like dolphins at any movement from behind the screens.

With little else to do but wander the streets of town, Maman and I would browse the quiet market stalls where the local African artisans sold their wares, beautiful things, beaded jewellery and intricate filigree work. Through the eyes of a child the Africans appeared to be so much happier and friendlier than the Arabs in Morocco. Life here seemed very simple. The streets were full of laughter, for they laughed a lot, laughed at the sorts of things that I laughed at. They were straightforward, demonstrative and less sophisticated than the people I later grew to know in Indochina and it occurs to me as I think back that perhaps it was because life was so uncomplicated that they found the time to enjoy it.

Mine was a sheltered, protected childhood, for I was protected in a way only a mother who has known the pain of losing a child could protect. I barely remember my little sister, Margaret, except the days after her death from pneumonia at eighteen months old: my mother, my security, my rock, crying hysterically, brushing me aside as I tried to climb onto her knee; then later, pale and exhausted, clutching me so tightly that I struggled to be free. It seemed that from then on I lived a life cut off from the world outside of my mother's devotion, that wherever we lived my life was much the same, with me occupying my time alone or with Maman, doing my own little thing, never very much.

It was exciting between posts to return to France where the school classes were full of pupils of my own age. But even there I was lonely, for out of school hours I was not allowed to be anywhere other than with my parents and it was difficult to make lasting friendships. My weekends were spent sitting politely in the drawing rooms of their friends or traipsing along after them to the theatre or on evening promenades. Besides my mother, all I had for companionship were my animals. I had to be content to occupy my time alone.

Mine was a childhood of looking over the fence at the fun other children seemed to have, hearing the shrieks of laughter in other, larger families. It was a happy enough childhood, I suppose, but solitary.

The trip out to Indochina had seemed interminable. It was September 1936, and I was an awkward teenager stuck with my parents for weeks in the lonely first-class section of the steamer *André le Bon*. Though I had heard something of the mystery and exoticism of the Orient I knew little about the country we were going to, and had even less idea of what to expect. At the busy, sultry port of Saigon, my first impression was of crowds and heat and dirt — though we stayed only long enough to change ships for the nightmare last leg of the journey. Then, for four and a half days, we were strapped to our bunks as the coastal steamer *Mon Kai* was tossed in a savage South China Sea, until relief came, in sight of the silt-laden channel that led to the port of Haiphong, Tonkin.

The train carrying us the 110 kilometres from Haiphong to Hanoi was slow, the air in the carriage humid. The glare of the Tonkinese sun had softened a little across the miles and miles of flat rice paddy, fields of vivid green and the patchwork of low earthen banks in every direction. Water buffaloes with enormous horns lumbered along, little white birds hopping about on their backs, pecking at their hide. A small boy perched astride the thick neck of one of them waved at the train as we passed, and I waved back. Slim figures bent double and dressed in what looked to be brown pyjamas dotted the landscape, their conical straw hats like private pagodas miraculously staying in place, sheltering them from the sun.

The train whistled as we passed each small village of *paillotes*, raised bamboo huts with thatched roofs. Papa said we were crossing the highly populated Red River Delta, where every year torrents of muddy water poured down from the surrounding mountains into the mile-wide Red River, leaving behind rich, fertile, silt-laden plains where much of the country's rice was grown.

Leaning across, my mother patted my knee. The small, decorative hat perched on the back of her head seemed ridiculously inappropriate to our new circumstances. She smiled.

'*Ça va mieux?*' she asked. Do you feel better?

'*Un peu*,' I replied. A little. I didn't really. A steward arrived with a tray of drinks, and the cool lime juice revived me more than my sleep. I closed my eyes again until, with a final long blast of the whistle, the train creaked and groaned to a halt.

We were in Hanoi. The platform was mayhem, a confusion of luggage and passengers, an olfactory cocktail of armpits and coal smoke. Grimy hands clutched at the bag I carried until my father, in his major's uniform of khaki and *képi*, waved away the porters. Our driver found us and we followed as he showed us to the relative calm of an army staff car. He pulled out and slowly negotiated a tangle of rickshaws, their skinny pullers jostling for fares among the passengers on the sidewalk.

Progress was slow at first, though there were few cars in the streets. Hanoi echoed with the rhythmic background *creak, creak, creak* of rickshaws — *pousse-pousse*, as I would begin to know them. Barefoot coolies trotted doggedly along in the sun, sheltered passengers perched high behind them. As we glided down a wide boulevard lined with flame trees, I turned my head to admire a group of Annamese girls, giggling together as they walked, their long, high-necked tunics, or *ao dais*, split at the sides to reveal ankle-length loose trousers in soft pastel colours. Amongst the local population a few Europeans walked the pavement, men in white linen suits, women in fashionable, slim, ankle-length dresses; occasionally there was a Buddhist monk, bright in saffron robe and gleaming head; and an old Mandarin, tugging at his beard in deep thought, sedately strolling, black robes flowing, a black umbrella tucked firmly under one arm.

Near the centre of town we turned down one side of a serene lake, where an arched bridge crossed to an old pagoda on the tiny island at one end. Facing the lake was a row of ochre and white two-storey villas, as typically French as those I knew on the other side of the world, each with a small front garden and a brick and wrought-iron fence. At one of these the driver pulled up and we got out to explore our first home in Indochina.

Three

Hanoi, Enchanté

'*Pho-o-o-o*', '*Gio-o-o-o*', '*Nem Ran-an an*'. The calls from the street vendors and the overpowering aroma of *nuoc mam*, fish sauce, filled my nostrils, reminding me I was hungry. I knew Maman disapproved of me eating in the street. She viewed the rudimentary dishwashing facilities with disdain, the enamelled basins of cold water used to rinse bowls and chopsticks over and over, before being sloshed into the street gutter and a new refill of water taken from the municipal tap at each street corner. But Maman and her friend were happily immersed in sifting through a huge pile of silks. I had money in my pocket. If I was quick I could slip over and devour a delicious bowl of *pho bo*, my favourite noodle soup with beef, and Maman wouldn't notice.

We were in the Vieux Quartier, the Old Quarter of Hanoi, 2 square kilometres of streets dating from the fifteenth century, most no more than lanes and each named after the artisans who lived and worked there. Maman often forgot the time as she explored her favourite streets — Cotton Street, Jewellers Street, Brass and Copper Street, Lacquer Street and so many others. This one was the Rue de la Soie, Silk Street, a favourite haunt of the ladies, with its endless display of the most beautiful *ao dai*, dresses and embroidery through which to browse.

It had become one of our regular evening strolls. Starting from the main residential district, along the grassed verges of Le Petit Lac[1], we might stop at the terraced café which spilled out over the cool, still water of the north end of the lake, where big multi-coloured carp came to peer inquisitively up at the customers. Then we would saunter across the road and into the artisan area, where the sweet frangipani fragrance by the lake evaporated into the smell of simmering food, and the tranquil calm of the water was overcome by the clamour of milling people and the singing calls of street vendors hawking for customers.

Maman was still in the shop, bargaining over the price of several metres of pale blue silk. The shop owner was full of bonhomie, for he felt the price he would get from this European woman would be good. At the next counter the conversation was more heated, as an

---

[1] Now known as Hoan Kiem Lake (Lake of the Restored Sword).

Annamese customer bargained with acrimony down to the bare bones of the value of the silk.

I cast my eyes around for one of the fruit merchants who strolled the streets in their rural dress of brown or black pants, hip-length tops, sometimes brown, sometimes coloured, and mollusc-shaped hats, a bamboo pole on their shoulder sporting a large swinging basket at each end loaded with two or three types of delicious tropical fruits. I would buy two tiny bananas for Poupette, who was in her usual place on my shoulder, her tiny paws only occasionally clutching at my hair to steady herself. And just a bag of lychees for me today, to help while away the time as Maman shopped.

Poupette, my macaque monkey, was a delightful little creature and like my best friend. She shared my food, and my bed too, curled safe and secure under the mosquito net. I would open my eyes in the mornings and see her comical face watching me unblinkingly for the first sign of wakefulness. Gentle and well mannered, she was welcome everywhere, even at the stables where she had become a sort of mascot.

For Maman and Papa, the races had been an integral part of the settling-in process. At the Bagatelle Racecourse they began to find a place in the social arena of Hanoi. Papa's eye for horses, developed when he rode with the cavalry during the First World War, was keen. Now he and two of his new friends, Maurice Jusserand, the Managing Director of the Banque Franco-Chinoise, and Jean Crepin, a successful importer and entrepreneur, had formed a horse-racing syndicate. Eventually they built a sizeable racing complex together, close to the racecourse on the outskirts of Hanoi. Starting with half a dozen well-performed horses and a few untried youngsters, the number in training would soon increase to twenty-four animals.

My love of horses grew quickly and I spent most of my out-of-school hours at the stables helping feed, groom and ride track work. At the races I learned to recognise hundreds of horses by sight, along with their breeding, age and performances. Bagatelle and the stables became my second home.

Our racing complex was adjacent to the Great Lakes District which bordered the dykes of the Red River, a paradise of secondary dykes too narrow for traffic but perfect for exercising horses, with firm tracks for slow pace work and water in which we waded the horses. There were islands to explore, and guava and lychee trees which bore delicious fruit seemingly all year round growing wild on the banks.

Later, much later, I walked those lovely, lonely dykes with a beautiful and passionate French girl. There was a grove of trees where the branches were so old and heavy that they hung like a draping curtain to the ground, all soft grass, warm and sweet smelling. The fruit was ripening on the trees and the only sound was of fish breaking the surface of the water. She was brown all over, with long hair, and I thought I was in the Garden of Eden.

* * *

At the racecourse a strong-boned bay frisked around the parade ring as my father watched admiringly.

'She is magnificent,' he said to the head strapper. 'I have big hopes for this filly.'

Papa was in his element. Behind us a betting boy hovered and my father gave him instructions to place a bet on the *tote guichets* under the grandstand.

We made our way back to a table on the immense terrace, past huge concrete urns shaped like bird baths, 3 metres wide and cascading with brilliant bougainvilleas. Maman was there under a large parasol shading a table, laughing with some friends. Below us we had a view of the last hundred metres of the racecourse and the winning post, and of the perfectly manicured lawns and flower beds and shaded alleyways of brilliant flame trees. Later we would join the punters, owners and trainers in the cool of the main building behind the terrace, where the crowd gathered at the conclusion of the races to celebrate or drown their sorrows. There was a carefree ambience in Hanoi then, and the orchestra would play and the revelry continue until all hours of Sunday night. This was Bagatelle, one of the pearls of the Orient, modelled on the Bagatelle of the Longchamps racecourse near Paris.

It was here at Bagatelle that I first met Marie Claire. She had become a regular visitor and had joined my parents' usual circle at the post-races evening dances. With her happy and vivacious manner I could not help but notice her. She was in her late twenties perhaps, or early thirties, very attractive and married to an army major who was reputed to be anti-social. We never once saw him.

Marie Claire was an excellent, if extrovert, dancer. I was sixteen years old the first time she dragged me out of my quiet corner into the glare of the dance floor. I was acutely embarrassed and unwilling, for my dancing experience was limited to the disastrous *soirées* aboard the ship, when I had left my partners obviously unimpressed. Marie Claire, however, did not seem to mind. Our first effort was a shambles, but later that first evening she came for me again. Soon I began to relax.

In the months that followed she taught me all the latest dances, from the Lambeth Walk to Latin American. I came to love her steamy renditions of the Latin dances. She wore the most diaphanous of gowns, and her shapely legs and feet, shoes buttoned across the instep, were sure and precise. It was easy to follow the fluid movements of her body as she pressed herself closely against me. Her Tango was nothing if not erotic, and to my chagrin I often felt an unwelcome stirring in my groin. If Marie Claire noticed, and she must have done, she showed no sign of offence. As the music ended she would whirl me back to my seat and the refuge of the edge of the tablecloth that neatly and thankfully hid my embarrassment.

I looked forward to Sunday evenings, to her merciless teasing and outrageous flirtations with my rather sober self. But in the end Marie Claire's husband was posted away from the city. She reappeared only occasionally after that, returning by train for a social weekend. Finally she stopped coming altogether and I missed her greatly, but life went on.

My family had settled quickly and well into this new country and we were all supremely happy. Since my father's unit was based at the Citadel, the old fortress in Hanoi, he worked regular hours and was home every evening. For Maman it was wonderful to have such a 'normal' life after her lonely exiles in Morocco and even Madagascar where there were fewer French people with whom to mix.

Bep, our Chinese cook, was the lord of our household. My mother often heard him ordering around Thi Hai and Thi Ba, our two house girls, as though they were lesser mortals. Occasionally she would intervene — difficult, as she didn't speak their language and at such times they preferred not to speak hers. Bep was a wonderful chef, a great relief to my mother after her struggles to train the green help she'd had elsewhere. She learned not to interfere in Bep's domain, even the time when she discovered him rolling little meatballs, one in each hand, straight onto his bare chest. She had simply retired quietly upstairs again, back to the dinner party, without revealing her presence.

I had heard my parents talking about us all staying on after Papa's tour of duty ended. They seemed quite taken with Indochina. I felt it too. There was something captivating about the place. But still, as I matured I was becoming more aware of the way we lived in the colonies. I didn't think a lot about it, but I began to notice things, little things about the French and the people whose country we occupied.

The French authorities regarded themselves as being on a *mission civilatrice*, a mission to civilise and develop Indochina, and indeed much had been done to build infrastructure — the roads and railways, the attractive cities with beautiful buildings and fine boulevards. But developing and maintaining a colony was expensive, and the brunt of the cost fell upon the people, in the form of high rents and taxes. To carry out the work of development, control and order had to be maintained, and it had been traditionally accepted by the French that force was the most effective way of doing so. French law-and-order enforcement had been hard, and often cruel. There were vastly different standards of pay for French and Annamese people performing the same jobs, and although in a way this had to be the case to attract French people to come to the colony, it was a source of great discontent among the Annamese.

My school, the Lycée Albert Sarraut, was the elite French language secondary school in Hanoi. About half the students were Annamese, and they were almost all the children of well-paid government officials. I had discovered, however, that the French government provided only a small amount of non-compulsory primary education for the locals, the ones who couldn't pay. There was a vast difference between the haves and the have-nots.

The Indochinese at school were difficult to befriend at first and tended to keep to themselves. They were competitive, worked much harder on the whole than the French students and did very well, many winning places at the Sorbonne in Paris. The wealthiest students paid their way to university. Gold was everything in Indochina and while the rich Indochinese had enormous amounts of it in the vaults of the banks, the poor had nothing.

Most of the Indochinese students at school were obvious Nationalists, some with Communist tendencies, and among my contemporaries at school were some of Vietnam's future independence leaders and top party officials. There were would-be revolutionaries not only among the students, but among the staff. Two teachers at my school — Maurice and Yvonne Bernard, a French husband and wife — would later disappear over the border into China. They were openly members of the Communist Party and would discuss their political beliefs with anyone who would listen. They said the Communist Party, as part of the politically legitimate Front Populaire, was very strong in France.

My history teacher, who also taught at the Lycée Thang Long, was rumoured to be a Communist with a police record for subversive activities. But I could not think of *Professeur* Giap as a subversive. I felt a real rapport with him; I think we all did. He was a bubbly and enthusiastic Annamese who, partly because of his lack of stature, seemed hardly older than we were. He had a round, good-natured face and was always dressed in a white shirt and tie under an immaculate white suit. He had a passion for Napoleon, whose battles he seemed to know in great detail. Yet he taught us history in a balanced way, and injected every historical episode with fervor. Unlike the Bernards, he never alluded to current politics in class. Even if he had it would not have worried us. Many students, including myself, had leftist tendencies, socialist sympathies, for the colonial system in Indochina did nothing to encourage native capitalism. Besides, it seemed obvious to me that the rich had too much and the poor too little. One just had to look around.

I had no thoughts about my history teacher's convictions. I liked and respected *Professeur* Giap immensely. He taught us the history of the French Revolution with a composed passion, but spoke little of the history of Indochina, although it must have been foremost in his mind. I was not aware of his deep-rooted resentment of the foreign occupation of his country. I had thought little about the fact that the Chinese had occupied Vietnam for a thousand years, that from then until the time the French arrived in the 1860s the Annamese had fought a continuous and aggressive battle against foreign domination, that there had virtually never been a time when a foreign power was not trying to swallow their country. I was not aware that it was the students of Vietnamese history and intellectuals such as Giap who were now leading the resistance. I did not yet understand why the Annamese were so different from the Laotians and the Cambodians who lived in the protectorates in the western part of what we called Indochina, how much more determined and competitive they were, how their struggles with foreign aggressors over the centuries had instilled in them resilience, toughness and self-sacrifice. To me the Annamese were graceful and often charming.

I did not think of myself as an aggressor. I remained blissfully unaware that not far beneath the surface of this seemingly idyllic life in Indochina there was seething discontent, an undercurrent of revolution.

Had such a notion entered my mind, the idea that my history teacher, Vo Nguyen Giap, was himself destined to carve a great niche in history, would have seemed impossible. But this lively *professeur* had a big future. In the years to come he was to take an unruly bunch of guerrillas and mould them into a highly effective army. He was to become the general who, alongside Ho Chi Minh, would lead the Vietnamese people to victory in a struggle of epic proportions, first with the French military and later, against enormous odds, with the massive United States (and allied) military machine. *Professeur* Vo Nguyen Giap was destined to become internationally renowned as one of the greatest warriors of the century.

Four

Coming Out

Heavy stone walls towered over me as I walked through the main gate of the Citadel. The old Annamese fortress in Hanoi, built in the early 1800s by the Emperor Gia Long, had been extensively redesigned and extended by the French to house the French Colonial Army. In the courtyard I looked around, trying to find my bearings. This vast complex of 180 acres was now the headquarters of the Colonial Infantry, the Artillery and ancillary services. It was a maze of barracks and headquarters, commissariats and workshops, offices and parade grounds.

This was September 1939 and with school finished and war in Europe I had joined the army reserve with visions of returning to Europe to fight. It had not seemed a big decision. I had no intention of becoming a career soldier, but the war Papa had said would never happen had begun.

He was furious that Germany, a supposedly civilised nation, had raised its military fist again. For me, joining up seemed the right thing to do. Maman was quietly unhappy about my decision and though I loved her dearly, this was my opportunity to escape the confines of home.

Perhaps my father's sway had got me into the army under age. It was still seven weeks until my eighteenth birthday and the rules were normally rigid. My head was full of notions of valour and duty and the evils of the German Empire. It did not occur to me that dark and troubled times lay ahead for Indochina, that army intelligence was, with growing concern, watching the brutal antics of the Japanese in their conflict with China immediately to our north. This concern had quietly led to a major recruitment drive.

I entered the army enthusiastic and, I thought, with my eyes open. I had seen military life before, but still it did not prepare me for what was to come. The change from my cosseted existence at home could not have been more stark.

I was a second-class soldier, the bottom rung on the military ladder. There was no peace nor privacy, from the moment of the jarring reveille, through the morning throngs of naked chests and buttocks of every hue, through the loud mouths and crowding armpits of barrack life, through the clattering meals and prodding medicals, and the endless, sweaty, punitive physical training. For a week I was lost among the throng, alone among many. Then salvation arrived.

Born in the High Pyrenees, Claude Mary was a true Catalan. A career NCO of ruddy complexion and fiery temper, his eyes were as sharp as his tongue was quick. We were opposites, for I was tall and still gangly with youth, he shorter but strong and thickset. I was quiet and shy, he forceful and exuberant, but still our friendship grew quickly. Eleven years my senior, he had worked under my father's command as paymaster and knew him well. Through the eyes of a seventeen year old, Claude Mary was worldly, all-knowing, and a fine friend to have around in those early uncertain weeks.

When I topped the entrance exam for Officer Training School, Claude congratulated me. But later an earthy conversation over a drink at the mess left me in little doubt that he had further education in mind.

'If you want to be an officer,' Claude explained as he lit a Gauloise Troupe, 'we'll have to make a man out of you —' he looked me squarely in the eye — 'at *the* place in Hanoi. The *Maîtresse de la Maison* is very particular about who she lets in. It's mostly high-ranking military and administration.'

'High-ranking! Forget it,' I protested. He made it sound like a club, as though membership would be some sort of social asset. The prospect terrified me, and Claude was enjoying himself.

'Don't worry,' Claude crooned teasingly. 'I mentioned your pedigree and arranged a special interview. Wear a silk shirt and be on your best behaviour. You will be fine. Trust me.'

I almost choked when he told me the cost of the exercise. 'Twenty piastres!' As a second-class soldier I received the princely sum of 1 piastre per day, the standard pay for all new soldiers, regardless of race. I had been in the army just over three weeks and had collected two pay packets, a total of 14 piastres. The idea of blowing my first month's pay in a bordello did not inspire me.

'Ha,' Claude snorted at my reticence. 'These are high-class girls. Guaranteed to treat you well. You want to try it with a street girl and catch the pox?'

'I don't even have 20 piastres,' I retorted.

With a flourish he produced a 50-piastre note from his pocket. 'You can repay me some day when you earn some decent money.' I took the note. There seemed to be no excuses.

Everything had to happen very quickly. In a little under two weeks I would be leaving the Citadel to report at the Officers' School in Tong, west of Hanoi, for nine months' intensive training. Claude arranged an introduction for Friday.

'That's it?' I asked in surprise. 'Right there?'

Claude looked at me, incredulous. 'You mean you don't know what is right under your nose?'

The building was familiar to me, but I had assumed it to be the residence of a general or a high-ranking administrator. The house was large, rambling and grandiose, surrounded by an enormous manicured garden. And it was right there, right on the apron of cleared ground that surrounded the Citadel, not far from the north gate.

I wondered how this splendid residence had become such an establishment. Perhaps Claude was right. Perhaps the proprietor did have links with the top.

Claude knocked confidently at the front door as I shuffled up nervously behind him. The door opened and a late-middle-aged Annamese woman greeted us and showed us into a plush waiting room. I looked around at the velvety furniture, at the elegant rosewood cabinets displaying ivory and jade figurines. Behind me there was a sharp *click, click* of high-heeled shoes on polished floor and I turned to meet the *Maîtresse de la Maison*.

'I am Jo,' she said, as though no further introduction was required. I mumbled something and she looked me up and down with piercing black eyes that seemed to see right through me. Mercifully, Claude carried the conversation. I was unlikely to impress.

I sat perched on the sofa dumbly, watching the woman. She was a *métisse*, a woman of mixed French and Annamese descent, perhaps fifty. Her figure was small and delicate, her jade-green satin dress exquisitely embroidered with tiny water lilies, and she wore a long string of expensive-looking pearls. Her heavy make-up suggested that the years and her lifestyle were taking their toll. Beneath her sartorial elegance and careful grooming she had the look of an opium addict, for her skin was crêpey and her lips painted a deep ruby red to disguise the tell-tale darkness of heavy dependence.

She turned to me with quiet poise and a hint of matriarchal knowingness. Had she and Claude already spoken of me? Suddenly it occurred to me that she knew I was a virgin, that this might offer me special status. Perhaps that was why Claude had said not to worry about my rank. Vainly I willed my cheeks not to redden. Blushing was a European habit that intrigued and amused the Annamese, and I felt more discomfited than ever.

But the madam's voice had softened at my nervousness, and the arrangements were soon agreed. The *Maîtresse de la Maison* rose gracefully to show that our interview was at an end.

The weekend flew, and I spent it digesting the humiliation of my 'special status'. Jo welcomed us warmly on our return, and with little ado two Annamese girls appeared beside her. Beautiful and dressed in flowing *ao dais*, their dignity and serenity seemed at odds with their vocation.

'This is Lua,' said Jo, presenting her to Claude, and then, turning to me, 'And this is Nguyet.' Squeezing my arm lightly, she added, 'She will take very special care of *you*, Michel.' I flushed uncomfortably. My embarrassment was complete.

Nguyet sat down close to me on the *recamier*, her thigh resting against mine. Her smile was sweet and reassuring and she knew exactly what to say, in excellent French, to make it easy for me. Soon, with a nod from Jo, she took my clammy hand and guided me from the room. Feeling more schoolboy than young man, I followed her humbly up the deep red carpeted stairs, into a room on the top floor.

There was barely a moment to take in the sumptuous furnishings, the large, intimidating, velvet-covered bed glaring at me from the centre of the room.

The door clicked closed behind me and I turned to find Nguyet already loosing her long black hair from its plait. She shook it around her shoulders and it was all shiny and sweet-smelling in its blackness. I opened my mouth to say something and she put a finger to my lips. Polite conversation was at an end. The first awkward moments I had dreaded were as fleeting as the few seconds it took for her *ao dai* to slip to the floor over pale magnolia skin. I had never seen, let alone touched, the naked female form, and its beauty took my breath away. Slim fingers were at my shirt buttons and caressing my still-smooth chest, smiling brown eyes gazed up invitingly into mine. Taking my hands, Nguyet guided me to her small, round breasts, pressing my fingers gently into their soft perfection. Then, stealing them away, she dropped to her knees and caressed my belly with moist lips. Her fingertips danced teasingly over my body and the sudden rawness of my desire took me aback. I felt like a spectator being taken along for the ride, and Nguyet carried my ineptitude with the grace of the professional that she was.

Downstairs Claude welcomed me as though from a trip to darkest Africa, though I felt uncomfortably like me again, a reserved young man very ill at ease in a bordello. But crowing beneath my awkwardness was a new pride. I *was* a man. Claude had been right. I could not go off to battle a virgin, a mere boy, to lie dying in a trench somewhere with my life blood seeping away.

Then I laughed at myself. I had no immediate expectations of going into battle. But just in case . . .

The success of the exercise established, Claude congratulated me heartily and suggested a whisky soda to celebrate. I declined, for in my immense gratitude I had given Nguyet a 10-piastre tip. But opium was less expensive than whisky on the bill of fare, so I proposed an adjournment to the *fumerie* instead. I had heard much of the experience of opium smoking and, emboldened by my success upstairs, felt another dose of euphoria would cap off the evening well.

In Indochina the practice of smoking opium was viewed variously from *chic* and fashionable to *déclassé* among the Europeans, depending upon how long one had been in the country and with whom one associated. The opium trade went back a long way in Indochina, and the opium wars with China were an integral part of the country's history. From the early days of the French the market had been controlled by a government-run opium monopoly which traded locally and now supplied pharmaceutical companies all over Europe. I had never seen my own father smoke, but I had heard much of opium's spiritual merits and therapeutic properties, even that it was helpful against colds and flu.

A sweet haze hung in the air in the dimly lit hallway at the back of the house. We were ushered to one of six smoking rooms. Inside, the ceiling, painted matt black, seemed to suggest infinity. The walls were a deep red with gold chimeric figures and Chinese characters wishing health, wealth and I knew not what else. Another display of ivory and jade figurines glowed in one corner. And two large wooden couch-beds, intricately carved and inlaid with mother-of-pearl, lay at either side against the walls. The room was empty of other smokers.

Having directed us to take off our shoes, Jo produced two satin smoking gowns and handed them to us. Apparently one was expected to disrobe for the occasion, the gowns being an accessory to the introspective and spiritual state to come. For the second time that evening I was without trousers and shirt. In the black, red-trimmed robe, I climbed onto a fine woven mat that covered the hard wooden bed and eased my head back onto an uncomfortable leather headrest.

The older woman called Hong who had greeted us at the front door had brought a tray, and was sitting on the floor in the semi-lotus position, one leg folded under supporting her body, the other acting as a prop to steady her. She lit the oil lamp and the flickering light danced across the lines of her face and illuminated the contents of the tray. I gazed at the three silver filigree opium pipes, each nearly 2 feet long with small porcelain bowls set a third the way from the ends. There was a highly decorated, lacquered bamboo container like an inkpot in which lay the thick liquid opium, and a long needle with an ivory handle. With practised fingers the woman began spinning the needle, working and mixing some opium resin near the flame of the oil lamp, dipping again and again into the liquid opium until the sizzling ball was the right size. Then with one final mix she deftly pushed the opium into a small hole in the bowl of the pipe, pressing it into a miniature doughnut shape, and handed it to Jo for a demonstration. I watched carefully as the *Maîtresse de la Maison* held the pipe at an angle above the flame of the oil lamp. The bead was bubbling gently and she took a couple of quick, sharp draws, then inhaled, long and deep, until the drug was finished. It could not have looked more simple.

The old Annamese prepared another pipe and then, easing the top of the pipe into position near the flame, handed it to me. Cautiously I took my first draw from the ivory mouthpiece. The taste was acrid on my tongue and as I tried to take another draw my body suddenly racked. Burning smoke flooded my throat and lungs. The little doughnut of opium caught fire and I coughed expulsively, gasping for breath. Through my distress I was dimly aware of Claude's guffaws and Jo's tut-tutting, as she reminded me that it was the break between the two draws that caused the opium to catch fire, that I mustn't stop drawing for more than a second.

Patiently Hong remixed the remains of the pipe with new opium and I tried again, only to cough and gag and once more fail to reach the final long draw. Claude, I was comforted to see, performed similarly, so, buoyed by his lack of success I persevered. But at the end of another round of dismal attempts, we both conceded — we were utterly defeated.

Jo smiled in resignation and clapped her hands for Hong to bring a tray of Chinese tea. The pale, fragrant liquid was served in tiny porcelain cups, the volume far too delicate to soothe our burning throats. I downed several, including the dried blossoms floating on the surface.

Outside, the sultry warmth of the night did nothing to clear my head and Claude, too, was uncharacteristically quiet. The guffaws I expected at the sight of my heaving form suddenly bent double were not forthcoming, for I turned to see him stagger and then, as if in sympathy, retch heartily onto the damp grass.

I had enjoyed my sojourn with the gracious Nguyet but, apart from being beyond my means, the idea of paying for sex did not appeal. I had discovered I was functional and the immediate challenge had been overcome. The opium smoking, however, had been a dismal episode. There was something other-worldly waiting to be experienced and I was determined to try again. Next time, however, I would do it on my own.

Claude considered his duty towards my education complete.

Jo was present again when I next called, and gently insisted I become her guest until I got the opium right. She stayed with me once more, smoking constantly, clouds of bluish smoke filling the air about her. We talked together like old friends. She had been addicted to opium for almost twenty years, she told me, and to feel comfortable and alert had to smoke thirty pipes each day. Her words should have cautioned me, but I was young.

That evening, success once again eluded me. Perhaps I stayed too long and tried too hard. Out in the still night my path back to barracks wavered, my head spun, my gut heaved. I asked myself why I had done it. Would it ever be worth it? But next morning, fully recovered, I told myself it had to be.

At the weekend I was to travel to Tong and would not be back in Hanoi for months. There was time only for one more visit to the *fumerie*. I was less self-conscious this time, and very determined, and in the hazy ambience of the opium den the now familiar ritual of drawing and coughing, spluttering and recovering, gave way at last.

On my second try and quite suddenly, everything fell into place. The small round clouds of smoke appeared as I puffed, and the ball of opium bubbled gently until it disappeared. Gradually a sense of peace and total happiness descended upon me like a soothing balm. My entire body relaxed into a state of sheer contentment and the den became a cosy cocoon, a sanctuary from the rest of the world. There were no hallucinations, no revelations, just a slightly disembodied tranquillity and peace of mind.

It was everything I had hoped it would be.

In the early hours of the morning I thanked Jo for her hospitality and patience, for helping me achieve my aim at last.

'You have more to aim for in your life than opium smoking,' she said quietly. 'I wish you luck with your course and you must come back and see me when you are an officer. You will always be welcome in my house.' She smiled, a warm, enigmatic smile.

I had begun to loathe *Capitaine* Tomasini. The little Corsican had done it the hard way, working his way up through the ranks over twenty years. The idea of us becoming officers after a mere nine months of service incensed him. He was like a true-to-size version of Napoleon upon his horse at the head of the column, and he was determined to make us pay for our commissions in sweat.

So this was officer training. Every bone in my body ached. Day after day we had been doing this, trudging up and down through the steep hilly terrain, each of us leading one begrudging mule loaded with a heavy piece of artillery. Every two hours Tomasini barked the order for us to halt and unload the animals, to set up and load the field guns ready for firing, then barked another order to dismantle and load up again. At the end of each exercise, and equally predictably, our commander checked his watch with an exaggerated gesture, shook his head and spat, 'Too slow, you lazy oafs. Get moving.'

They were long days, returning at dusk after ten hours walking, to attend to the mules, to feed them, water them and rub them down with fresh straw until their coats were clean and dry. Only when the equipment was cleaned and stowed were we free to look after ourselves. My tiredness had already taken its toll when I staggered off to bed one night with my rifle, instead of returning it to the armoury. That effort cost me two days of solitary confinement in the cell block over the following weekend. It was the last time I made that mistake.

I was now part of the 2nd Battery of the 4th Regiment of the Colonial Artillery, a battery my father had commanded before his promotion to major. In the whole gruelling day the only bright spot was breakfast — not the army breakfast, but good old Ma Lee's breakfast, which could be had for 3 and a half piastres if one slipped out of barracks into town early enough and returned in time for roll call at seven. Now, at the rank of Corporal First Class, my salary had dramatically increased to 20 piastres per day and I could easily afford the indulgence Ma Lee bestowed: a large bowl of piping hot coffee with creamy fresh milk and two crusty bread buns, still hot from the baker's oven, dripping in delicious butter. It was a far cry from the military breakfast of watery coffee and leftovers on a slice of bread.

Tong was an unassuming little town, built around the military base that served to keep the 5000 troops off the streets of Hanoi yet within 60 kilometres — close enough to be useful. Ma Lee was one of many enterprising people who had settled in the district to cater to the needs of the military. The streets were a mass of stalls. Every second bamboo eatery served alcohol and hosted its own flock of girls to entice the surfeit of hot-blooded young men in uniform. The Annamese girls appeared delicate and swanlike, floating gracefully and unobtrusively along the bars with a demure and virginal air, beckoning only with their eyes. But venereal disease was rampant, as my father had warned me, and I succumbed to these girls only in my imagination.

Instead, I discovered some of the other opportunities the locals offered to take a soldier's money. Gambling was a passion among the Annamese. Even the purchase of fruit or market wares could be performed with a wager, and many vendors kept a bowl of dice next to their abacus. I tried it a few times, a sort of winner-take-all, loser-pay-double affair with the odds stacked heavily, but through sleight-of-hand imperceptibly, in the vendor's favour. Though it made shopping more interesting, it was not a particularly profitable way of buying one's bananas. Though young, I had begun to get a feeling for Annamese culture, and noticed that their love of gambling seemed rooted in a belief that the gods of fortune controlled their destiny. Gambling was almost a ritual of faith in the notion that what would be would be.

As 1939 ground into 1940, the dreaded marches following the arse of Tomasini's horse became less frequent and the time in the classroom lengthened. The technical side of the artillery enthralled my mind as mathematics always had, and there was new interest for us in the form of solid sessions on regional affairs, in particular the perturbing behaviour of the Japanese military.

Japan had invaded Manchuria in 1931 and by 1937 had occupied the major centres of Peking, Tientsin, Shanghai and Nanking in China. It had taken time for news of more than the barest details to filter through to Hanoi, but now we knew that in the weeks following the fall of Nanking in December 1937 the Japanese military had embarked on a brutal rampage through the city, raping, torturing and slaughtering its citizens. Those who were machine-gunned to death escaped lightly. Others not so fortunate were used for bayonet practice, disembowelled, burned alive, castrated or hung by their tongues in an orgy of cruelty. It lasted only a few weeks. But in that time over 260 000 Chinese civilians had died an appalling death.

I personally found it difficult to believe that any army was capable of such bestial acts. Surely the stories were exaggerated. I did not feel threatened by events to the north of us. Japan was at war with China. What could they want from us?

In class I learned how rapidly things were changing, that since the outbreak of war in Europe, Japan had become increasingly belligerent, that Indochina was now in a difficult position. Despite having declared itself neutral at the outset of the Sino-Japanese war, the French government had been allowing supplies, much of it aid from the United States, to pass via the Yunan railway through Tonkin to Chiang Kai-shek's nationalist troops fighting in China. Japan had lobbied Hanoi intensely but failed to have the rail link closed, and had recently bombed the Tonkinese border section of the Yunan railway, damaging the line and causing casualties among the rail workers.

Like many other soldiers of my age there, I had expected to stay in Indochina as some sort of reserve force to be sent to the *European* front if and when required. But as tension mounted in our own region we remained in Indochina, while in Europe France was crumbling under the weight of an inexorable German onslaught. The future for France looked bleaker every time we heard something, though up-to-date news remained hard to come by. The daily newspaper from Hanoi somehow never reached provincial towns, and radio receivers were enormous, multivalved devices that only a few well-established families could afford. Then in March 1940, as the situation in our own region became more heated, Headquarters began to send a young information officer from Hanoi on a weekly sojourn to Tong. His brief was to report all the latest events, spiked with a good dash of propaganda for patriotic effect.

That same month a Japanese mission had come to Hanoi to protest about China's supply line through Tonkin to the Governor, General Georges Catroux — with disastrous effect. Neither party conceded anything and Japan responded with further embittered air raids, dropping bombs 'accidentally' on the Indochinese side of the frontier. Catroux ordered French anti-aircraft units in the border area into action and in April Japan retaliated with intensified bombing of the railway. Japanese generals in position in South China rattled their sabres and an aggressive anti-French media campaign began.

The French government was in no position to bargain. Their military forces in Indochina were not prepared for war. Ready to deal with the odd local uprising, yes, but in no way equipped to defend the country against the Japanese. As Japan massed her military might in the northern border region of Tonkin, Governor Catroux had few cards to play. The airforce in Indochina was virtually nonexistent. In the whole of the country and including the *garde indigène* — an Annamese force which was more peace-keeping *gendarmerie* than a combat force — there were only 50 000 men under arms. Around half of these were support staff, and fewer than 11 000 were French. Catroux estimated that supplies and munitions would last not much more than a month of fighting. His only hope was to play for time and appeal for help from Britain and the United States.

In a private meeting with the Commander of the British Far Eastern Fleet in Saigon, Catroux was told the

British could not provide military support because they did not have it to give. The US Undersecretary of State told Catroux that the United States would not go to war with Japan if Indochina was attacked, but that a purchasing mission to buy military supplies would be welcomed as with any other friendly country. Governor Catroux urgently dispatched such a mission.

Then, on the 18th of June 1940, after four days without a word from the French government in Paris, Indochina received the news that France had accepted an armistice with the Germans. French Indochina went into shock. Suddenly the country which had been kept militarily and economically dependent on France was cut off from her government on the other side of the world.

The realisation that the meagre forces in Indochina would be left alone to deal with Japan was met with alarm and disbelief. At home my father's reluctance to accept what had happened soon turned to outrage and anger. And for those in the French community who allowed themselves to dwell upon their position, the stories of Japanese atrocities in Nanking and elsewhere now became haunting images.

The day after news of the armistice in France, the Japanese presented an ultimatum to Catroux. With Japanese troops threatening at the border, the Governor had twenty-four hours to accede to the demands. Catroux found himself with little alternative. With no hope of help from the outside world, and weak and ill-equipped at home, he assented to the demand that the transit of supplies to China be stopped. Hoping the concession would appease the Japanese, and still bargaining for time, he flatly refused Japan what she really wanted: free passage through Indochina for her troops, as well as access to and use of French aerodromes in the colony. If nothing else, he hoped to be able to arm his forces with the material bought from the United States, and be ready to fight by October.

Catroux was in an invidious position even without knowing Japan's grand plan. His 'no' was never going to be acceptable: the French held the key to all Japan desired. The passage through Indochina was geographically vital to enable her to invade Southeast Asia. From Indochina she could strike Burma, Malaya, Singapore, the Dutch East Indies and the Philippines. Paris was in enemy hands and Japan was now well aware of just how weak France was.

As the sun was setting on the halcyon days of French Indochina, I was sitting my final examination. It was a pompous sort of affair, with fully brassed senior officers from Hanoi officiating. About eight of us passed, and we received our postings along with our exam results. I was to report within thirty-six hours to the Lang Son 155 mm Battery, to the northeast of Hanoi near the Chinese border.

Twenty-two feet of steel barrel, aimed at the frontier to China. I walked around the great marine gun, touching it, stroking it, trying to resist the temptation to fiddle with the firing mechanism. We had four of these imposing weapons, and I was responsible for two of them. The guns were designed for accuracy and distance and boasted a range of 32 kilometres. I could not help but be impressed by them. Originally the guns had been based at the port city of Haiphong to repel naval attacks, but now they had come by rail to this purpose-built siding, far from the coastal emplacement for which they were designed.

I had been surprised to be charged with the 2nd section of the battery. I was only a reservist, eighteen years old and straight out of officer school, yet I was left to set up and maintain the two guns, to supply and store the ammunition, and ultimately to fire them. But I did not dwell on the desperate state of the defence that had earned me such responsibility.

I didn't seriously believe the Japanese would attack us. Still, I went about my business, finishing protective-bunker earthworks around the guns and completing the ammunition dump on the south side of the hill flanking our position, securely storing a thousand rounds of shells and charges in their airtight marine containers. I singled out a couple of observation posts at the highest points overlooking the sparsely populated hilly region near the Chinese border, where only a few subsistence farmers grew rice on terraced paddy fields. Each had a panoramic view of the frontier we would cover with our guns. I was enjoying the science of it all. I worked out by triangulation the coordinates of strategic objectives such as bridges and road junctions, and established a diagram to direct fire within seconds without further calculation. A handful of pilot shots into no-man's territory and I was ready.

Lang Son was a straggling, leafy sort of town set on a high, green plain surrounded by rolling hills. The railway through town continued to Dong Dang and the 'Friendship Gate' into southern China. Since the French government had stopped the official haulage of weaponry to the Chinese, Lang Son had become a profitable haunt for those who had got into the armaments game. Along with the recent influx of soldiers, the usual bars and fan-tan houses of town were sprinkled with shady characters: German bag-men, dubious-looking Americans and international villains in general, all keen to court the attention of the Chinese government agents.

I preferred the lively, smoke-filled ambience of the Officers Club. After closing time Gaston would join me, bearing a Pernod with *glacé pilée* for me and a fresh lime juice for himself.

Gaston had many friends outside of town. On weekends we'd walk to one of many surrounding villages where fifty, sometimes a hundred people lived quietly self-sufficient lives. In the homes of his friends I enjoyed being a part of the gentle rituals of Vietnamese hospitality, although I understood little of the conversation. Gaston would always enlighten me as to the village affairs on our way home.

Gaston was greatly amused by my monkey, Poupette, and he was one of the few in Lang Son in whose company she relaxed. Though prone to mischief out of doors she was a gentle, well-mannered little thing and only rarely did she disgrace herself in the homes of our hosts. Her one weakness was for the red paper streamers bearing messages of good luck in gilt ideograms that adorned some houses — though she knew I thoroughly disapproved of her wearing them. Chickens and ducks roaming the streets were another temptation to play, and I would regularly have to scold her and whisk her from her one-sided games to her place upon my shoulder.

There were late-afternoon trips of discovery into the hills above town too, and there Poupette could run free, exploring jagged limestone caves and sanctuaries, Gaston and I laughing as we pursued her along the small, tortuous tracks that had no apparent pattern and seemingly led nowhere. She was interested in everything, the scuttle of a lizard, the flustered flight of a bird from the undergrowth, the smell, even the taste of the flowers. They were happy afternoons, just the three of us, full of conversation and good humour.

In Lang Son's military camp I had quarters of my own and Poupette approved of the arrangement, for crowds made her jumpy. In the privacy of our room she could relax, lounging across the back of an armchair where, when I sat down, she could comfortably inspect and groom my hair.

I was young, naive, and enjoying the army in my own quiet way. I did not give enough consideration to the consequences of what was happening around me, either in the Governor's Palace in Hanoi or in the corridors of

Vichy power in German-occupied France. Having had a taste of life as a private I appreciated how things had changed for the better for me, in the short time since I graduated, and was quietly pleased to be a fully fledged army officer. I did not realise that my initiation had not yet begun. Nor that it would be so callous and brutal.

Five

Three Day War

Pounding the dirt track through the lonely outskirts of town, it was as if I was running from the knowledge of what I had done, escaping the memory of the morning. Being forced to preside over the execution of my friend Gaston, to order the cutting down of his fine-boned body, to put the last bullet in his handsome head, had crucified me. Though I had known him only since I'd been in Lang Son, the bond between us had grown quickly. He was a friend who had seemed above it all. I had broken his trust in the most unspeakable way and felt myself vile and contemptible.

I had been given the afternoon off and was fleeing. I barely noticed an old woman tottering out onto the street balancing a chicken cage on her head, nor her startled shriek as I almost collided with her. All I wanted was to get as far away as possible, somewhere in the hills where I could lose myself and begin to deal with the trauma. At the foothills I kept on, head thumping and gasping for breath, up through the woods. Suddenly there was a heavy tree branch in my hands and I was flailing it around, screaming in rage. Unsatisfied, I swung the branch hard onto the solid trunk of a tree, jarring my hands and sending splinters biting into my fingers.

'Why?' I yelled as I hit again and again and again. There were no answers.

Exhausted, I flung myself down. There in the isolation of the woods I set my emotions free, emotions that I had stifled for the sake of France, for the sake of the Vichy regime, for the sake of my own neck. I grieved for Gaston, for the person I knew he was and the way in which fate and the political events of the world had ended his life so cruelly. I grieved for myself because I knew the person I was and I loathed the person I'd had to be.

I lay on the ground for a long time, filled with self-pity and dwelling upon my own misfortune. I had joined the army at seventeen, revelling in the opportunity of doing something for my country, of doing something for myself, of seeing the world from anywhere other than from the protection of my mother's wing. But the world was not turning out quite as I had imagined.

The travelling theatre troupes which I had patronised so keenly, I would learn, were Communist sympathisers too — ‘letter-boxes’ for the Communists. Beneath the exotic white-and-red painted faces were the eyes and ears of the Communists, watching and listening for them, assisting them, harbouring them, passing clandestine information across the country, conspiring with them. Yet to me these were wonderful, hospitable people. I could not imagine them as sinister — but apparently they had been the enemy. I had been fraternising with the enemy.

I thought about the hours and hours I had spent in conversation with Gaston, talking into the early morning, about everything, about nothing. He had been a well-educated fellow and I’d always thought that the barman’s job at the Officers’ Mess was beneath him, that he should have been more than a corporal in the French Army. Our discussions went round and round in my head. I had never had the faintest suspicion he was a Communist. We had talked of the plight of the lower classes or any such topic of the moment, but never of any hard-core political issues. Gaston had never asked me what was happening in the field, as one would expect from a spy. I never for a moment believed he had tried to pick my brain.

The execution at Lang Son changed me for ever. In the years ahead I would try to block it out. But I never did. I could not. I would carry it within me, always.

In Hanoi there was another crisis looming. Governor Catroux had been dismissed, regarded by the French colonial minister as being too pro-British and independently minded.[2] The concessions he had made to the Japanese had been badly received in Vichy, for the French government disliked the Japanese even more than the Germans. More importantly, it was less afraid of them and could not understand why Catroux had given way to them.

His replacement, Vice Admiral Jean Decoux of the French Navy, had since made it clear that he was resolutely against further appeasement of the Japanese. However on 2 August 1940, with Japanese forces still massed at the border, he too was cornered by an ultimatum to allow Japan to cross Tonkin and occupy Indochinese airfields. Japan claimed her objective was merely to secure a buffer zone to China. Using the best traditions of delaying and parleying and with no other option, Decoux suggested the Japanese take up the matter with the Vichy government in France.

Once again Vichy appealed to the United States for help. Once more the request was refused.[3] Indochina was alone in the world and her government in France was under the thumb of Japan's allies, the Germans. French Foreign Minister Baudouin was convinced that Indochina could not be defended. Though Cabinet split

---

[2] On his dismissal Catroux left Indochina and later joined Charles de Gaulle's Free French forces to fight in North Africa and the Middle East.

[3] In doing so, US Undersecretary of State Sumner Welles told Vichy that the United States 'appreciated the difficulties with which the French Government was faced and did not consider that it would be justified in reproaching France if certain military facilities were accorded Japan'.

over the issue, at the end of August 1940 the Vichy government signed a face-saving 'Accord of Principle' with Japan. The agreement recognised French sovereignty over Indochina and respected Indochina's territorial integrity, in return for France's recognition of Japan's dominant interest in the Far East region. France would discuss economic conventions and the granting of military facilities to Japan in Indochina. Japan promised to evacuate Indochina as soon as China had been defeated.

So, though we did not know it, the Vichy government had already acceded to all Japanese demands, the most important one being its 'confidential' pledge to allow Japan to station troops outside cities and provincial capitals in Tonkin.

The tables had turned completely. Now it was the Vichy government which was making concessions to the Japanese and it was the Governor in Hanoi who was furious.

'If we must run the risk of losing Indochina,' Decoux declared to Vichy, 'it is better to lose it in defending it rather than by betraying it.' He was not the puppet the Vichy government had taken him for.

Refusing to implement the accord, he began obstructive tactics, and early in September took advantage of a border skirmish to cancel all talks with the Japanese. The Vichy Foreign Minister intervened and tension reached breaking point.

With the strength of the Japanese 5th Army preparing to strike across the border with China, a dispatch arrived from Intelligence. Japanese field commanders were preparing to move and we were to leave Lang Son for our field positions.

For me the timing could not have been better. Let the Japanese come. I was ready to fight. I wanted to fight. I did not much care if I died this week.

We left for our battery. Across the Chinese frontier ten divisions, a massive army of over 100 000 Japanese troops, were positioned along the length of the border, ready to strike. Governor Decoux had received the final ultimatum: agree to Japanese demands by midnight of 22 September 1940. Decoux must have once more considered the odds. Including support units such as ours and some small bastions of *garde indigène*, our frontier force had a strength of 4000[4].

So far Decoux's stalling tactics had failed, and as the deadline ticked out he dispatched his Chief of Military Office to the port city of Haiphong to resume negotiations with General Nishihara. But it was too late. The Japanese field commanders considered the bureaucrats in Tokyo soft in their dealings with the French, and were impatient and eager to begin their assault. Though Decoux and Nishihara signed an acceptance treaty that night, the Japanese field commander of the 5th Division, General Nakamura Aketo, had already taken things into his own hands.

[4] Of the Foreign Legion regiment, eight companies, some 1500 men, were deployed north of Lang Son, with only one company remaining to man fortified positions on the outskirts of town. Six companies of Colonial Infantry moved to field positions and the six batteries of 75 mm mountain artillery covered the hilly district northeast of Lang Son.

* * *

The night of 22 September 1940 was quiet and still. Keeping watch in the earthen trench that was the No 2 observation post, I still didn't believe that the Japanese would attack.

The first jarring explosions shattered the night. To the north, mortar traces immediately began to arc through the sky and staccato gunfire cracked through the middle distance. The field telephone rang — a line I had laid overland myself — and through the crackle came the report that the Japanese had launched a major assault on the Lang Son/Dong Dang front.

Somehow, the news released an enormous safety valve for me. At last there was somewhere for my pent-up emotions to go. Let the battle begin.

But there was nothing I could do until dawn. Sleep was impossible. Occasionally a monosyllabic check message cracked over the telephone. Yes, everything was ready. Time crawled — three, four, four-thirty and still I could see nothing, and then at last a faint glimmer of light appeared from the east.

Above the distant echoes of war the birds were singing early-morning odes to the world, unreally, as though it was just a normal day. Light bathed the rolling hills in pinks and golds, and the long shadows cast by the first rays of the sun made a tapestry of the colours, illuminating an unsettling scene. Japanese troops were spread over a wide front, some engaged in close combat with French forces, the white *képis* of the Foreign

Legion units vaguely identifiable alongside the Colonial Infantry.

I would avoid that area, concentrate on the horizon to the west.

Training across the crimson dawn, I saw a textbook target bearing slowly down upon us. A large column of Japanese soldiers, on foot and marching down the main road, was flanked by a fleet of vehicles and small armoured tanks. Checking my pre-set coordinate table I gave an order to gun No 1 for a pilot shot. The massive weapon launched its first shell on a perfect line, but it landed 200 metres short of the road. The next saw the 155 mm shell explode right on the road in front of the column. Working quickly I ordered the second gun into action and watched with elation as the explosion kicked up on the road to the rear, hopelessly trapping the trucks, tanks and equipment. Now we had a chance to do some real damage.

That day the four huge marine guns battered the Japanese column for hours. From my vantage point on the hill I watched the pandemonium with an increasing sense of confidence that, despite the huge odds against us, we would be able to hold out. Japanese intelligence had failed its troops badly and our mighty guns had proved themselves. Though it was impossible to assess the troop damage with accuracy, the destruction of Japanese vehicles and equipment in the column had been enormous.

Night fell and with it an eerie quiet. Relieved from my post, I hunkered down in the main bunker at the battery.

We had not heard anything from the eastern front, and I looked forward to the news.

I fell asleep, loaded with expectations for the following day.

Before dawn I was back at my observation post, scanning the horizon, picking out the abandoned remains of the convoy to the west, still smoking and smouldering. Nothing moved around it. On our northern field of fire all was quiet. There were no troop movements anywhere. I found myself flat, hollow, unsure if I was disappointed or elated. It appeared the Japanese had retreated, yet I was in the mood for more. There was nothing to do but wait for a report from Headquarters.

When the news came it was all bad. Overnight our infantry had withdrawn and the Japanese had followed them in their southwesterly retreat. On the eastern front, too, the Japanese troops had moved south, completely out of our field of fire. I was bitterly disappointed. Our great guns had already been rendered totally obsolete.

For us, it was all over. In anger and frustration Captain Bouvier ordered a shot on the outer limit of our perimeter. There was nobody to hit, but somehow it eased the tension.

That day, the 24th of September 1940, nothing at all happened until a high-flying aircraft circled our battery in the late afternoon. It was an ominous sign. Our own air force was virtually nonexistent, and we had been spotted by a Japanese reconnaissance aircraft. Darkness descended into another restless night.

At daybreak nothing had changed. Unable to contact Lang Son for information and direction, the mood was quiet. The gunners mooched about with nothing to do, cigarettes dangling from their bottom lips. Though they knew they had almost certainly fired their last shot, they cleaned and polished the guns and prepared the ammunition. As I paced around making quiet mental preparations for the order to retreat, two Japanese Zeroes appeared, flying low and swift over the hills towards us. There was no time.

In seconds, and at an altitude of no more than 50 metres, the Zeroes flashed over the last of the hills. Flat on the ground, my face in the dirt, I was vaguely aware of someone shouting, then the staccato of machine guns over the engine noise. Almost simultaneously four deafening explosions blasted our position and a shower of debris dropped over us. As quickly as it began, it was over.

Cautiously I raised my head and saw the Zeroes disappear into the distance towards China. Figures stirred, and faces peered over the top of the bunker. Someone was cursing roundly but there were no screams of agony, no urgent calls for assistance. Picking my way around the bomb craters for a quick head count, I was amazed to find everyone present and accounted for. The guns were intact and there were no casualties besides a few cuts and bruises. It was incredible, a marvellous stroke of luck.

This strike stressed our vulnerability — yet there was still nothing to be done but wait.

* * *

Not until the early part of the afternoon did we at last make contact with Lang Son. The news was now disastrous. The Japanese had broken most of our lines of defence and besides a couple of Foreign Legion units desperately holding their positions, Lang Son was almost ready to capitulate. Worse was the news that two large columns of Japanese infantry were advancing on our own position in a pincer movement.

The battery evacuated quickly. Loaded with whatever they could carry, the men headed off down the railway line, hugging the culvert for security. I remained behind with a team of three Annamese gunners and Marcel, a stocky French corporal with a lopsided grin. We were to destroy the guns and ammunition and follow in retreat to the provincial capital of Bac Ninh, some 80 kilometres to the south.

There was little time. Destroying the guns was easy, a question of loading the instrumentation of all four guns into the barrel of one, and firing. Then there was the ammunition. Surely any boy scout could blow up an ammunition dump.

Mentally revising the safety manual on pyrotechnics, I heaped a stack of crumpled paper at the entrance to the dump, leaving a 3-metre tail outside. Four containers of powder charge were opened and I sent Marcel and the men to the shelter of the railway cutting, before cautiously lighting the tail. It ignited and I sprinted for the cutting, the warnings in the manual about not allowing naked lights within 200 metres of storage facilities flashing through my head.

We lay there and a minute passed ... two ... then three. Something had gone wrong. Had it gone out completely or was it just smouldering, ready to creep the last few inches and send the whole lot up? Hesitantly, reluctantly, I tiptoed back towards the dump.

The ether-like stench from the open marine containers holding 200 kilograms of powder each was overpowering. At the entrance I found the tail. All the paper had burned, but that was it. What had happened?

I recalled the crew and we opened another half-dozen containers, threw bags of powder on the ground and built another heap of crumpled paper, bigger this time and with a longer tail. If I was on edge before, this time I was petrified.

'We'll be in the cutting if you need us,' said Marcel sardonically.

My heart in my mouth, I lit the tail once more and bolted, throwing myself headlong into the cutting. Again we waited ... one minute ... two ... three minutes — and nothing.

Marcel looked at me and grinned widely out of one side of his face.

'Now what?'

What the hell had happened? Every minute wasted left us a minute closer to being captured by the Japanese. The longer I waited to make sure it was safe to return, the less time I would have to try it again. I had to forget the safety procedure.

I raced back, my assistants following with waning enthusiasm. We opened yet more containers, slit bags of lamellated powder and spread the contents all over the ground. This time there was no paper trail, but a thick powder trail 50 metres long. I sent the men back, got ready, lit the trail and sprinted for the cutting. Marcel reckoned I made the 80 metres in eight seconds. The fireworks started in ten.

There was no waiting around to enjoy the spectacle. Heads down and in the cover of the cutting we headed south at a trot. Behind us 800 shells and about the same number of marine containers of gunpowder began to detonate, fierce explosions and hissing fragments shooting in all directions.

Hours later our pace had slackened a little — but still we could hear the results of our handiwork cracking and blasting in the distance.

The march was long and hard, through difficult country. After twenty-four hours and having walked all night, I took my first bite of the half-loaf of hard, mouldy bread I had absently picked up before leaving. I was ravenous. It was all I had to eat and it seemed utterly delicious, washed down with a sip of muddy paddy field water. With each kilometre getting longer and another day's march ahead, I thought of the route marches behind Tomasini's horse. They had been just afternoon strolls compared with this.

In the late afternoon of the 27th we reached Bac Ninh, forty-eight hours after bolting from the ammunition dump. Our unit was camped at the local junior school, where we had a classroom of our own, complete with straw mattresses laid out on the floor. I chose one and collapsed into it. It was blissful, like the premier suite at the Ritz.

An army staff car pulled up at the school the next morning. It was General Massimi, Commander in Chief of the Artillery in Tonkin. He had driven out from Hanoi to deliver a morale-boosting speech. Surely it would have to be the speech of his career.

The men fell in and we listened expectantly. Before us was a man showing no sign of being resigned to the idea of defeat. His eyes were hawkish, keen, and he seemed fired up, excited. His congratulations on our efforts we accepted with misgiving. There was a worrying spirit of optimism about his praise which I did not share. The odds were well against us.

He paused for a moment, then delivered his orders. We were to reorganise and join the infantry of the Bac Ninh garrisons to counterattack the Japanese as they approached.

But we were artillery! The idea appalled me. We had no infantry training and inadequate arms for infantry combat. Our only weapons were obsolete mousequeton carbines, World War I vintage, with forty rounds of ammunition each. Our Intelligence had little idea of the strength of the Japanese forces descending upon Bac Ninh, yet our orders were to go forward and counterattack with a meagre force of three or four hundred. As General Massimi outlined his gallant plans I could only imagine the disaster that lay ahead. But no one asked for my opinion.

With no duties for the rest of the day I was given a few hours' leave. It was one of those typical late September afternoons, warm and sultry with no rain in sight, and I wandered into town. Bac Ninh had been the centre for production of mother-of-pearl inlay for hundreds of years. The artisans in the street waited for custom, squatting on the footpath or sitting behind rickety desks. Their loose-fitting shirts and trousers looked faded against their shining, black-lacquered wares, and the inlays of mother-of-pearl shell glistened like fish scales. I idled along, stopping to contemplate some of the finer pieces. It was as though the Japanese were not bearing swiftly down from the north, as if the region of this town was not soon to be the place of a bloody battle in which the French colonial forces would be massacred by the new Asian imperialists. I tried not to think about it, immersing myself in the ordinariness of the market scene, the everydayness of it all.

The bustle of the morning was over and the stalls were mostly devoid of customers. There was an air of tranquility about the place.

As my eyes wandered over a shining copper and brass display, a soft voice behind me queried, 'Michel?' Wondering who could know me in this place, I turned around, and my heart skipped a beat. I had not seen her for over two years but I could not mistake those shining blue eyes and that *bouche moqueuse*, that teasing mouth. She smiled. It was Marie Claire.

I hugged her. 'I'm so happy to see you,' I said truthfully. 'You look wonderful.'

She wore a softly draping straw hat and from beneath it she looked up at me with a shy but certain radiance.

'Let's walk,' she said, and together we walked slowly up the street, exchanging news of the last two years.

At the end, where the stilted bamboo dwellings of the working people began, we doubled back towards the centre of the small town. Marie Claire's husband had gone with his battalion four weeks ago to reinforce the defence in Lao Kay in the far northeast of Tonkin. She'd had no news of him. So we spoke of the old days at the Bagatelle races, of the people we had known and of the Sunday night dances. Cherished memories warmed through me, memories of her whirling me across the dance floor and of her holding me so close in the tango that I could feel her every soft curve through her thin silk dress. I realised, not for the first time, that I had never been happier than when I was in her arms.

The centre of town, where perhaps we would part and go our separate ways, loomed close. I slowed to crawling pace. There was a pause in the conversation and in the humidity of the afternoon Marie Claire took off her hat and fanned her face a little

'I'm going to the cinema this evening,' she said. 'There's a new French film showing and I've heard it's very good. Will you come? We could have something to eat afterwards.'

Of course I would.

She gave me her ticket so that I could ask at the box office for an adjoining seat. I said *au revoir* and walked away casually towards the theatre, using my every effort to avoid breaking into an undignified trot. There was an influx of troops in the town. What if the film was sold out?

At the little café bar adjacent to the cinema I met Marie Claire shortly before seven. She looked gorgeous in a dark blue cocktail dress, not unlike those I remembered her wearing in those carefree Bagatelle days.

Perhaps the film was overrated, or perhaps our interest in the cinema had waned for the time being, for we lasted no more than half of the film. Marie Claire's hand seemed to move easily to my inner thigh and she stroked my leg briefly as she leaned across.

'Shall we go,' she said. It did not seem like a question.

Outside, the street was dimly lit and nearly deserted. Marie Claire slipped her hand into mine and we walked slowly. She stole a furtive kiss, convincing me that this was some cruel dream from which I would soon awaken. I was not yet nineteen and Marie Claire was a mature and beautiful woman. Why would she be interested in me? Ahead were the brighter lights of the street stalls where we had planned to eat, but as we passed the haphazard tangle of tarpaulins and tent poles, the braziers and sizzling woks, she showed no sign of noticing. I did not remind her. We walked some more, then suddenly we were at her door.

It was dark as we entered and I struggled to make out any furniture so as not to stumble. I hesitated, there in the entrance hall, then felt two slim hands slide up my chest and around my neck in the blackness. A pair of soft, full lips caressed and then gently parted my own. This was no dream. Fingers were at my buttons, kisses across my chest, the blue cocktail dress fell to the floor. My fumbling hands began to explore — her face, her neck, her arms, then further, to sacred places, beautiful, delicious places.

We never reached the stairs.

Early morning light filtered through the drawn curtains as I woke. We were in the drawing room. Marie Claire was curled up naked at my side in a deep and peaceful sleep. I found a white linen cloth on the coffee table. Lovingly I covered her, pausing for a moment to look at her face. It seemed to me soft, delicate, the face of an angel. Suddenly I knew for sure what I had suspected so long ago. I was in love with Marie Claire. A verse came to mind: '*Le coeur a ses raisons que la raison ignore.*' It was one of the romantics — Blaise Pascal? Guy de Maupassant? I thought Pascal. No doubt my heart had its reasons and it seemed no other reasons in the world could alter my love for Marie Claire.

I kissed her, barely touching the curl of hair on her brow, and left her to her sweet dreams.

Going about the business of allocating daily duties around the army camp, organising the day, some sense of reality returned. The atmosphere was tense and everyone was discussing the immediate future. What would the next few days bring? Since yesterday afternoon I had barely given a thought to the Japanese bearing down upon us, about returning to the battle front as untrained infantrymen on a suicidal mission.

The sun was well up in the sky when news came through the railway's telegraphic system. Our orders had changed. There had been a cessation of hostilities. At 1400 hours that day a train was due to depart Bac Ninh for Hanoi, and all troops were to be aboard it.

A wave of relief swept over the men. We would not be going back to battle, at least not for the moment. All I could think was — *Not today. Surely not today.*

I fled the camp as soon as I could, rushing up the Rue de la Gare.

Marie Claire opened her front door, looking fresh and cool in a morning dress. Sitting beside me on the settee she spoke calmly and softly, stroking my hair gently, lovingly, her fingers spread.

'Tomorrow will be another day, *cheri*,' she said. 'We still have almost three hours together. Let's not spoil a moment of them. Come.'

She took my hand and led me upstairs, where those precious moments ran down fast. Afterwards we lay entwined, damp and spent on the bed, the ceiling fan revolving slowly overhead as if every grinding turn was marking down the seconds we had left together. Marie Claire's efforts to console me were tireless. It would be all right. We would see each other soon, perhaps in Hanoi. There would be many other times.

I kept glancing at the wooden carriage clock on her bedside table, willing it to stop, but it raced mercilessly on . . . 1.15, 1.30, 1.35. Suddenly it was time to go. A last embrace, a promise to be together soon, and I left, not daring to turn my head to look back.

Hurrying to the station, I prayed the engine had broken down or the Japs had blown up the line. But no, there it was, smoke from unseasoned timber belching from the stack of the old locomotive, carriages overflowing with troops, whistles blowing, officers shouting. Marcel was standing beside the train, grinning as I sprinted up the platform. I vaulted into the carriage and he followed me in.

'I won't ask,' he said, and slammed the door behind us.

Two o'clock, dead on time, a couple more sharp whistles and the convoy stretched painfully out from the station, tearing me away.

Six

Of Peacocks and Tigers

I had never seen my father so disturbed. His face was serious, his mouth set hard and determined.

'It's a disaster,' he said again. He was pacing up and down the room, fingers clenched, then unclenched, frustrated and angry. 'Indochina is being walked over by the Japanese. In France it is the Germans. The army is in disgrace. The French people are in disgrace. What can I do? There is nothing.' He turned to look at me, exasperated. 'It is up to you. You must get out.'

Maman, however, could not contain her elation at my return. As my father raged about the house she kept touching me, clucking about me, offering me things to eat.

'You, Michel,' Papa said, 'you will go to England and join de Gaulle and the Free French forces. With the

Japanese here you will be demobilised and I will arrange your passage to Singapore. There are freighters . . .' His voice trailed off as if he had suddenly remembered something. Then he picked up his *képi* and was gone.

French Hanoi was reeling. For days there was total confusion. Bits of news filtered through, body counts were done.

The French had lost more than 800 soldiers in Tonkin. Of these 130 were Foreign Legionnaires who had fought to the last cartridge, only to be machine-gunned by order of the Japanese commander. Two had survived their wounds, been rescued and nursed by Annamese locals to return to Hanoi and tell the story.

An agreement with the Japanese had been signed by Decoux, under duress, on the night the assault began. Such were communications, however, that it took days to stop the attack on Tonkin. Since then the Japanese had been all apologies in diplomatic circles. The whole affair had been a dreadful mistake, they said, the result of an independent action by the Commander of the 5th Division, General Nakamura Aketo. He would be severely dealt with.

So for now, peace had been restored. The Japanese command had ordered the bulk of their troops back over the border to South China, but they were still there, hovering, and Decoux was pressed into resuming negotiations.

I'd like to think it was the determination the French field commanders had shown that now caused the

Japanese to moderate their demands, for in the final agreement they were given use of only three disused airfields, and the permanent force of Japanese troops was to be limited to 6000 men in Tonkin. The transit of Japanese troops would be limited to 25 000 men at any one time and the requirement for a port facility was dropped.

My father's plans to get me out of Indochina were bold and unsettling but, besides that, coming home to Hanoi had been like re-entering the cocoon of my former existence. Maman's devotion to me was total. The story of Gaston's execution had spilled out of me, leaving her outraged and distraught, and her words went a little way to appeasing my self-loathing. Immediately she demanded of my father an investigation, a request he quietly ignored.

I did not tell my mother everything that had happened to me over the last month, but it occurred to me that it had been a lot. It began in early September when I had lost my little monkey, Poupette. She had playfully disturbed a nest of bees, and she was attacked *en masse*. Though there was little I could do, I had nursed her through an agonising death. Then, within four weeks, I had killed a best friend, been to war and back, fallen in love, mentally prepared first for death in battle, then for flight to England to join the Resistance.

But a day later it appeared I would not be leaving Indochina at all. The Japanese Navy was blocking all shipping through the South China Sea to blockade supplies to China, and only small fishing craft were allowed within 50 kilometres of the coastline. Papa had thought he could get around this but there was no transport to be found in the foreseeable months. In any event, with the French still in authority there had been no demobilisation of reservists. And so it was that three days after returning to Hanoi I was ordered south to Cambodia.

Hanoi railway station was a *mêlée* of uniforms and luggage, as 400 soldiers waited in disarray, sprawled along the length of the platform. The train was late and I scanned the faces of the men in search of my old unit. They were all from reservist ranks but there was no one else from mine. The only person I could find in authority was a dispatching major. We were going to Cambodia, he said, as a plugging contingent, in case of heavy losses at the Siamese frontier.

I was deeply disappointed. This seemed an unnecessary little fracas, a border dispute that had been brewing since December 1938 when the pro-Japanese militarist Marshal Phibul Songgram came into power in Siam. His government had renamed the country Thailand and in June of 1940 signed a nonaggression pact with France, in which France had agreed to renegotiate the Thai–Indochina border. But France had since fallen and, encouraged by Japan, Marshal Songgram's demands for territory had increased to the extent that Vichy had met them with a flat refusal. Thai troops, equipped and trained by the Japanese, were now in position along the border.

It was a long trip — south by rail to Saigon, then by road west to Cambodia. Crossing Cochinchina we passed through the heavily populated Mekong Delta, where crowds of people in baggy trousers and tunics assiduously went about their daily work. In every direction there were small figures, some pushing carts, others carrying sacks, bending double in the fields or tottering under heavy carrying poles, the weight of their burdens reflected on their faces beneath limpet-shaped hats. There, we were still in Annamese lands where the ambience was typically Chinese, but as we crossed the border the joss houses, dragons and paper good luck streamers suddenly vanished. In Cambodia there was an Indian, almost Middle Eastern essence to the countryside.

The lush green of Cochinchina faded as the landscape began to change. It became drier, dustier, a savannah-like country of acacias and bottle-boled sugar palms, areca palms and bamboo groves. There was barely a soul to be seen, and the few people we did pass appeared to have little to do, for many were squatting or sitting by the road, cheerfully regarding us as we drove by. The women covered their breasts with a wrap — though outside of towns not always — and carried their babies on their backs in a sling. In the small villages, houses were of bamboo and thatch, on stilts, though much of life appeared to be lived in the open. Domestic animals wandered unrestrained, and we slowed down to negotiate pigs and ugly yellow dogs that sauntered casually across the road.

We came at last to our base in Kompong Cham, a small town on the Mekong River. Here we'd find trade an altogether more relaxed affair than in Tonkin, and the markets imbued with hotter, spicier, more pungent smells, redolent of Indian curries. There were more shaven heads in Cambodia, and more skin visible. It shone a burnished bronze in the sunlight.

The round-faced Cambodians I found genial and friendly. They stared unabashedly if they were interested, laughed heartily if they were amused. Yet there was a meditative, renunciatory air about them, and they lived very simply.

The country was less populous than Vietnam, where the industrious Annamese followed only a highly diluted form of Buddhism. The Cambodians — and, I learned later, the Laotians — followed the doctrines of Buddhism to the letter. Buddhas sat in portly vigilance everywhere, in statue, in relief, on canvas. Buddhist monks in flowing orange robes walked the streets pensively under fringed umbrellas, their little boy attendants trotting dutifully behind. I learned that every man spent at least a year of his life in a Buddhist monastery, where he was conditioned to living a life of poverty while remaining, it was plain to see, supremely happy.

Cambodia was a French protectorate and apparently very comfortable to be so. There were few plantations in the country and the bulk of the population lived their own quiet lives unaffected by the small French presence. In the development stakes, the Cambodians were virtual nonstarters, and very content to be so.

Finding ourselves miles from the Thai border, we occupied ourselves organising a voluntary Cambodian home guard, along similar lines to the *garde indigène* in Tonkin. Gradually enrolment increased and eventually the recruits grew into a small but reasonable law-and-order unit. In the process there seemed no pressure, leaving the opportunity to explore the surrounding country and learn more of the local population.

The moon in her last quarter hung high in the tree canopy. The night was clear and heady, the perfumes of virgin forest exotic. Maurice and I had been on this lark several times now. Night hunting trips brought excitement in this, the most peaceable of places.

The biggest skirmish we had yet encountered on our patrols of Kompong Cham was between the owner of a local dog — typically ugly, yellow and undernourished — and the owner of a walking chicken dinner. Yet out here in the jungle, hand torches strapped to our shoulders, clutching powerful but inaccurate short-barrelled Mousquetons, our senses were alert. We were listening for the eerie call of the peacock. I had no real desire to bag one. It was just a good excuse for adventure.

It had been a relief to find Maurice L'Huillier among the reservists sent to Cambodia. He had been at school with me in Hanoi and like me was a youngster with patriotic sentiments about the war in Europe. He too had enlisted in the army at the outbreak of war, and had quickly risen to the rank of sergeant. We had joined company on this mission and become good friends. Tonight, however, we were both on edge. We had lost our bearings in the faint moonlight and the jungle was alive with unfamiliar sounds. It was after midnight and we had no clue which way to turn.

There was nothing to be done but sit it out until dawn.

Beneath the luxurious branches of a low-canopied, spreading Banyan tree we found sanctuary. After a little trial and error, the trunk of the tree, smooth and complex, offered perfect mouldings for the spine. We settled for the night.

In the distance the weird call of a peacock echoed unnaturally through the darkness, and I remembered, uncomfortably, the words of the locals — 'Where there are peacocks there are tigers.' Daybreak seemed a long way off.

There was a little desultory conversation about what a good spot we'd found, and I stretched my legs out and eased my head back into a more relaxed posture. I closed my eyes.

Suddenly I was on my feet, pounding through the undergrowth, a piercing, shrieking yowl resounding in my eardrums. Maurice thundered along close by me — driven, both of us, by the idea of our crashing boots drowning out the pads of the tiger as it bounded after us in pursuit.

The backs of our necks prickling as if brushed by the warm breath of a large animal, we ran and ran, like terrified hares.

Five, perhaps ten minutes later we slowed to a jog. And stopped, hearts pounding.

Straining to hear beyond the sound of our panting, I listened for the telltale crack of a branch that would give the animal away.

'*Merde*,' Maurice gasped at last. 'That was too close. It was right above us, in the tree. A tiger, do you think?'

'Or a panther,' I puffed.

Either way, the appeal of resting under another tree for the night had evaporated.

'Let's just walk,' I said. And so we walked briskly on until we found a track.

A short way along the trail, a glow of light flickered through the trees. There, alone in a clearing, stood a thatched bamboo house set high on stilts.

Rural people usually kept a small oil lamp burning at night for security and convenience, but it did not mean anyone was awake. We walked a little closer and a dog barked hysterically. Pigs grunted and then chickens squawked indignantly from within the slatted shelter beneath the house.

It seemed all hell had broken loose. The door of the house opened and a small figure peered out. We stepped clear of the shelter of the trees.

'*Bonsoir*,' Maurice said as we approached, as if it was the most natural thing in the world to be calling on someone at one in the morning.

An old man climbed down a precarious ladder and, as though he had been expecting us, greeted us courteously and invited us to ascend.

Inside, the room was warm, welcoming, and faintly agricultural as the aromas of the resettling animals beneath wafted up through the floor. A large wooden bed stood sentinel, the only piece of furniture, and in one corner was an earthen oven next to a shelf of utensils tied to the wall.

An elderly lady draped in a sarong roused herself and began to brew some tea. From the second room a younger couple emerged, and greeted us sleepily, smiling all the time. The old man showed us to a grass mat, then disappeared down the ladder.

We sat cross-legged, awkwardly exchanging pleasantries with the younger man, digging deep into our meagre Cambodian vocabulary.

Soon the old man returned carrying a newly cleaned and plucked chicken. He handed it to the woman with a few words of suggestion, and squatted to serve the tea she had made. We held the tiny cups in two fingers and began stumblingly to explain our presence. Our host, we were relieved to find, had some rudiments of French, at least more French than we had Cambodian. He had picked it up years ago, he told us slowly, working as a lumberjack for a French timber company. The other couple were his daughter and son-in-law, he continued, and there the conversation paused. It didn't seem to matter. Everyone was smiling, I felt welcome, even relaxed, and it occurred to me again that these people had a natural grace and hospitality that I'm sure could never be learned, not even in the finest French schools of etiquette.

We ate the chicken dinner from leaf-lined baskets, all of us, feasting in the dead of night as though it was the customary hour to do so. By 3 a.m. we had finished, and the host was insisting we sleep in his bed. I was embarrassed at his generosity, but afraid also that it might be impolite to refuse. We accepted and with great ceremony the women picked up the grass mat from the bamboo-slat bed, flapped it about and turned it over. Our bed was ready.

Settling to rest that night, I wondered whether I could find it within myself to be so generous to unknown callers arriving on my doorstep at such an ungodly hour.

The rooster beneath us began to crow raucously, rudely. I cursed the bird. It seemed I had just closed my eyes and I found myself lamenting that *it* had not been the basis of our meal a couple of hours earlier. The household was stirring. It was time to rise.

As we were leaving that day, I thanked the old man profusely, pressing some money into his weathered hand. He shook his head, refusing it again and again. From my belt I removed my hunting knife in its leather sheath and presented it to him. A flicker of delight danced in his eyes, but again he shook his head. It was an honour and a pleasure to have us as his guests, he said. I took the knife out of the sheath and grasped his fingers, wrapping them around the handle. His face crinkled into a wide smile as he succumbed, thanking me over and over. I was so glad to see his joy.

I would leave Cambodia all the richer for the experience.

I wish I could have stayed longer, learned more of the country and her people. Instead I would take with me an understanding of the misty-eyed fondness I had seen in a friend of my father, an administrator returned from a posting in Cambodia. He, like me, had been beguiled by the country's demure charm, and talked reverently of others who never returned at all, who chose to go native and spend the rest of their lives living serenely, surrounded by the tranquil influences of Buddha. I think of those people and it is hard for me to imagine how the 1975 atrocities of the Khmer Rouge could occur in such a placid, peaceable country; though perhaps it was just this quality of gentleness that lent itself to conquest and subjugation.

The clashes between the Thai and French armies in late November were a prelude to a nineteen-day war in January 1941, but it all happened without me. Of course it was Japan, the mastermind of the dispute, who would emerge the real winner. She had encouraged the Thais and provided military instruction and armaments. When things turned nasty she stepped in to arbitrate. In the process Thailand was given most of the disputed territory and Japan secured for herself a guarantee from France to receive 80 per cent of Indochina's rice exports. The episode concluded as planned, with Japan boasting of its 'peacemaker' role on the world stage. The self-proclaimed Protector of Asian Nations had struck another blow against European domination.

But for now I had finished with the military. By late January 1941 I had my army release papers, and had returned to Hanoi. The cold weather was creeping in with the damp of the *crachin*, the fine, chill mist that penetrated the bones, but it was good to be back, soaking up the familiar, resuming old habits, taking a leisurely stroll by Le Petit Lac.

There was a sharp breeze and I regretted I had not brought a jacket. It seemed quieter than I remembered. An enormous frangipani stood naked, bare of its leaves until spring, and I missed the flower sellers with their multi-coloured mounds of blossom. Towards the northern end of the lake, near the old quarter, a boy eyed me hopefully, his bamboo shoulder pole slung with swinging cups and teapots and pipes.

'*Nuoc voi nong an thouc khong*?' he sang: hot tea smoke tobacco. I bought a small wad of tobacco and, rolling my own, resumed my walk. Ahead of me two young lovers were ambling along. They were wearing coats and their hands were entwined in the pocket of one of them. Seeing them reminded me again of Marie Claire.

I had already decided to stay on in Indochina, and make it my life. We were not yet aware of the real intentions of the Japanese. When this war with China was over they would get out of Tonkin. And besides, adjusting to the new regime had not been difficult — the Japanese presence in Hanoi was barely noticeable and the French framework of administration, police and army control remained undisturbed. On the surface nothing really seemed to have changed, and I had no wish to see beneath the surface.

In Cambodia I had whiled away my spare time reliving every minute of those precious hours with Marie Claire, dreaming of being with her again. On Sundays now I set out eagerly for Bagatelle with my parents. Marie Claire had promised to see me in Hanoi, and if she was here this was where she would be. The vision of her haunted me. Each of those afternoons I scanned the faces beneath the hats of the racing crowd, searching for my love. But she was not there. My guarded inquiries turned up nothing. No one had heard from her for months.

Perhaps she was still in Bac Ninh.

It was about 30 kilometres to the little town, but it may as well have been a fraction of that for I hardly noticed the distance. That Saturday morning my heart was pounding as much over the image of Marie Claire as from the exertion of negotiating my bicycle around the potholes in the road. In two hours I was in Bac Ninh, pedalling slowly along the wide, empty street towards Marie Claire's villa.

In front of the building I stopped, got off my bike, laid it against the wrought-iron fence. I grasped the top of the gate unsteadily for a moment, opened it, then walked the few steps to the front door. Rang the doorbell.

Would she be there?

For what seemed an eternity nobody came. Then footsteps. The door opened slowly and a beautifully dressed Annamese woman, glittering in gold jewellery, stood inquiringly. My heart sank. It was obvious. Here was the new lady of the house.

Marie Claire had gone away, she said. Her husband's battalion had been posted to somewhere in Laos at the beginning of the dispute with Thailand, and Marie Claire had followed a couple of weeks later. No, she wasn't sure where. So many postings, one lost track. She was sorry she couldn't help.

Darling Marie Claire, a thousand kilometres away. My legs turned to wood. It was a long ride home, as if I knew that I would never see Marie Claire again, never hear from her, never hear of her.

I missed the races that weekend, trying to find an escape. A week passed, then another. I had accepted an offer of university sponsorship from the biggest civil engineering firm in Indochina, Les Grands Travaux d'Extrême Orient (GTEO) — training plus twenty hours' work per week, and half-salary while I studied. I didn't give it a great deal of thought. The die was cast. I was to become a civil engineer.

I had begun work for GTEO on the Mint building for the Banque de l'Indochine. It was a full schedule and there was little time for socialising.

Slowly, gradually, a trickle of good sense returned. Life began to settle to normal. Except that nothing in Hanoi really *was* normal.

It was not obvious, but it was there sometimes in the eyes of the Annamese, in little snippets of conversation, in expressions, in remarks. For them the image of the white man's supremacy had been shattered. That the Japanese could walk into Indochina in the presence of the French was incredible, unbelievable, *illuminating*. And the French felt it too, deeply, disturbingly. Beneath the optimism and bold, tough-talking demeanour of the average Frenchman there lurked a bemused despair: they had been humiliated by the Japanese.

In the middle of 1941, on the other side of the world, fate dealt yet another bad hand. The Hitler–Stalin pact was over. Nazi Germany had begun the vast undertaking of invading the Soviet Union, and was looking for assistance from its ally, Japan.

In an effort to entice Japan into attacking Russia's east coast, the Nazis forced the Vichy regime to sign a new accord with Japan. This accord for the 'common defence' of Indochina, gave Japan an almost free hand in Indochina. From then on the country's resources were bled to feed the Japanese war machine.

The first signs of the new accord appeared in the form of the Kempeitai, the ruthless Japanese military police. Japanese sources maintained they were there to co-ordinate troops in transit and seek out agents of the Chinese. But their intelligence network was also supporting pro-Japanese Nationalists and closely monitoring the French. An evil began permeating south through Indochina as more military bases were set up, and the residents of Hanoi began to realise that the intentions of the Japanese went beyond controlling supply routes to China. It was a ghastly realisation. Under our very noses the Japanese were marching inexorably towards war on the world. And we were powerless to do anything about it.

Hanoi awoke to an unusual tension on the 7th of December 1941.

Without warning, Japan had that morning attacked Pearl Harbor in the Pacific. Three thousand US servicemen were dead and the US Pacific Fleet lay devastated. Using southern Indochina as a springboard into Southeast Asia, Japan had launched air raids on Singapore and Hong Kong, and Japanese troops were already advancing on Malaya and the northern Philippines.

Japanese troops were back in and around the city of Hanoi, infiltrating, taking key positions, surrounding the French garrisons. At the Governor's Palace yet another ultimatum had been received: co-operate with the Greater East Asia Co-Prosperity Sphere or face the destruction of the garrisons and the imprisonment of the French civilian population in concentration camps.

Though the Free French declared war on Japan that day, after Pearl Harbor, for Decoux there was little room to manoeuvre, and no one to appeal to for help. He played his usual delaying tactics, but eventually he capitulated. There was nothing else to be done. By surrendering to Japanese demands he saved the French civilians from incarceration and the meagre military forces from almost certain annihilation. The French government would, apparently, be left in administration. Life would go on.

At the end of December 1941 I was studying for my first-year examinations as though Japanese troops were not slaughtering their way through the terrified residents of British Hong Kong and Malaya. Around me in Hanoi the mood was darkening. Many of the Annamese students I counted as friends had joined Nationalist groups now active on campus. In the latter part of the year, and despite my Nationalist sympathies, I felt the bond between us weakening. I tried not to dwell upon it, but among my Annamese contemporaries I could feel affability turn to civility, frankness turn to reticence, and intellectual circles gradually tighten.

Seven

Death and the Dragon's Head

Life in Hanoi was an intriguing tapestry, the threads of which wound their way through the streets and veiled the troubles of the city. From a sidewalk table of a favourite café, I could see a white-aproned *thi hai* pushing an elaborate bamboo baby carriage, sauntering down the Rue Paul Bert. Across the road a grubby but spirited urchin was selling sugar cane to two pigtailed Annamese schoolgirls in pristine uniforms, and a wiry rickshaw coolie lay back to rest under the shade of his green-fringed hood. A *métisse* glided past in softly draping elegance, stepping deftly aside to avoid a ragged old peasant woman labouring beneath a heavy burden. The old woman bore a pole across her left shoulder from which swung twin baskets laden with fruit, leaving her right side free to drag a small child by the hand. They crossed to the other side of the street and she dropped her baskets on the *trottoir*, resting momentarily while the little boy relieved himself in the gutter. The *patron du café* called to her and waved them away, then turned to me to take my order for another corn-based 'coffee'. At the next table men in white linen suits were talking business, and opposite a group of three Annamese girls chatted animatedly in their soft, clicky, singsong tongue. One of them called to the *patron* and they paid for their lime juice before all piling, giggling, onto the same *pousse-pousse*.

It was easy to believe, if one were of a mind to, that all was well in Hanoi. The political situation, though far from ideal, had thus far not affected anyone too much. The Kempeitai were keeping a low enough profile among the average citizens, so there was barely a Japanese face to be seen.

From Hanoi it was hard to imagine the Imperial Japanese Army sweeping ruthlessly across Southeast Asia. To the northeast of us Hong Kong had fallen in an orgy of rape and drunken pillage. To the southwest the Japanese had stormed the Malay Peninsula, taking Singapore by mid-February 1942 in a battle for the island that had lasted but five days. The island had been hailed as impregnable, a bastion of the British Empire in the Far East. Now it was a scene of devastation and misery, pockmarked with great pits providing mass burials for thousands of dead.

While I soaked up the ambience of a street café in Hanoi, British civilians in Singapore were locked up in the stinking hellhole of Changi Prison. They would be there for three and a half long years. Among the Allied soldiers now prisoners of war at Changi Garrison, nearly 13 000 were destined to die of starvation and brutality as slave labourers of the Japanese military. And all over the island there had been mass executions of innocent Chinese civilians, for no other reason than that the Japanese considered the Chinese sworn enemies. From all this, the population of Indochina had been saved.

France was still the colonial power in Indochina. Around us the Japanese onslaught had crushed other European colonial governments one by one, until ours was the only one left in Asia. We lived an unreal existence, our military bound and toothless against the Japanese incursion. None of us liked it, but to the French in Hanoi this was no 'collaboration'. It was not even co-operation. Short of committing the military to a fight to the death and the general populace to brutality and imprisonment, as had happened in Nanking, it was accepted that Decoux had done what he could. We saw the agreement as a nonaggression pact under which the French administration, despite being under constant duress, gave the minimum of concessions. Indeed, over the next four years every effort was made to delay acting upon Japanese requests, and many if not most agreements were broken — not officially, not immediately, but eventually.

There was a frail façade of normality in Hanoi. Though much of the indigenous population seemed unaffected and were happy to live their lives without the complications of political affiliations, others had quickly seized upon the Japanese incursion as an opportunity to rebel. The first had occurred in 1940, just after our retreat down the railway line from Lang Son, when a group of Nationalists had marched into the frontier town with the intention of replacing the French administration. Another group had led the first Communist insurrection in Bac Son, while in the south of Indochina the Communist Party had begun to organise uprisings. The trouble had been swiftly dealt with by the administration. But then throughout 1941 the Sûreté, the tough, unforgiving French intelligence police, had run a campaign of arrest of suspected revolutionaries, executing about thirty of them. This had produced the spark that ignited the ready flames of Nationalism in student circles at the University of Hanoi.

Our position in Indochina was regrettable, unfortunate, but in the sanguinity of youth I grasped at anything that inspired hope for the future. There were some encouraging signs. During my university years, colonial policy in Tonkin was being completely overhauled, and salary differentials between French and Annamese doing the same work were abolished. More Annamese were being trained for higher positions in the administration, and between 1940 and 1944 the number of Annamese in the middle and upper echelons of government doubled. There were major advances in education, more Annamese teachers, more schools built.

Within the university a new science department and a whole new campus were opened and in the field of Annamese art and literature new prizes and subsidised painting salons were introduced. These changes were part of a belated endeavour to win Annamese support, and many initiatives came out of Decoux's new concept of an Indochinese Federation: a mutually beneficial organisation of all the peoples of Indochina, under which the different traditions were to be respected and encouraged.

The Youth and Sports Movement was a vast undertaking in which one million young Annamese were given the chance to develop a sense of discipline and leadership. In a nation that traditionally venerated old age rather than youth, it gave young people proof that they could make a positive contribution. But the Youth Movement would also become a hotbed of Nationalism, and the paramilitary training given by the French was to later give graduates a head start in the rankings of the revolutionary army of the Vietminh.

During the years of the Japanese occupation the French administration also undertook a huge program of public works. As well as miles of new roads, many impressive edifices were built in the city. This was a busy time for Les Grands Travaux d'Extrême Orient, and so far I had worked on two important government buildings, the Mint for the Banque de l'Indochine and the large four-storey National Library. Imports had long since ceased and as those goods dried up we had to learn to improvise. There was plenty of cement from

Haiphong, but every week there was something else that was no longer available. Steel was difficult to get and tiles impossible, so we used a lot of timber. We had done without petrol since mid-1941 and vehicles were now fuelled by rice alcohol. There was no more paint so we used locally made stuff concocted from a fish-oil base. It took a week to dry and smelled repulsive.

Then, from mid-1942, the United States began using China-based bombers to conduct air raids on Tonkin. The targets were ports, bridges, roads and railways. As the transport infrastructure was gradually destroyed, so too were our supply links from the north to the south. But though the bombings presented new difficulties, they struck hope into our hearts. The Americans were coming. The war would soon be over.

At first the news didn't mean much to me. I had never known anyone with cancer and I never for a moment believed that my mother would not get well again. It was March 1943 when she was first diagnosed. I was twenty-one years old and Maman was still my best friend in the world. Mothers didn't get sick and die. I could not even conceive of it.

There were multiple consultations. My father found the best available specialist, the top surgeon. My questions were met with vague, evasive answers; still I was sure she would get better. She had always been so strong, living her life trailing Papa across the world, settling so easily into remote and unfamiliar places. We had been in Indochina for six years now, well past the end of my father's tour of duty. There had been no talk of wanting to return to France when the war was over. Here in Hanoi Maman had found real happiness.

The months passed and Maman began to look very ill. She did not get better. Without warning my father announced that he would sell off our racing interests. I was shattered. I knew Papa would never have done such a thing if he thought Maman would recover. The races at Bagatelle were their life together in Hanoi. Maman adored the horses, the fashions, the society that came with being an integral part of the racing establishment. Now our beautiful horses were going, along with the stables and the staff and all that had been so much a part of our life here. I became alarmed. Suddenly I realised my mother was dying.

Months passed, cheerless and bleak. No one ever admitted it, but the cancer was inoperable. As I tried to carry on with my second-year studies, Maman became bedridden, needing constant attention and supervision. Her pain became unbearable and with every passing day the will to live and fight on was slipping away. I could see it in her eyes. Then one night I overheard her telling Papa she wanted to die, begging him to help her do it. Her agony ate into me.

In October 1943 she was admitted to Dr Patterson's private obstetrical and gynaecological clinic in the Boulevard Gambetta[5]. There, with the help of heavy doses of morphine, Maman regained some composure.

---

[5] Now Tran Hung Dao.

Seeing her feeling a little better filled me with hope. The pain was gone from her eyes and she seemed so peaceful now. I pinned my faith on a miracle. But there was no miracle. My mother was wilting, fading.

She had always loved and supported me and in her time of need I resolved that I would do the same for her. I was at the clinic as often as possible, sitting by her bed for hours, bringing in my textbooks just to be near her. I was there at my mother's bedside when we had the biggest air raid so far over Hanoi. From the window I glimpsed what must have been at least thirty US bombers roaring over the city. I wanted to rush outside to get a better look, but Maman was whimpering and I returned to her bedside to hold her hand.

As the bombers let loose their deadly cargo the noise was deafening. The huge onslaught was destined for the railway yards and depot at Gia-Lam, just over the river across Pont Doumer[6] 2 kilometres away. With the railway yards went the rail transport junction between north, south and east. Almost as a postscript, the Gia-Lam Airport was bombed, and for poor Maman, lying helpless and unable to move, it was terrifying.

She was not talking much now, but it was enough, I think, that she knew I was around. I missed our conversations. I'd had no brothers, no sisters to confide in. My relationship with my father was different, a more distant sort of man-to-man affair. The idea of Maman dying was frightening, and though I tried to prepare

[6] Now Long Bien Bridge.

myself, there was a sense of unreality about it. I could not stand seeing her lying there wasting away, her once handsome features scrawny and gaunt, her skin pale and sallow, her normally coiffed hair hanging in long, limp strands around her face.

Maman died on the morning of 14 December 1943, and I was not there. I had stopped at a café with a friend, and was later than usual. The thought that she may have tried to hang on to say goodbye overwhelmed me. The sun was shining through the window of her room and she looked at peace. Too late, I bent to kiss her.

That day an intense and smothering loneliness descended upon me. For all those years my mother had been the one constant in my life, my anchor, my refuge. Now she was gone, and nobody could understand the bottomless abyss of that.

Standing with my grim-faced father at her funeral, flanked by two sombre generals, I could not hold back my tears.

Weeks after Maman's death my life was still in a vacuum. Alongside me my father, too, was grieving, but his was a private affair. It was not something we could talk about. I had always related better to women, and felt the loss of being close to someone intensely.

On the verandah of that grand old house, I hesitated, my hand on the huge dragon's head of the brass knocker. Would Jo still remember me? It was so long ago, October 1939, four years since I had last visited, four years since I had indulged in opium's sweet liberation.

Unusually, it was Jo who opened the door. Time had not been kind to her; another four years of her heavy opium habit had etched themselves into the thickly painted canvas of her face. But her eyes were the same, and they lit up in recognition when she saw me.

'Michel,' she said in delight, 'where have you been all this time? I had thought you would never visit me again!' Then she looked at me, and — 'Come,' she said quickly. Without another word she guided me to the rear of the house, to her own private room, and sat down on the couch beside me. 'Tell me everything.'

After a while she took my hand and her unexpected touch meant the world to me.

I took the opium pipe she offered thankfully. It was a beautiful thing, fine silver filigree along its shaft, and I held its porcelain bowl to the flame of the oil lamp as Jo issued a few words of advice. In a few seconds I held the mouthpiece to my lips. There was no reticence this time. I was looking for escape and I drew the smoke deep into my lungs, finishing the pipe in one draw. Jo looked on in approval and handed me another. A deep calm began to permeate my body. For the first time in so many months the smothering veil of grief began to lift.

That night, in the sanctuary of Jo's den, the sadness eased from my shoulders. I felt comfortable, secure. Jo could not be there all the time, for she had business to attend to, but during my few hours in her company she seemed to know just what to say.

Later, as I was about to leave, she took both my hands in hers and said, 'My home is your home. You must come any time.' I was very thankful.

During Maman's illness we had moved to a small apartment over a haberdashery shop on the south side of the Rue Borgnis Desbordes[7], where we would be close to the clinic. It was not far to Jo's house and I found myself returning the next night, and the next. In our apartment I had a downstairs room with its own entrance, and with my father safely upstairs I was free to come and go. And so I continued to slip out quietly at nine each night, returning to bed for a four-hour stretch at around three in the morning. This became routine.

Using an alternative entrance at Jo's, I was able to enter and leave as I pleased. I did not understand why I had been granted this privilege, for arriving without an appointment was normally strictly forbidden. Discretion was guaranteed, and indeed so professionally did Jo run her premises that never during any of my visits did I see any of her clients.

I spent my time in the sanctuary of Jo's private den at the back of the house. I had no inclination to go upstairs again, but occasionally the younger girls, the working girls, would come and visit. They were gently spoken and kind, pleasant company. The first time Nguyet popped her head in I had a moment of embarrassment, for she teased me about not having visited her again, saying that I had not found her attractive. But it was

---

[7] Now Pho Trang Thi.

only a tease, a gentle one, and we became quite good friends.

In the refuge of Jo's house it was easy for clients to forget there was a war on. Imported goods had disappeared from the city, yet at Jo's there were still home-grown pleasures to be had. For this *Maîtresse de la Maison*, trade had never been better.

But for the rest of the population, the war was eating relentlessly into everyday life. There was no coffee and no wheat flour at all. Our bread was made from an unpalatable mixture of rice and cornflour. Had it not been for the innovative work of the Pasteur Institute there would have been no medicine, for even those imports had long since dried up. Inflation was rampant, with prices up 400 per cent. Some Chinese shopkeepers ran an efficient black market, but for the average Tonkinese the prices were way out of reach. Civilian vehicles had disappeared completely from the streets, except for the buses, which were kept running on charcoal. Even rice alcohol fuel was now rationed for use only by the military. There had been talk of heavy pilfering, since the Foreign Legionnaires discovered that at 98 per cent proof the fuel could be mixed to make all sorts of potent and inebriating drinks, and thousands of litres had disappeared from transport units and depots. When the High Command realised that it was difficult to find a Legionnaire standing to attention, it mixed a lethal poison into the rice alcohol and the party was over.

Perhaps because Jo was a *métisse* with contacts in the highest of circles, she heard things from all sides. I rarely tired of her conversation, except perhaps when she spoke of revolution. She had real concerns that the revolutionary movements, the pro-Chinese Dong Minh Hoi, the Communist-led Vietminh, the Nationalist VNQDD[8] and the pro-Japanese Phuc Quoc, were more active than I imagined. I dismissed her worries. From what I could see the middle classes were rallying to Decoux's reforms. She disagreed.

'The middle classes are the minority elite,' she told me. 'The real power is with the peasants because they are the masses. Once their strength is harnessed by the Nationalists or the Communists, there will be no stopping a full-scale revolution. They will be the ones who will decide the future of this country. You will see. Nothing is the same as it was.'

If Jo was right, I preferred not to dwell upon it. I didn't come to see her to hear prophecies of doom, and told her so. She laughed.

'You live in a world of your own, Michel. You choose not to see what displeases you. I can understand that. You are young. But when the time comes you must listen to the advice of your elders, particularly me! I shall see to it that you do.'

In my little world of silence and grief, of cold and fading flesh as Maman was dying, I had met a girl who had been a tonic of warmth and compassion, of rosy-cheeked vitality. Her name was Mireille Reynaud. The

---

[8] Viet Nam Quoc Dan Dang, the Vietnamese Nationalist Party.

eldest of three children, Mireille had recently finished her secondary education at the exclusive girls' school Les Oiseaux. Her family were planters, her grandfather having taken up a concession in Tonkin from the French government in the 1880s. She lived with her parents at Son Cot, their concession of 4000 acres of rice paddy fields nearly 80 kilometres northwest of Hanoi. Mireille was at Dr Patterson's clinic attending her mother, who was awaiting the birth of a fourth child. The baby was late and she had been there for days. Out of the circumstances in which we met, a certain intimacy developed. But when the baby was born and they had all suddenly left for home, it had seemed like a long way away.

I still hoped to see her again after Maman died. But Son Cot was 80 kilometres away, and despite the kindest words in her letters following my mother's death, it had not been enough.

Jo, though, always found time for me. Now, as the weeks passed, Jo had become my sounding board and advisor. So I confided in her about Mireille too, about my lingering affection for the girl I had met in the clinic waiting room. I did not see her often, I told Jo, for Mireille came to Hanoi only on shopping trips with her mother. Jo's response was ready and firm.

'I am very happy for you, Michel,' she said, 'but you must wait until this wretched war is over before you commit yourself to anyone.'

It sounded just the advice my mother would have given.

* * *

Over the many hours we spent together that year, Jo and I spoke of philosophy and poetry, of Confucianism and Buddhism, and the religious ways of the world. I told her about my childhood, the years in Morocco and Madagascar, about the loneliness and the turtles and my little donkey Bourico. We spoke of France, of Indochina and of the future and what we hoped it would be. Beneath Jo's sophisticated, brittle, intelligent exterior was a soft and deeply caring inner core. I was puzzled at her obvious affection for me, but never did I dare ask her the one question that turned and turned over in my mind — I was too afraid the wrong word would bring down the shutters on her soul. How, why, had she become the owner of a brothel?

It was Hong, the weathered old woman I had met on my first visit here four years ago, who gave me my answer. She had been with Jo for thirty years and had seen a lot of things. One night she was in her usual place, sitting unmovingly on top of the ebony couch, her betel-stained teeth just visible in the dim light. She was speaking to me of a time many years earlier, and of the young French officer with whom Jo was then desperately in love. For two and a half years they were together, said Hong, then when his tour of duty was over he ended the relationship and returned to France. Jo had been left behind in Hanoi with nothing but a baby son and a broken heart.

Alone in the world with little Jean-Jacques, Jo had found the oldest profession in the world the easiest way, perhaps the only way, to re-establish herself. She wanted great things for her little boy — a good education, university — and for that she needed money. But she was concerned about Jean-Jacques growing up in the unsuitable environment of her business. And so, for the time it took to put away a nest egg for him, she placed the child temporarily with foster parents in the countryside near Nam Dinh. There, she visited him often.

'She loved that little boy so much,' said Hong, 'and hated being away from him. But what could she do? He was happy enough in the country, and those people were good to him.'

But a cholera epidemic swept suddenly through the Nam Dinh region. The child became critically ill. Nothing could be done to save him, and Jean-Jacques died at the age of six.

Jo had been inconsolable, blaming herself for her child's death. She still carried the guilt, Hong said, and yearned for the love of the son she had lost.

'And you know, Michel,' Hong confided, 'Jean-Jacques would have been exactly your age now. I know Jo sees in you the son she would have had.'

It was March 1944 and I had a big year ahead. In third year of university I had been assigned to a new Public Works Department project of my own, the supervision of the building of the filtration and purification plant at Bac Mai, to supply potable drinking water to Hanoi and districts. It was a position of real responsibility. When that project was complete, I was to take up an assistant position on the construction of the new post office and telephone exchange in central Hanoi. This was my last year at university and final exams were set for early 1945. Despite this I was in Jo's *fumerie* until all hours, consuming about eight pipes a night. I had even begun to crave opium during the day. Over these few months I had, to some degree, become addicted. Now I had to stop this opium dependence and concentrate on my work.

As I had hoped, Jo was there to help me and promised to make it easier. She refused me any more opium and the concoction she brewed looked like stewed grasshoppers, tasted appalling and made me feel sick. I took it as instructed, twice a day, and reported to Jo every second day. And though it was an unpleasant business, it was not enduring, for my addiction was not yet heavy. I had my Cotabs, cigarettes made from a locally produced light tobacco tainted slightly with opium. It wasn't much, but it helped.

Within three weeks I was back to normal, both physically and emotionally. I was ready to get on with my life.

While I had been embroiled in my own problems, the cauldron of Indochina had simmered on with discontent. The demands of the Japanese military were slowly draining the country, and all the while the people of Tonkin were getting hungrier. On the surface the Japanese paid an agreed price for what they took. They opened an account in a bank in Japan in the name of the vendor, and theoretically paid what was owed in yen into that account. But since there was no way of getting the money out of Japan, and no opportunity to buy Japanese goods or transport them to Tonkin, the accounts were worthless. In reality the Japanese paid nothing. At the end of the war these bank accounts were frozen and the money lost.

From behind the closed doors of the Governor's Palace the diplomats from Tokyo continued their cat-and-mouse negotiations with the unco-operative Decoux administration, which was powerless to stem the outgoing tide of resources. A good stock of rice had always been kept in the government granaries, a reserve to feed the people in case of a bad season. Now the Japanese military were requisitioning rice from the reserve stockpile to feed their armies. The granaries were being emptied and a bad season was looming. Tonkin was in danger of starving. Those with money could still purchase the staples of life on the black market. Those without money were already finding it difficult.

News of the war in Europe was patchy, and details were hard to come by. Radio Hanoi was silent on the subject and there were few radios powerful enough to pick up the BBC World Service from Yunan or Calcutta. The government administration had contact with France, but to avoid reprisals from the Japanese did not publicly broadcast news of Allied successes. Still we knew that the Allies were getting the upper hand in Europe, and this did much to bolster the mood of the European community. The war in Europe was turning against the Germans, we'd heard, and the subject of French politics, almost taboo whilst the Germans were occupying France, suddenly became the popular topic of conversation. The talk was all of Charles de Gaulle and the Free French. Even the Vichyites became Gaullistes, out of prospect if not principle. Everyone had begun speaking of resistance from within Indochina.

Until now there had been little in the way of civilian resistance to the Japanese. There was a Free French resistance in Calcutta, supported by the British, and another over the border in Kunming, China. In Tonkin a few Frenchmen still risked their lives operating a radio intelligence network for the Allies. However the French made up only about 2 per cent of the population. We were isolated and had nothing to resist with, so a resistance movement anything like the scale of the one in France had been impossible. Little of practical value could be achieved until the British began air drops of arms in the countryside.

Now suddenly the mood changed. Even Governor Decoux, an ex-Vichyite, began to negotiate with de Gaulle. Soon General de Gaulle appointed General Mordant to lead both the civilian and military resistance and, to disguise Mordant's role, Decoux made him Vice-President of a new Council of Indochina.

At last the civilian resistance movement in Tonkin became an organised affair. My father had kept me up to date with these developments and now I jumped at the opportunity to be involved.

I became second in command of a civilian undercover group of platoon strength. It seemed somehow all the more exciting because of its covert, clandestine nature. Each of us was code-named. For my tall, lanky stature I became 'Charles' after *le grand* General de Gaulle, and our group commander was 'Bernard'. There was a strict code of communication. We were to have no contact, no knowledge or relations of any kind with any other resistance group. We were sworn to secrecy among the only resistance members we knew — our group. Only our group leaders had contact with the central command committee, which acted under direct orders from General Mordant. At least, that was the theory.

In practice the idea of resistance had caught on too well with the long-frustrated French civilians in Tonkin. Everywhere I went people were talking too much. We had been forcefully drilled that utmost secrecy was crucial to a resistance network, but among the civilian units there were some very careless and inexperienced men.

In August of 1944 the Allied forces stormed into Paris and set the tricolour flying again in the capital. France was liberated, free at last. From the deep recesses of a cupboard, my father produced a bottle of Veuve Clicquot that he had saved for the occasion. It was presented tenderly to our young *bep*, Cong, to be put on ice, and that night our small apartment was full of *bonhomie* and high humour. There was no dancing in the streets, but behind the closed doors of Hanoi's villas the ecstatic French were celebrating. The end of the war was near.

Eight

Crumbling Empires

Calcutta had advised an air drop scheduled for 0100 hours. In the dark, in a ditch that ran alongside a bomb-damaged and disused section of the southbound railway line, the whole platoon was present and ready. Eighteen of us had bicycled the 20 kilometres from Hanoi, staggering our departure times so as not to attract attention. All was quiet as we listened for the sound of an aircraft.

This was the stuff of the resistance movement, and I was revelling in it.

The drop zone was one of ten that we knew of, each a kilometre long and all mapped along the rail lines for easy identification from the air. The signal torches were in position, simple resin-impregnated linen affairs, fastened to the end of metre-long bamboo poles and set at 100-metre intervals. We'd had several such missions and we knew the drill. At the first distant drone of the aircraft engine we would light up the drop zone.

Within ten minutes of schedule the aeroplane loomed low out of the blackness and passed overhead in a reconnaissance run. It disappeared into the dark again, circling slowly, to return at 200 or 300 metres' altitude and disgorge from its rear the 50-kilogram canvas-wrapped bundles. Without parachutes they thudded one by one in rapid succession into the earth.

Snuffing the torch markers quickly, we recovered the cargo — twenty bundles of arms, ammunition, emergency rations and medication. The sealed ration boxes and some of the ammunition we buried beneath a nearby culvert for retrieval the next night, and we loaded the Stein light machine guns and whatever else we could onto the carrier frames of our bicycles, to take back to Hanoi. Every shred of evidence of the night's work was buried or concealed, including the excess packing and the torches that could be used again if need be, although it was rare to use the same drop zone twice.

Ahead lay a stealthy ride alone or in pairs, carrying the weapons back to 'safe houses' across the delta or in Hanoi. I rode alone and once more I was in luck. Pedalling quietly over the delta plain and through the outskirts of town with the weapons and supplies, I barely saw a soul. At my designated address in the French quarter I cached the cargo, where it would remain until the day it could be used.

We counted ourselves fortunate to be getting these drops, organised through the British Force 136 or the French working with them, from Central Air Command, Calcutta. Competition with the military resistance had been stiff. Under General Mordant, the military resistance was led by two other Generals, Alessandri and Sabattier. They were more experienced than we were, better organised, and barely tolerated our civilian outfits. It was an attitude that had already led to much ill feeling among some of the unruly, would-be partisans.

While the resistance movements gathered momentum, the Japanese were losing ground on almost every front and the mood in European circles was buoyant. To the west of us the British were driving the Japanese to the wall in Burma. To the east the remains of the Japanese Navy and Air Force were being pounded, as island after island was reconquered by the Americans as they advanced towards Japan. In the excitement of the time it was hard not to be swept away by the notion that the Americans were coming. The US troops were going to land with their armada of landing craft as they had done on the coast of North Africa, and the French Colonial Army, backed by our partisan resistance force, would mount a surprise attack on the Japanese rear. The Americans would fight their way inland and we would fight our way out to meet them. Together we would set Indochina free.

That was the dream, but the reality was to be far different. There would be no help for us from the United

States. President Roosevelt had already declared in the United States that he would do nothing in support of French resistance groups. Indeed, as part of his anti-colonial policy he had made it clear he wanted the French out of Indochina completely. It would have shattered our visions had we known of it.

So while the British Force 136 worked alongside our resistance movement, in the mountainous northwest region of Tonkin a group of American OSS[9], under Captain Archimedes Patti, was supporting another resistance movement. This Communist-inspired Vietnamese guerrilla group called itself the Vietminh, an abbreviation of Viet Nam Doc Lap Dong Minh Hoi, (League for the Independence of Vietnam), and it was led by the founder of the Indochinese Communist Party, Ho Chi Minh. In its determination to evict the French from Indochina, the United States was supplying and training the very guerrilla force it was later to spend ten tragic years fighting, in what would become known as the second Vietnam War.

Though we knew nothing of this, still perhaps we had good reason to be optimistic. The concessions made to the Japanese had left a bitter taste in our mouths, but French sovereignty over Indochina remained intact. Importantly, we still had an army, and the current reformist administration had done more for the people of Tonkin than any before it. Now we had a resistance movement and with it a real hope of being a part of a

---

[9] The Office of Strategic Services, the predecessor of the CIA.

glorious victory that would help to erase the lurking shame we felt at having been forced to kowtow to the Japanese. But in our enthusiasm we chose to ignore the fact that one vital ingredient in the success of a resistance movement was missing — the active support of the Annamese population.

As the war turned against Japan, we found ourselves bottled up with 50 000 angry Japanese soldiers who had been in transit through Indochina and now had nowhere to go. And yet I saw careless, foolish members of the civilian resistance flaunting orders and bringing arms, supplies, even parachute silk into Hanoi to show off to friends. It became a game of high spirits and one-upmanship played incautiously and with little thought to the fact that at stake were the lives of our compatriots. And between times they talked and talked.

From beneath straw coolie hats and cork *casques colonials*, eyes followed the khaki uniforms that up until now had been rarely seen in the streets of Hanoi. In the side alleys faces appeared warily at windows to peer down through long poles of washing suspended above the street. At the outdoor tables near the food stalls people looked up from their bowls of *pho* to nudge each other and whisper. Children stopped their street games and old men their conversations, to stare openly. The Japanese Imperial Army was making its presence felt.

The build-up of Japanese troops in Laos had been an early warning, and my father had seen Generals Sabattier and Alessandri move 2500 troops of the French military resistance out of Hanoi in response, dispersing them in the countryside in small contingents to reduce vulnerability in case of an attack. But up until now the regular army, and indeed the French administration, had been slow to react. For so long they had hung on to power, and been on almost constant alert throughout. The end of the war seemed so near.

Early on the 9th of March 1945, the High Command even downgraded the state of alert ordered upon the garrison. But then came the telegraph reports that large Japanese military convoys were converging upon Hanoi, and there was a sudden scramble to prepare the defence.

I was working in my room that evening when I heard the rumble of heavy vehicles in the street. It was about 9.30 p.m. and I took the stairs two at a time, almost colliding with Papa coming to call me.

A chilling procession of open army trucks, packed tightly with Japanese troops, was driving slowly and with lights extinguished along the street past our apartment. There must have been hundreds of vehicles, thousands of troops, heading towards the Citadel in a seemingly endless convoy. With rising alarm we stared, each of us doing mental calculations as to the chances of the defenders as they waited in the fortress, less than a kilometre away.

Just after 10 p.m. gunfire shattered the night. Blasts of artillery fire followed at short intervals, the windows rattled, and my little dog, Coquette, took refuge under the sideboard, whimpering in fright. I remained by the window, listening, my thoughts with the French and Annamese combatants. There was nothing we could do to help them. The uneasy truce between Japan and France was at an end.

Papa sat down at the table, his head in his hands. Between us we had many friends among the 2500 military in the Citadel, and he knew the garrison commander, Colonel Guyot, well. The Annamese fighting troops my father had commanded when we first arrived in 1936 were in the fortress, along with the maintenance unit he presently directed. With little experience in combat, his men would be fighting now. Frustration and helplessness engulfed us.

The night sky over Hanoi flickered with the glow of stray fire and the buildings resonated violently with the sounds of battle. On through the small hours the walls of our apartment shuddered with the deep boom of the 75 mm field guns, just inside the fortress. The stout wooden gates would be open and through the heavy iron grilles of each, the guns were firing anti-personnel shells at zero elevation. We sat listening, guessing at what was happening. Each time there was a lull we prayed that the Japanese had withdrawn, but they were collecting their dead and wounded and reforming with fresh troops to attack again and again.

Nearby the infantry regiment deployed along the perimeter of the Citadel was standing fast, repulsing the Japanese soldiers. It was difficult not to imagine those forces rolling in, teeming waves of resolute humanity, surging forward under covering fire from their rear, scrambling up the walls of the fortress, then picked off by the defenders, crashing back onto the aprons of the Citadel to be swallowed by another wave of suicidal troops. For them, death in the name of the Emperor was the highest of honours.

I wondered how long it would last. The Japanese troops would be taking severe losses, Papa said, but he was concerned for the French ammunition stocks.

Dawn broke over a city frozen in fear. There had been little respite. At around 8 a.m. our *bep*, Cong, appeared with the usual roasted corn 'coffee' and rice buns. We had little taste for either. Not long after, the field guns fell suddenly silent.

My father sat stock still, waiting. His face was ashen.

'If that's the last of the 75 mm ammunition,' he said grimly, 'it won't be long now.'

The small arms fire continued, but he knew that the loss of the field guns would see the Japanese try to broach the main gates of the fortress.

Our worst imaginings were indeed being played out in graphic reality. At the front line command post Colonel Guyot lay bloodied and dying. Around him in the mayhem many of his subordinates were dead, shot or bayoneted, while others struggled desperately in hand-to-hand combat.

Through the morning and into the afternoon, the soldiers in the Citadel continued the fight; then late in the afternoon, two thunderous explosions resounded over the top of the battle as the French blew up their fuel dump and equipment depot. Papa turned to me, his face pale, unshaven, appalled.

'It's over,' he said.

Breakfast the next morning was a sombre affair. A deathly silence had settled over Hanoi. In the city's old fortress over 200 Frenchmen lay dead, nearly 300 injured. The Citadel had fallen.

Papa and I were coming to terms with the fact that this could be the last time we would see each other. Papa had been ready at his usual hour. He ate at the dining-room table dressed in full military uniform, a black bag packed with essentials at his side. I knew he would go.

His was a non-combat unit quartered within the walls of the Citadel, and the survivors would now be interned. As an officer, his place was with his men.

When it was time to leave, Papa clasped my hand and shook it firmly.

'*Bonne chance*, Michel,' he said.

'*Et toi*, Papa.'

Then, without another word he turned, picked up his bag and walked out of the door.

From the window I saw him stride purposefully down the deserted street towards the Citadel. He did not look back, and as I watched him go it came to me suddenly how much, despite his brusque manner, he meant to me. Before he got as far as the corner he was surrounded by a Japanese patrol and marched away with a bayonet at his back. I was on my own.

* * *

An army vehicle cruised down our street, a Japanese soldier intoning through a loudspeaker, first in Annamese then in halting French.

'Hanoi is in a state of martial law. Everyone must remain inside. Tomorrow all arms, cameras or radios must be surrendered to the nearest Japanese post before curfew time of 6 p.m. Anyone found on the streets after that time will be shot.'

I stayed put for the day, but by the following morning I could wait no longer. Quietly I slipped out of the apartment in search of my unit leader. I made my way through the back streets, streets that were normally full of Annamese conducting business and gossiping, eating meals, performing ablutions, all with apparently little desire for privacy. Now it was so quiet it seemed not even the birds were singing. There was not a soul around, nobody. The emptiness was unnerving.

Like everyone else, 'Bernard' was home, but not at all pleased to see me.

'What are you doing here? Are you crazy?' he said as he shunted me quickly through his front door.

I had come, I told him, to see what he knew, to see where we would go from here.

'We are going nowhere for now,' he said. 'The Kempeitai are everywhere, rounding up all known or suspected civilian resistance members. If you want advice, you should lie very low, or better, get out of town completely.'

So I slipped home through the deserted streets, feeling eyes everywhere. I now realised how foolish I had been, that the Kempeitai would torture, probably kill any resistance members they captured.

I considered my position. Practically everyone I knew was connected either with the military or with the resistance. For the time being I could have safe contact with no one in Hanoi, and the idea of being cooped up with Cong, for any length of time did not appeal. I could think of only one alternative. I would go to Son Cot and seek shelter, at least temporarily, with Mireille's family.

Night fell. A rucksack on my back and dressed in dark clothing, I pushed my bicycle out into the empty street. At the end of the road a military truck rumbled past, and further on came the rhythmic footsteps of a Japanese patrol. I ducked behind an abandoned street stall, cursing my squeaking wheel.

On the outskirts of Hanoi dark figures dashed about here and there under the cover of night. In front of me was an 80-kilometre journey, out west through the paddy fields of the Red River Delta.

Pedalling out across the flat fertile plains I thought about the reception I might receive. I had begun to realise that if there was a group considering themselves the elite among the French in Indochina, it was the planters. They lived in a world apart, a little like the Mandarins, the governing class of learned men who ruled Vietnam before the French arrived and who had amassed great wealth through tax collection from the peasants who worked their land. The Mandarins, having eventually agreed to collaborate with the French, had been left in ownership of around 80 per cent of the arable land in Tonkin. Of the remaining 20 per cent, much was owned by the privileged French planters who had obtained concessions from the French government in the late 1800s.

Here in Tonkin the planters cultivated rice, not rubber, although in truth they did not cultivate anything. Like the Mandarins, they divided their land into plots of 5 to 10 acres, and local peasants did the work of cultivation and production. The planters were paid in rice, a percentage of the yearly crop.

In the colonial backwater of Indochina the planters were lords of all they surveyed. They lived the life of the landed gentry in England, the gentleman farmers of France. They were the aristocracy in European circles, masters of their own little kingdoms, and their wealth and property were sizeable. Planters such as the Reynauds were the real *colons*, mostly third-generation families who considered Indochina their country, their home. In contrast, many of the French in Indochina, including the administrators, were in the country for only a short tour of duty of around two and a half years. Some were very dedicated to advancing the interests of Indochina during their term in office. Many others, however, had little affinity for the country or its people and had come simply to advance their careers.

Mireille was born in Tonkin and spoke the native language fluently. Her family had everything: their own electricity, a beautiful house, expensive furniture, servants by the dozen. Mireille had lived her life in colonial privilege. It was all she had ever known. There was little doubt that I would not, now or probably ever, be able to keep her in the manner to which she was accustomed. But at the time it had been the last thing I was thinking about.

It was after two when I pedalled up the long driveway to the Reynauds' house. It stood before me dauntingly, a large, rambling French colonial homestead trimmed with a wide verandah, alone in bucolic isolation, moonlight bathing pale walls and washing over large, manicured gardens. I parked my bicycle against a palm and walked hesitantly up the stone steps to the front door. I did not expect to be well received anyway, let alone at this hour.

Indeed, Monsieur Reynaud was none too pleased to see me. But as a good Christian, and under the circumstances, he could not refuse me shelter. I was given a room and a bed, and felt safer and very thankful for it.

In the morning Mireille was delighted to find me at breakfast — but at the first opportunity she lamented that all was not well at Son Cot. Her father had been 'difficult' these last few days, she said, and everyone, from the family to the servants, was uneasy.

I soon realised that Son Cot was not the safe haven I had hoped it would be.

Apparently, the increasingly desperate Japanese Imperial Army had recently been requisitioning everything it could get its hands on. Roving groups of bandits, too, had lately caused trouble in the region. The Reynauds were in an invidious position, and feeling acutely vulnerable.

A few days after my arrival they decided to move to a neighbouring property. The Guillaumes were the oldest and wealthiest family of planters in the district. In this isolated existence it seemed only natural that, in a time of crisis, the families should join together for security and morale. No one knew what would happen next.

For the youngsters there was a time of illusory happiness, a time of excitement and laughter together with so many people in the Guillaumes' sprawling plantation house, Les Banians. Three families, including that of Charles Guillaume's younger brother, were now in residence.

With almost thirty Europeans, including the younger children, there were not enough beds, so we made our own. A dozen of us, aged from fifteen to twenty-three, slept together in a large room we dubbed 'the dungeon', our bed a mass of straw covered with sheets. We thought we had it made. Living all together like that, we could not help but forget the circumstances and enjoy ourselves.

For two weeks our evenings were filled with mahjong or cards, innocent fun, music from an old gramophone and late nights of talking and high spirits. During the days we lolled around or gambolled about the extensive grounds. Under the same roof as the girl with whom I was falling in love, I was supremely happy with my new situation, and did not think about what might happen tonight or tomorrow or next week. The setting was as wide and opulent as a *Gone with the Wind* extravaganza. Yet we were living the final act of a sumptuous production, before the curtain came down for the very last time.

The finale came on 27 March 1945, the day a small convoy of Japanese military vehicles rolled slowly up the long driveway to the house.

An officer of high rank and two juniors marched up the front steps to summon the three planters. Soon after, we watched the six of them stride across the yard, in the direction of the rice silos. Next, the planters were standing in the wake of the departing Japanese, each clutching a piece of white paper and speaking in urgent tones.

Though the Japanese had requisitioned every kilogram of rice held on all three concessions, a sense of relief washed over us all. At least the business had not been settled by rape and pillage, as it had been in Nanking. I remained optimistic. The requisition had been inevitable and the rice had gone to the Japanese. I considered the bigger picture. France was now free from the clutches of Germany — surely before the end of the year the war in the Far East would be over. The Japanese would be gone and there would be other crops.

But the respite lasted only three hours.

That afternoon a group of small, heavily armed men looking not unlike peasants arrived on foot in the grounds of the house. Our spirits plunged. These had to be what the provincial French called 'bandits' — in fact Vietminh guerrillas who claimed to have been resisting the Japanese — though up until now there had been few Japanese in northern Tonkin to resist. The most effective part of their organisation, apparently, was the propaganda network.

Like the Japanese, they had come to requisition the rice stocks. Unlike the Japanese, their approach was more conciliatory. The last harvest had been bad, they said. Rice was needed urgently to feed the people. The guerrillas were firm but polite and promised to return the following day with vehicles to empty the silos.

The planters were in an impossible position, caught between the Japanese and the Vietminh. Either group would turn nasty if it didn't get what it wanted. The situation was critical. That night there was an emergency meeting in the dining room. Life was of prime concern and the decision was made. Before dawn the next morning we would all leave for Hanoi.

It was a night of frantic preparation, the wives tearfully sorting through possessions in the house or that they had brought with them from their properties. Agonising decisions had to be made about what to take and what to leave behind. It should have been easy: there was little room in the vehicles for possessions — a few photos, the best jewellery, maybe a favourite ornament that could be tucked away in a suitcase, but that was all. Survival needs were the priority: food, clothing, medicine.

Faced with no such decisions — my bicycle would simply have to stay — I was called to the dining room. The three planters were alone there. They were discussing the dangerous journey to Hanoi. Between them they had an enormous amount of cash and to take it all would be to risk it all. The safe in the house would doubtless be ransacked and the only alternative was to hide a financial reserve on the property.

I did not know why I was asked to assist. Perhaps Monsieur Reynaud was not as confident about the future as he appeared. Perhaps he could foresee that one day, whether he approved or not, I would become a member of his family. Or maybe he sensed that he would never be going back to Son Cot, that tomorrow morning they would all be leaving their old life for ever: their land and beautiful grounds, the houses and a lifetime of furniture and contents, an armoury of handsome hunting guns and expensive antiques. All would be left behind for the taking. Perhaps he was already making plans to leave Indochina.

I had never seen so much money. How on earth could someone have so much money in the house? Wads and wads of 500-piastre notes lay in three separate areas on the dining-room table. Even taking into account the enormous number of servants and labourers on the payroll, it still seemed an extraordinary amount. I made a quick mental calculation. There would have to be a thousand notes here, half a million piastres, perhaps half a million dollars in today's currency. And that was just what they had in cash.

A dozen large glass jars appeared and into them we stuffed half of the wads, with an inventory note in each, and then sealed the jars with wax.

To keep them out of the way the servants were called to a meeting, while the rest of us slipped quietly out into the night. In silence we padded out across a moonlit field, perhaps half a kilometre, to a small wooded area. Lines of sight were taken on the house and a spot designated. I had the shovel and began to dig.

Behind me, voices were low, the mood bleak, sombre, prophetic. Perhaps the three men already knew that their lives would never be the same again, that this was the end of their era.

In the palest of dawns a quiet convoy of six cars, groaning with people and bulging suitcases, drove slowly away from the plantation house. In the back of the Reynauds' Fiat I sat squashed between Mireille and her two brothers. Taped to my body I had the equivalent of about $50 000, a share of the family's money to carry into Hanoi for them. No one said anything.

As we drove out of the front gate Mireille's mother turned to look back for the last time. She did not cry out loud, but the tears were falling steadily down her face, flowing onto the wide collar of her dress. Mireille leaned across me to take a last look herself. I squeezed her hand. It was the last time we saw the plantations. Nobody went back.

Nine

Under Mikado

The morning streets of Hanoi were almost devoid of Europeans. Here and there a white-suited figure dashed fleetingly and with head well down on some errand about town, but for the most part French civilians were keeping out of the way, hoping not to be noticed. The markets were open and though the crowds were a little thinner, for the Annamese it appeared almost business as usual.

It had been a tense journey and the Fiat pulled up quietly outside my apartment. I peeled the Reynauds' money from my body, and bade the family farewell. But I had no wish to leave them.

The dog was there to greet me as I opened the front door, joyous and hysterical. I was relieved to see she had been well looked after by Cong in my absence, but there was little else to welcome me. There was nowhere to go, nothing to do.

From a French point of view, Hanoi was at a standstill. The city was under martial law and there was a new curfew in place, from 6 p.m. until 6 a.m. The Japanese had taken over everything — the government buildings, the power generation plants, even the water filtration plant I'd been working on. Now there was no job to go to. Les Grands Travaux d'Extrême Orient had come to a grinding halt and every building project was abandoned. Most developments had been financed by the government, but now there was no government. Everyone in the administration, French or Annamese, was out of work.

In the Citadel where my father was, the number of imprisoned military personnel had doubled to around 5000. The newcomers were those fortunate enough to have been captured in the nearby Delta region and relocated to Hanoi. Others further out in the provincial capitals were in concentration camps run by small units of the Japanese Army, where incidents of brutality and cruelty were endemic. In other regions of Tonkin, mostly in the north between Cao Bang and Lang Son, the Japanese had taken no prisoners, military or civilian.

While I had been delighting in the sanctuary of Son Cot, there had been a bloodbath on the northern border. At the small forts lining the Chinese frontier entire garrisons of French and Annamese troops were massacred. The families of French nationals were rounded up by Japanese troops and executed like war criminals. At Ha Giang they used French women and children as shields to storm the fort, bayoneting them when they had served their purpose. At Fort Brière de l'Isle, when the garrison surrendered the entire company had been machine-gunned *en masse*.

My old stamping ground of Lang Son had met with tragedy yet again. Since 1940 when I was there, the fort had been restored and improved; and the garrison had put up the strongest defence against this second Japanese assault. But the garrison commander had been captured by the Japanese, and along with the civilian *Résident Supérieur* he was brought alongside the walls of the fort and asked to order a surrender. Both men refused to do so and were beheaded there and then.

Inside the fort, supplies were running low and the doomed garrison had only one hope: the fighter squadron of the 14th US Air Force — General Claire Chennault's 'Flying Tigers'. Based in Yunan, they were only 200 kilometres from the northern Indochina border. In the last month before the Japanese attack, liaison officers from the squadron had made contact with Sabattier's French Resistance forces, mapping supply drops and offering air support and assistance.

But unknown to the French, Chennault had since received strict orders from General Wedermeyer's headquarters: no arms, ammunition or supplies were to be provided to French troops under any circumstances.

In Lang Son the besieged French defenders called desperately for support from the Americans. The last radio message from Lang Son intercepted by Sabattier's French Resistance HQ was, 'Still holding three-quarters of Citadel. *No water*. Request air support and supply drops. Where are the Americans?'

No Americans came. Three days later the garrison was overrun by the Japanese. What followed was a massacre: the whole garrison, some 1500 to 2000 men, was slaughtered. There was but one survivor, left for dead in a bloody pile of tangled bodies.

Without American assistance the French military resistance forces fared no better, suffering appalling casualties. According to de Gaulle's memoirs, of the 12 000 French and Annamese troops who were not immediately slaughtered by the Japanese, 4200 were killed in combat during their difficult and circuitous retreat to China. A further 2000 perished slowly and painfully of sickness and starvation. As demoralised survivors left their dead comrades behind to rot on jungle tracks, they too were asking themselves, 'Where are the Americans?'

But with the war almost at an end, the anti-colonial President Roosevelt remained determined that the French should not return to their pre-war existence in Vietnam.

Meanwhile, the British did what they could for their French allies, travelling all the way from Calcutta, operating their transport planes at maximum range inside enemy territory, without fighter escort, and despite rebukes from the Americans about overstepping their theatre of operation. It was not enough.

Of all this we still knew nothing. In Hanoi the civilian population was trying to make the best of a difficult situation, but even the basics of survival — rice, fruit and vegetables — were getting harder to find, and prices were rapidly rising beyond the reach of the average citizen. Extravagant memories lingered, of stalls brimming with red-lacquered ducks, crispy webbed feet and glossy pigs' trotters, first-rate shark fins, bowls of semi-hatched eggs with apertures cut into the sides to advertise degree of incubation, and baskets of tiny, diaphanous baby octopus. With Japanese requisitions, food supplies in the city were becoming critically low.

The Annamese-language press, firmly under the scrutiny of the Kempeitai, had made much of the French using rice stocks to make fuel, and there were reports that extra rice stocks had been collected by the French in case of an Allied invasion. Nothing was mentioned in the newspapers about the Japanese requisitions, and the blame for the food shortage was placed squarely in the court of the French. Nationalist sentiment, it seemed, was being rallied by revolutionaries released from prison by the Japanese. Tonkin was fermenting with discontent and the mood in the hungry provinces was volatile. Without a real administration, anarchy broke out.

It was my second day back and Cong, despite having worked for us for five years, was being strangely distant with me. We had no telephone (few private residences did), and the prospect of our remaining cooped up for any length of time together looked grim. But at around two in the afternoon, the doorbell rang. Cong announced that it was Monsieur Heissler — George, my portly and somewhat extrovert friend from university was there on the doorstep!

'Heard you were back,' he said, cheerful as ever. He settled himself into the most comfortable chair. 'Thought you might be interested in what's been happening around town.'

In the three weeks since the coup on the 9th of March, he told me, the Kempeitai had been vigorously rounding up known or suspected civilian resistance members. Somewhere in the region of 450 had been arrested in the first week, most of them now imprisoned in Hanoi Central Prison (later branded the Hanoi Hilton by American POWs). Those suspected of higher rankings had been taken to Kempeitai headquarters at the former Shell Company building, a large five-storey complex in the Boulevard Gambetta. There were generous rewards being advertised for anyone denouncing activity prejudicial to Japanese security.

I wondered whether 'Bernard' had followed his own advice and got out of town as I had. But only much later could we know of the fate of those who'd been taken to HQ. They were to be locked in the infamous 'monkey cages', tiny bamboo cages not even high enough to stand up in. At regular intervals, day and night, they would be taken out for interrogation and tortured. Around forty of them would not survive the experience.

Now George told me that a proclamation had been posted all over town. All French citizens under the age of thirty must register immediately with the Kempeitai and obtain a 'clearance certificate'. That sounded like an ill-disguised ploy to root out people like me, and I didn't like the sound of it at all.

George lowered his voice to be out of earshot of Cong.

'Things seemed to have quietened a little,' he said, 'but I wouldn't be showing your face outside of these walls.'

I contemplated my position. For the duration of the war I would have to live with the immiscible cocktail of boredom and tension, not knowing if or when my name would come up in the torture chambers of the Japanese Kempeitai.

'It could be worse,' said George, who had always been too laid-back to consider joining the Resistance. Then, 'How about I organise a game of bridge here tonight?'

I was cheered by the prospect, and it was agreed.

George said he'd bring a couple of our friends with clearance certificates, and he left me to arrange refreshments: dinner and breakfast, sustenance for an all-night game until the curfew lifted in the morning.

While Cong went shopping I had a quiet afternoon nap.

Cong appeared on cue with a tray of drinks as we all settled around the table. He no longer bothered with drink orders, as there had been no imports into Indochina for four years and everyone drank the same thing. We called it 'paddy cassis soda', a concoction of brown rice alcohol, black currant liquor and soda. It was a warming brew, despite the ice.

Everyone had news, if not of themselves then of mutual acquaintances. Most of it was bad, but we were pleased to be together, and there was an underlying spirit of optimism: if we could make it through the next few months then the war would be over and the damned Japanese would get out of Indochina.

It was close to ten o'clock before I opened a pack of cards, and we settled to a serious game of rubber bridge, at 5 centimes a point to keep the bidding honest.

At a little after eleven the front door of the villa crashed open. Heavy boots came tramping through the entrance hall and up the stairs. The door to the apartment flew open — and a small Japanese sergeant strutted in, pistol drawn. He was flanked by six armed soldiers.

Had someone from my unit talked at Kempeitai HQ?

I glanced at Cong, who had withdrawn to the other doorway. His face said it all. I had been betrayed, sold out by my own *bep*.

I thought immediately of the gun in the desk. On the morning my father had left for the Citadel he had tossed a 9 mm Browning into the top right-hand drawer. Worse, on the top shelf on the back wall of the room was a briefcase my father had acquired, engraved in gold lettering, 'US Air Force'. It lay atop a pile of ten of my ordnance maps at 1/100 000 scale, which I had put high up and out of Cong's field of view. Marked in red and blue crayon were possible escape routes to China, safe houses and location of depots where arms and ammunition collected from air drops were buried or stored.

I dared not glance in the direction of the shelves. Perhaps their disorder would make the incriminating material less likely to attract attention.

The sergeant quickly identified the desk, strode over and wrenched open the top right-hand drawer. Seizing the pistol, he swung around to glare at me accusingly, and in broken French asked if it was mine. I shook my head and he lunged forward, smashing the butt of the pistol hard into my right cheek. I felt for my handkerchief to stem the blood and my little dog, Coquette, up until now maintaining a low profile under the dresser, flashed out from her hiding place.

In fury she leaped at the sergeant's face and sank her sharp teeth into his hand on the way down.

The air was thick with Japanese expletives. Bleeding, the sergeant pursued the dog around the room, trying to get a clear aim. In the fracas I contemplated bolting but the door was firmly blocked by three of the henchmen, now with arms drawn.

Coquette darted in every direction under the furniture, then, like a bolt of lighting, through the legs of a soldier at the door. She was gone. Faithful little Coquette. I never saw her again.

The sergeant was furious, and wanted revenge. He checked my guests and two of them quietly produced the correct papers and were gruffly motioned aside. George too produced some papers. But he waved them about, being unwisely voluble about having been cleared by the Japanese authority. In a temper the sergeant snatched the papers from his hand and tore them up. George was outraged — but was quickly calmed by a gun to the temple.

As for me, there was no point protesting. I didn't have any papers and the Japanese didn't even ask my name. One prod in the back and I was marching out the door, George right behind me.

At the crossroads where we should have turned left towards the central prison, we crossed the road instead and were frog-marched to the right. A few hundred metres and we were at the main police station on the corner, across from Le Petit Lac. The guard outside barely glanced sideways as we were shoved through the big carriage gate and across into the entrance of the building. A glimmer of a chance appeared.

These men who arrested us must be from the army, not the Kempeitai, which had a ruthless reputation. If Cong had reported us here, at the army-occupied police station instead of Kempeitai headquarters, perhaps the army would deal with us. It was the dimmest of hopes, the thinnest of straws.

In the bowels of the police station we were herded down a brightly lit corridor flanked on one side by a whitewashed brick wall, a row of small cells on the other. I barely noticed the inhabitants, watching glassy-eyed as we passed, for the stench of stale urine assaulted the senses, reaching deep into the nasal passages. At the last of the cells we stopped and a soldier released the bolt of the heavy, barred door and pushed us in.

The cell was tiny, a police lock-up designed to hold a man overnight, and we surveyed our accommodation in dismay. It was 6 feet wide by 6 feet long. Half of the floor space was taken up by a 6-by-3-feet concrete bunk, leaving the same area again as standing room. In the corner an open 50-litre drum took up more room. It was empty but far from immaculate and I assumed from the evidence clinging to its inside that it was to be our toilet. There was nowhere to wash.

I looked at George and his face was unnaturally bleak. It was me who had got him into this mess. There was nothing I could do for him but try to be good company.

It was quiet outside. We heard nothing from the other cells. Our cell was at the end of the corridor and nobody passed. We talked round and round in circles. We took turns at lying on that hard, narrow, concrete bench, trying every position. Then we just sat on it, backs to the cold wall, waiting for something to happen. But nothing happened. All that long night we waited, parched from perhaps one too many paddy cassis sodas, hungry for the evening meal that Cong had never brought.

Neither of us had a watch. Only cheap Japanese timepieces were available in Indochina and their reputation was so poor hardly anyone bothered to own one. But how I wished I had one now. It was impossible to tell whether it was day or night.

Finally, after what seemed way past breakfast time, there was a rumble at the top of the corridor. Something clanked at the adjoining cell and a soldier appeared, dragging a small trolley carrying an open-ended kerosene tin. It was filled with water, an empty tin can hooked on the side by a piece of wire. The guard filled the can and passed it to George's outstretched hand. There was a clunk as the can hit the bars and George tried to manoeuvre it through to his lips. It wouldn't fit. The guard spat something in Japanese and we realised we were expected to drink with our face pressed against the bars, holding the tin can outside.

The bars were cold against my face. I was very thirsty and slurped awkwardly, spilling water on the floor. It was enough to infuriate the guard and he struck me hard across the knuckles with his truncheon. The rough edge of the tin smashed into my lip and I dropped the precious can of water. Muttering, the guard picked up the tin and replaced it on the wire hook. There would be nothing more to drink for now.

George regarded me sympathetically.

'Okay,' he said. 'So what were you expecting, the Metropole?' My mood lightened. It could have been worse. George's sense of humour had remained so far intact, an attribute worth a great deal in the circumstances. Nothing could be said however, to ease our growing hunger.

An hour or two later the same guard returned with a basket. From it he picked two small balls of brown rice, one each, about the size of a lime, and wordlessly passed them through the bars to us. Again we carried out the ritual of watering from the can through the bars, and this time I did not spill a drop. The guard left and it was the last we saw of anyone for many hours. We could only assume the rice ball was a late breakfast, and hoped for something more substantial for dinner. Every moment I was expecting to be collected and transferred to Kempeitai headquarters.

Still no one came for us.

There was unlimited time to talk, a lot to talk about. George was a pharmacy student and before he'd dropped in I hadn't seen him for a month. He had a boyish charm and an active love life that never ceased to amaze me.

Between yarns I began to devise a Machiavellian plot to escape. There was a small equipment cache near Hoa Binh, southwest of Hanoi. If I could persuade the Japanese to send us with a small patrol to recover it we might have the opportunity to escape, or perhaps be rescued by a Resistance group.

George was unimpressed, and flatly refused to be a part of it. My position, however, was less happy than George's, and I was convinced of its merits.

The alternative, it seemed, was interrogation and

torture, probably a painful death. When the guard returned with what was probably the evening meal, I tried hard to communicate that I wished to speak with his commanding officer. He showed not a bit of interest, and probably did not understand a word; his expression did not change and I may as well have been conversing with the brick wall opposite.

After doling out another rice ball each, no bigger, no smaller than last time, he left.

Gnawing hunger set in. Another day passed, and another. Each time a guard appeared I tried in vain to speak with him, but there was no interest in us.

No one else came, and my plans to escape went nowhere.

It was just as well. The scheme would have immediately connected me to the Resistance and my request would have been channelled to the Kempeitai. The pile of compromising ordnance maps and the US Air Force briefcase in my apartment would have been discovered. At the time, however, I was convinced I would be tortured anyway.

The briefcase had been there since January. My father had been with a small party on a tour of inspection near Ninh Binh, south of Hanoi, when a US bomber crashed near the coast 20 kilometres east. Learning of the accident they had driven to the scene, to find the plane wrecked and all the crew dead. They had gathered anything they could find, including a set of mission orders, the flight plan, name tags from the bodies and a Colt .45 revolver with ammunition. They stored everything in the large leather briefcase and my father took it to Army Intelligence in Hanoi. Intelligence was interested only in the documents and the name tags. The Colt .45 my father had locked in a safe box at the Banque Franco-Chinoise. The briefcase on the shelf at home was empty.

In our fetid little cell we began to scratch a mark for each passing day on the wall. The corridor light was left burning constantly but we learned to distinguish day from night by the interval between rice balls. During the day the time between meals was shorter, perhaps six hours: between 11 a.m. and 5 p.m. The night interval was excruciatingly long, for the breakfast/lunch meal seemed to come so late. Determined to maintain some sort of regimen, we established an exercise routine to keep muscle tone. Two steps along, a little hop and a jump onto the concrete bunk, two steps on the spot, a jump down and two steps back again. We were like tigers in a tiny circus cage, except hungrier and with nothing to look at outside.

Within a week the shortage of food sapped us of energy and we could barely muster the resources to bend and stretch. We sank into a lethargic routine of cat-napping for short periods, talking or playing noughts and crosses with saliva on the smooth, grey concrete, then falling back into another fitful sleep. How I wished we had brought a pack of cards.

The door was never opened. Not once. At first George had hoped that the 50-litre oil drum in the corner might be our salvation. 'We'll soon fill that,' he'd declared. 'And then the little *salaud* will have to open the door to empty it.' His optimism had been shortlived. We only used it about three times in the first week for the only solid matter that reluctantly emerged, and after that only for urinating. Despite our best efforts, forlorn on a small amount of water per day, evaporation ensured the thing never got more than a quarter full.

By the end of the second week our stomachs had adjusted to being empty. We were still hungry but it was no longer painful. I gave up trying to communicate with the guards. I gave up any plans to escape. Boredom was killing us. On so few drinks a day, wasting saliva on games on the wall was not sustainable. George devised another amusement, competitive farting, with merit awards for loudest, longest and most melodious. I took up the challenge and after a few misfires improved my performance, with any worthwhile rendition punctuated by the shout, 'That one for the Mikado!' But I was no match for George. And despite his encouragement, my ambition waned.

We were by now crawling with lice. We itched unbearably, but at least scratching gave us something to do, kept us moving. We had adjusted to our hunger, our stink, our filth, or maybe we just didn't care any more.

After ten weeks we stopped marking the days on the wall. It just didn't seem to matter any longer. We were getting weaker and weaker. We gave up everything we had determined to do to survive. Another month went by, and another, but time meant nothing to us. We sat propped and dazed on the concrete bench staring at the wall opposite, no longer seeing each other, skin hanging from weary bones. We stopped scratching. Itching had become a state of being. We were in a stupor. I had ceased to wonder about our fate, ceased to think about dying. The Japanese could have unlocked the cell door and marched us off to a firing squad and I might have appreciated the gesture. But they didn't come for us.

Ten

Famine and Feast

There had never been two men before. I stared through the bars and tried to focus. Even that was difficult. For over five months I'd had little to focus upon besides George, who was not a pretty sight and hardly worth the effort. Through my state of torpor I heard the unfamiliar jangling of keys, and vaguely wondered if I was hallucinating.

This morning there was the usual guard, and with him the sergeant who had arrested us. I watched numbly as the door was unlocked for the first time since our incarceration. It swung open and the ill-humoured sergeant snapped something indistinguishable and waved us out. George got to his feet, too quickly, and fell dizzily against the bars. Taking it easier, I stood up slowly and made my stumbling way out of the cell. My knees buckled and my heart pumped painfully with the sudden exertion. Still giddy in the corridor, I was barely interested in our fate, but vaguely aware we were heading towards the front of the building, where I imagined the interrogation rooms to be.

It all happened very fast. The guard shoved me in the back and I lurched forward again as I was thrown off balance. A harsh and painful brightness seared my eyes and I covered my face, blinking behind my hands, confused and half imagining our interrogation under lights was beginning. The pushing continued and then suddenly there was nothing.

When I looked up there were no Kempeitai to be seen. The light was from the morning sun, the glorious morning sun. We had been pushed out of the courtyard and through the gates, and we were standing on the corner, looking across to Le Petit Lac in front of us. The Japanese had disappeared, and only George was standing there behind me, his huge smile disproportionately wide in his gaunt, scrawny face. He clapped me on the back, with more gusto than I thought necessary, and we fell into an ecstatic embrace.

'Let's go to my place,' I said, for it was only around the corner, a few hundred metres away, and we had no desire to walk far.

'It's so quiet,' George remarked. 'Where is everyone?'

I had noticed it too. Only a couple of Annamese walked past us and they gazed at us with dull eyes. We must have been a sight — unshaven, unwashed and unchanged for five months, unsteady on our legs, leaning on the wall of the building to regain some composure. I looked about in search of a *pousse-pousse*. There were none.

Like a couple of hopeless drunks, we worked our way along the wall and back past the heavy wooden barrier gates. It took a long time to reach the corner and we turned at last into Boulevard Borgnis Desbordes.

'*Mon Dieu!*' George gasped.

We stared down the road in disbelief. This had to be a nightmare. The street, which even at this early hour should have been bustling with people and oxcarts, cyclos and rickshaws, was deserted. In their stead were dead bodies, perhaps a dozen of them, scattered where they had dropped along the path between the corner and my apartment. Some appeared to have died in their sleep, others lay twisted in grotesque positions where they had fallen. All were Annamese. All were emaciated.

We passed close to one of them and I noticed a flicker of movement — a wasted old woman who had fallen awkwardly on the pavement in an impossible position. Between us we managed to arrange her limbs more comfortably and shuffled on as fast as we could, turning thankfully into the apartment building.

It was no homecoming. The entrance door to the building was missing and the door at the top of the stairs had been ripped from its hinges. The apartment was devastated. Everything was gone, our possessions, the furniture, even the shelves and light fittings. Electricity cables had been gouged from the walls and there was a gaping hole in the lounge-room floor where a couple of square metres of floorboards had been ripped out. The hand basin and taps had disappeared from the bathroom. The place had been stripped of everything that could conceivably be removed.

'Can you make it to my place?' George asked.

There was little alternative. Downstairs I poked my head into the little haberdashery shop at the front that had once done a steady trade. It too was ransacked. There was not so much as a button left.

Grimly, we set off along the street. At the next corner another wretched scene awaited us. Sprawled on both sides of the street were crumpled human forms, dead and dying of starvation. Dozens of them lay along the road in the few hundred metres we had to cover before turning into the avenue where the Heisslers lived. The only sign of life was a couple of young Annamese hauling a two-wheeled oxcart, crisscrossing from one side of the street to the other, with another two youngsters picking up bodies. The corpses were being thrown up onto the cart where they landed every which way, in a tangle of wasted arms and legs.

As we stood for a moment, appalled, one of the bodies showed a sign of life as it was moved. The boys propped the poor soul gently into a sitting position against a wall and continued on their way, the oxcart squeaking along the otherwise deathly silent street. As we passed the man I stole a look at his gaunt, wizened face with its glassy expression long past despair, his stick-like legs and arms poking from ragged clothes now many sizes too large for him. Tomorrow, I guessed, he would be heaved onto the oxcart with the others.

'*Merde*,' said George.

I said nothing. My throat had jammed shut.

We shambled on as best we might, stepping around the corpses rather than over them, and the sight of George's family's comfortable villa, front door intact and looking otherwise normal, was a great relief. The door was opened by George's sister who, ignoring his unsavoury condition, flung her arms around him, shrieking with such delight that his mother and father came running, to continue the rousing reception, shuffling us inside and thrice bolting the door.

Sandwiches and grilled corn coffee appeared, a feast to our eyes. We could do it little justice however, and ate daintily.

'You must eat ... *You must eat*,' his mother fussed. Over five months our stomachs had shrunk to nothing, and we could manage very little.

While we nibbled, we heard how the Heissler family had discovered that George was detained at the Number One Police Station. Every fortnight thereafter Nicole had delivered a parcel of goods to the station for her brother. The first parcel had contained a comb, toothbrush, toothpaste, soap, even shampoo, and then it was mostly food, purchased at great expense from the Chinese black market. Nothing had reached us. Although most of the little victualling extras were not part of the normal Japanese diet, no doubt the guards had appreciated them.

The ersatz coffee was bitter and strong and life-giving after months of dank-tasting water. We sipped at it gratefully while George outlined our past five months. I had met his parents several times before and they seemed pleased enough to see me again — but then, as the questions and answers tumbled out, I sensed resentment: it was through me, after all, George had got into trouble.

But we too were hungry to *know*. What had been happening in the outside world? Why had we been so suddenly and summarily released? Why was there such horror in the streets? Then we heard of the atomic bombs, and of the unconditional surrender of the Japanese. We heard some local news — of life under the Japanese; of how the French civilians were still keeping a very low profile, scarcely venturing out of their homes. And we heard how thousands of people had come to be dying in the streets.

The Imperial Japanese Army had commandeered every grain of reserve rice from the government granaries, grain which was always held aside as insurance against a bad season. As well, for several years the Japanese had required some rice planters to grow other commodities, such as jute and oil crops, and then since the Japanese coup there had been no French technicians to keep the dykes in the fertile Red River Delta in good repair. Now the latest rice harvest had been all but destroyed by floods.

As the starving peasants flocked from the provinces to the city hoping to find relief, the Japanese had released no rice to feed them. The most they had organised to manage the situation was the conscription of a few hundred youngsters to haul the oxcarts and pick up the day's corpses, and the digging of huge dumping pits on the outskirts of Hanoi. This great famine had been raging for four months, and hundreds of thousands of people had died of starvation.[10]

Madame Heissler was wringing her hands, saying that it was all too dreadful, that they felt helpless to do anything about it. They were all so short of food themselves, perhaps if there had been only hundreds they could have helped a little, but there were thousands out there in the streets ... There was an awkward silence, then she continued.

'But now that the war is over, *plais à Dieu*, things will sort themselves out. George, you smell appalling. You must have a bath. Come, *mon petit chou*.'

George was swept away by his doting female kin and I was left alone with Monsieur Heissler, twinging with envy that George had someone who cared. There was no mention of a bath for me.

Awkwardly, George's father and I spoke for a while. Then, when no one reappeared, he suggested that perhaps I should seek medical attention.

The two hospitals in Hanoi, the Général and the Militaire, he said, were still controlled by the Japanese, for their use exclusively. He knew that a group of Sisters of Charity were running a small hospital away from the centre of Hanoi in the former building of the Ministry of Tourism and Information.[11] Perhaps I could get in touch with them.

---

[10] There are no accurate figures, though estimates range from the French claim of 600 000 to the Vietnamese figure of 2 000 000.

[11] Now the Museum of Fine Arts.

I knew where it was — a couple of kilometres away, nearly opposite the Mint building on which I had worked in 1941. So, taking my leave of Monsieur Heissler, I headed yet again out into the hideous streets.

Pausing often and resting wherever there was somewhere to sit or lean, I felt my will more than the strength of my legs carrying me. Around the base of trees and along the walls of buildings the frail and dying seemed to have gathered in emaciated little groups, perhaps finding some comfort in their togetherness. Once an old Annamese, or perhaps he was no older than myself, staggered sideways as he approached and fell heavily against me, his hands, strangely strong, grabbing my arms. For a frightening moment I thought we would both go down, never to get up, that we would succumb together to the same grotesque fate as the wretched corpses on the pavements. But then a small spark of determination flickered suddenly in his dull, grey eyes and he loosened his grip and lurched away.

It was a slow, painful journey, and it took the rest of the afternoon before I glimpsed the high wrought-iron fence I was seeking. Mustering the very last of my strength, I made my way slowly up the road and passed through the heavy grille of the carriage gate, slightly ajar, and then through a relatively well-kept garden, to a colonnaded porch. The idea of being turned away was frightening.

A sister in immaculate white robes and cornet appeared, and looked me up and down. I began my story but she put up a hand to stop me. She led me inside to a door under a staircase on which a sign read, 'Mother Superior'. There, in a small office, an elderly lady sat at her desk, her blue eyes brimming with kindness. For the second time I began my story. Again I did not get far. She stood up, her face radiating compassion.

'Come,' she said.

That morning I had woken to a living hell. The sun was setting on the very same day and it was as though I had ascended to heaven, where gentle figures in flowing robes fulfilled my every need. They scrubbed me, deloused me, attended to every bruise and sore on my emaciated body, then encased me in pyjamas smelling delicately of soap. They weighed me — 45 kilograms — and brought a small, fragrant bowl of rice and vegetables, before tucking me into a soft, crisp bed on the second floor, in a private room.

I lay a long time before sleeping, pondering again the extraordinary good fortune I'd had in being taken to the police station instead of to Kempeitai headquarters, trying to come to grips with the fact that it was over, that I was alive, that I was free. That I had lost every material thing I owned, that I had nothing but the threadbare clothes I had worn in prison — these things seemed of little consequence.

During my imprisonment I had not thought a lot about the Japanese. They were the enemy in a time of war. Except for the men who had arrested me and the cell guards, I'd barely had any personal contact with

Japan's countrymen. Now, consumed by the grim spectre of the famine and Tonkin's emaciated and dying population, I was overcome by a sudden loathing for the Japanese because they had let it happen.

For me, 16 August 1945 was a momentous day, and as millions of people across the world still celebrated, I wrestled with the pillow, the sheet, the blanket, until the early hours of the morning. I was physically exhausted and emotionally drained, wondering at what a difference a day made, at what it meant to be French instead of Annamese, and haunted by the tortured faces of the poor, desolate souls on the streets of Hanoi.

The early afternoon sun filtered through the leaves of the banyan tree, dappling the grass with rippled shades of green. Two sisters strolled across the lawn, heads bowed in deep discussion, while a small bird grappled with a determined earthworm near the bench on which I rested. I watched the bird hop about, happy that it too had found sanctuary in this place. Even the wildlife had suffered terribly in the famine, as every edible creature was hunted down for food. This haven from the troubles of the world had been my home for several days now, and already I felt the strength returning to my bones.

Outside the sturdy iron gates, in this peaceful corner of Hanoi all was quiet. The French civilians were still lying low and the Japanese seemed to have disappeared from the streets. No doubt everyone was wondering how long it would take for the Allied forces to arrive. I expected the French Army would soon be released from imprisonment in the Citadel — to facilitate a smooth transition back to peacetime — and desperately hoped my father had survived his ordeal. It would be good to see him again. Despite the charity I was receiving, I had never felt so alone in the world as I did now. I leaned back in my chair, absorbing the warmth of the day, trying to still my worries.

Somewhere in the distance cymbals were clashing, and there was an unlikely booming of gongs and drums. Curious, I strained my ears to listen. The commotion grew louder and I moved carefully over to the wrought-iron fence, craning my neck to look down the street. For a while there was nothing — then the clamour increased suddenly and a large, ragtag procession of people came into view. With a huge chorus of singing and shouting, they moved *en masse* down the boulevard, gesticulating and dancing wildly, their songs clearly revolutionary, nationalistic, anti-French as far as I could gather. They did not look like soldiers, for they were dressed mostly in clothing typical of the rural people, brown cotton pants and tunics. They passed the gate between eight and twelve abreast, waving hundreds of bright red flags, each adorned with the big yellow, five-pointed star that was the insignia of the Vietminh. Among them they carried an assortment of military weapons, including Thompson tommyguns and others of American origin. Where had these come from? How was it that the Vietminh were equipped with such modern weaponry?

The column passed for a good half-hour, I thought, though I had no watch, and perhaps there were 3000 of them.

These soldiers, it turned out, were the bulk of the Vietminh, many of whom must have crossed the border from Chinese territory in December 1944 under the command of my old history teacher, Vo Nguyen Giap.

* * *

I had now lived in Indochina for over eight years. For me they had been impressionable, formative years, years in which I had developed a deep, indefinable love for the country. Indochina had cast a potent spell on me and I was imbued with a passionate desire to hold onto my life in Tonkin, even though I knew in my heart that the country did not belong to me. They were years in which I had turned from a cosseted boy into a grown man who had already experienced more of what life could dish out than I would wish upon anyone. Deep inside me the turmoil had never abated. Perhaps because I had largely grown up in the colonies, I lacked the confidence I saw in other Frenchmen about who I was and what my place was in this world. It was as though I was a *métis* like Jo, half French, half something else, neither one thing nor another, never really feeling as though I fitted completely.

I loved the French way of life in Tonkin. For me however it was the spice of the Annamese that set such an interesting, colourful backdrop to the everyday. Their aesthetics intrigued me, the way their ancient culture afforded prestige to poets and philosophers. I admired their natural inclination towards harmony with the environment, their arranged excursions in the season to admire flowering trees, or moonlight upon a lily-filled lake. I could not help but sympathise with their position, for they had been fighting for their independence for a thousand years.

But things were changing. Though for the most part their polite grace remained intact, it had become more and more difficult to get close to them. Part of it was plain loss of faith and resentment over the Japanese occupation. But as the Nationalist movement had grown in strength, it too had sent powerful messages coursing through the Annamese community. The myth of French invulnerability was dead.

I had noticed it first at university, then it became apparent even with our house staff. I had always believed we treated our servants well. Certainly most French did not treat their servants as individuals, but in comparison they treated them far better than did the Chinese and wealthy Annamese. Cong had started off as my mother's rickshaw boy and had risen to a good position in the household. We had always got along well. Still, his betrayal had come as no real surprise to me.

When the vicious repression of Communists began, just after I joined the army, both *Professeur* Giap and the Bernards, the other Communist teachers at my school, had no choice but to get out of Indochina. Before he left, Giap had spent a short time in the Hanoi Library boning up on the rudiments of weaponry and revolutionary tactics, then he had fled Hanoi for the border. He left behind his wife and infant daughter.

The news some time later that she had been arrested and convicted of conspiracy against the security of France came to me first through an old classmate working in Sûreté intelligence. I never heard that she died in Hao Lo Prison, but that she did is now recorded in history. There are varying accounts of the way she died, but whether it was through torture, suicide or natural causes, it was a tragic event that would only have fuelled Giap's determination. It was to prove a disaster for the French, for Vo Nguyen Giap, animated and likeable teacher of French history, also found in himself a brilliant genius for military organisation and guerrilla warfare.

I had met Madame Giap, and the news of her arrest grieved me and left yet another open wound in my patriotism. I could not help but be disappointed and concerned that the past policies of the governments in France towards Indochina had been so largely directed at trading and defence. Certainly my forebears had, in seventy-five years, developed the country with roads and railways, avenues and beautiful buildings, improved hygiene and sanitation in the towns and done marvellous work researching and vaccinating against tropical diseases. The population had doubled since the arrival of the French and food production had soared through extensive drainage and irrigation and improvements in the old dyke systems. But still the French had been slow to alleviate the plight of the lower class of Annamese, particularly the *dan que*, the peasants. For them they had, as yet, done little.

The educated Annamese could do very well, and did, but there was little that the landless poor could do to get out of the hole they were in. As they had been for centuries, they were doomed to a life of labour, squeezed by the people above them, who were squeezed by the French or the Indochinese Mandarins and the influential class. The Catholic Church was there to preach God and love, and though on a spiritual level they were successful in some areas, from what I saw on a practical level they did little of substance to help the Annamese.

While we French were embroiled in our own problems over the years of the Japanese occupation, revolutionary fervour had been building. Though I knew a little of what was taking place in the Nationalist movement, as I sat there in the sisters' garden I was not yet aware of the magnitude of the change. Communists, such as *Professeur* Giap, who had fled Hanoi during the war years had found sanctuary in southern China and the border region of Tonkin. Vo Nguyen Giap had spent his time in China studying revolutionary tactics, and his power to galvanise interest, to engage people, was about to become one of his greatest assets.

Giap had returned to northern Tonkin a prominent member of the Vietminh. At the end of 1944 he had begun an urgent recruitment drive from the remote Chinese border region, in command of the Vietnam Liberation Army's first unit, the Armed Propaganda Brigade. Then, by April of 1945, he had become head of the Vietnam Liberation Army. His propaganda agents were working the Delta region during the famine: 'It is the French who are to blame for your hunger,' they cried. 'Victory is approaching, and soon the Vietminh will liberate you and form a new democratic government.'

The Japanese coup in Hanoi in March 1945 played perfectly into the hands of the Vietminh. Intelligence provided to the United States by the French Resistance dried up, leaving the Vietminh network the only source of information. The Vietminh's Communist leader, Ho Chi Minh, was well aware of President Roosevelt's anti-colonial attitude, and had everything to gain from helping the United States against the Japanese. There were very few Japanese in the northern region where the Vietminh operated, and it was easy for them to walk in and claim it as a 'liberated zone'. The relationship with the Americans was then built on providing intelligence and assisting downed American pilots out of Tonkin. In return the Americans supplied the Vietminh with the arms they so urgently needed.

Wherever they went the Vietminh identified themselves as part of the Allied cause, and the US weapons — like the ones they'd just carried past our gate — lent weight to their claim. For the starving masses who had suffered so terribly under the Japanese, the Vietminh represented hope for a brighter future.

The war had ended abruptly, on the 15th of August 1945, after the two atomic bombs were dropped by the United States Air Force on Japan, devastating the cities of Hiroshima and Nagasaki. In Tonkin no one was quite ready for it, not the Vietminh nor other anti-French groups like the Dong Minh Hoi[12]. But while the Dong Minh Hoi was still in China preparing itself, the Vietminh was already on the ground in Tonkin. Ho Chi Minh and Vo Nguyen Giap went into action. They knew they would have to perform a great illusion, convince the people that they had played a real part in defeating the Japanese, that this was their victory. They had to make themselves appear far larger, stronger and more ready to govern than they really were. And they had to convince not only the people of Indochina but also the government of the United States.

As I watched the revolutionaries through the bars of the fence that day, the passion I saw in their faces disturbed me. They looked like a people who would never give up their fight for independence, no matter the outcome of their current revolution. In my heart I hoped the French government sensed that too, and used this crisis to negotiate some sort of autonomy for the Vietnamese. There was no doubt in my mind that the time had come for real change.

Yet it would have been difficult to believe then that this fledgling army dancing past in the street, these ragtag guerrilla units built by my old history teacher, would grow under his leadership to prove invincible — one of the most passionate, the most determined armies in history.

---

[12] Viet Nam Cach Menh Dong Minh Hoi (Viet Nam Revolutionary League), a more moderate coalition moulded by the Chinese government, with which the Vietminh was at first affiliated.

Eleven

Revolution

It was hard to believe there was a revolution going on. In the heat of the afternoon, cocooned from the world in my pleasant second-storey room, I gazed out through the lush green treetops from my seat by the window. A small corner of an old terracotta-tiled roof peeped out from the foliage behind the hospital, and from the garden of the house shrieks of laughter from small children gave a comforting impression of peace and normality.

The sisters had little information of the outside world, but I appreciated their calm reassurance. I had been worrying about Papa, about what had happened within the walls of the Citadel over the last few months. Had there been beatings, brutality, starvation? Mireille, too, had been in my thoughts. Had she come to any harm?

Or was she worrying about me too? And Jo, poor dear Jo. What had become of her? Her house beneath the walls of the Citadel had been in the direct line of the Japanese attack.

It had been ten days since my release from the Japanese and under a strictly controlled weight-gain diet my strength was returning. I had been out already, just once, an arduous walk about a kilometre to the northeast wall of the fortress to see that Jo's gracious, rambling old house was now just a black, charred shell. Please God let her have survived.

If only Jo was still alive and I could find her, I felt somehow I could get news of my father. Jo's network was remarkable. I suspected she worked for French intelligence, though she never told me so and I never asked about it. Tomorrow, I thought, I will go to town.

The body cart must have already been through the next morning, for the streets were clear of corpses. Everywhere emaciated figures begged for food, but somehow their plight was less palpable, for there were more people around now. Some, the wealthier Annamese, looked as though the famine had hardly touched them. There were still few white faces about. Red flags emblazoned with the five-pointed gold star of the Vietminh were everywhere. Posters and banners adorned the buildings, written in several languages, none of them French. Their message was clear: 'Welcome Allies — Peace is Here' ... 'Independence for Vietnam' ... 'Vietnam for the Vietnamese' ... 'Out with French Imperialists'. There was a sense of expectation in the air, as though everyone was waiting for something to happen.

Incredibly, a few rickshaws had reappeared on the streets, though customers were scarce. Mother Superior had loaned me some money and I hailed a rickety *pousse-pousse* from the sidewalk. I asked the driver if he knew what had happened to Jo. He didn't, but, rickshaw coolies being reliable sources of information, I made certain he knew where to find me if he heard anything. I was accustomed to rickshaw coolies being thin and wiry, but sitting on this squeaking seat I tried to avoid the sight of the ghastly protruding ribs, the matchstick legs half-jogging along in front of me.

I had given him directions to Mireille's parents' house and, once there, I climbed thankfully down and tipped him handsomely.

Mireille opened the door!

Her pretty face lit up with pleasure. We had not seen each other for six months, and as she fluttered about me her distress at my pallor and thinness was satisfying. She wanted to know everything at once, but I barely had time to get a word in before her parents appeared. I had hoped they might be at least mildly pleased to see me, but they stood, coldly polite, supervising our conversation, so that our joy at seeing each other again was muted.

Gone was the intimacy I had felt with the Reynauds the night we escaped the plantations together, the night I felt at one with them as I watched their heartbreak at leaving behind, perhaps for ever, the life they had known.

That night I had felt accepted, one of the family. Now I sensed it was as before. They did not consider me suited to their daughter and they did not mind me knowing it. I was offered neither a meal nor a drink, and my visit was brief. I left the house disconsolate and disappointed.

Two days passed before the rickshaw coolie appeared at the hospital, asking for me.

It was only a short jog, perhaps half a kilometre, to the comfortable middle-class district where we stopped in front of an unpretentious two-storey house. I knocked on the door and it soon opened slightly, and a wizened Annamese face peered suspiciously through the gap. I could not contain my delight at seeing that it was Hong, and as her face illuminated in surprise I put my finger across her purple lips to stop her exclamation. I turned to the rickshaw coolie and thanked him. His eyes shone as I counted out the reward I had promised, the last of the money Mother Superior had lent me.

In a dimly lit room at the back of the house, Jo was sitting straight-backed, as I had seen her so often, on an intricately carved wooden day-bed. I entered quietly and she turned to look, and in an instant had leaped up, opening her arms wide and throwing them around me. I laughed as in her excitement she dropped to her knees, and staggered a little as she hugged my legs. I pulled her up again into my arms while Hong clucked around us. Here at last was a real welcome.

Holding me by the shoulders Jo stood back, tears in her eyes, and took a long look at me.

'Where have you been, Michel? When I saw your apartment ransacked I was sure you were dead.' Hong was pinching my ribs through my shirt with her hard little fingers.

'Too thin, too thin,' she growled. 'I get you something to eat,' and she shuffled off muttering happily to herself.

I felt suddenly guilty about Jo, that in the few months before my imprisonment I had been so busy with my work, studies and the resistance business that time had slipped by and I had not been to see her. Perhaps, too, I had avoided her because it made it that much easier to avoid the allure of opium.

Now I sat close beside her and the story of my imprisonment spilled out.

'How lucky you are,' Jo said when I had finished. 'So many have gone.'

'And you,' I replied. 'Your house is destroyed. How did you survive the Japanese attack?'

She laughed. 'It pays to have friends in high places.'

She mentioned no names but I gathered they had been warned of the attack at the last minute, by an officer of General Alessandri's Intelligence Section. Jo and the girls had fled the grand old house, her home of twenty years, leaving behind most of its fine furniture and ornaments. This house was one of half a dozen Jo owned in Hanoi, and she was easily able to accommodate her staff. But like most of the community they had been lying low, and since the Japanese coup she had been closed for business to all but a chosen few. All the more remarkable then that these friends of hers still kept her so well informed.

The Allies had split responsibility for Indochina at the 16th parallel, she told me. The British had been given the south and were landing their own forces there. Here in the north the United States was responsible, and a small delegation of Americans was already in town. They had arrived a few days ago and set up headquarters in the Hotel Metropole. She had also heard that a French military mission headed by Jean Sainteny had arrived on the same flight from Kunming. Sainteny and his entourage of French negotiators had been met by angry demonstrators outside the hotel and the Japanese had removed them 'for their own safety' to the isolation of the Governor's Palace. Japanese soldiers still guarded the gates and grounds, and nobody had seen or heard of the French delegation since.

I asked her why, if the Americans were there, they still hadn't released the French Army from prison. The streets were awash with Vietminh soldiers stirring up trouble and surely order had to be restored quickly.

'It's not as straightforward as you think,' she said quietly, kindly. There was a lot I still did not understand. 'I don't think the Americans see it quite like we do. I think they would be very happy if the French never returned to power in Indochina, and indeed it wouldn't surprise me to see them actively supporting independence for the country.'

That I could understand, for I had similar sentiments. But did they really want to see independence that way, by handing the country to the Vietminh? I was surprised. Fundamentally the Vietminh was a Communist organisation.

Ho Chi Minh had been actively playing *down* the Communist element, Jo said — he had been trying to impress both the Annamese Nationalists and the Americans. Also, Chiang Kai-shek's Nationalist army was on the way to oversee the Japanese surrender and maintain law and order.

'The Chinese!' I blurted out. 'But the Annamese hate the Chinese!' For a thousand years the Annamese had fought the Chinese. Surely they would have preferred the French to the Chinese.

'It is not easy to understand,' Jo said quietly. She bowed her head and her heavily made-up face was profoundly sad. 'There are difficult times ahead, Michel, for all of us. I don't think anything will be quite the same again. I want you to realise that.' She paused for a long moment, and then looked up, her black eyes glistening. 'No matter what happens I want you to promise you'll be careful and that you'll always keep in touch. For now, if your father is still alive I can possibly make contact with him, but don't expect to see him too soon. That way, if he is released in the next few days you can be pleasantly surprised. If not, then you know the situation.'

I gave Jo a note for my father as I left. I did not ask how she could possibly contact him, but I called in on her every afternoon to see if there was any news.

A week later she had a reply for me. I tried not to snatch at the paper as I recognised Papa's handwriting.

For a few moments my eyes gulped greedily at the words on the page, taking in at first bite the vital information that he was alive and well and hoping to be reunited with me shortly. It was an immense relief, and reminded me again of how afraid I was of being alone in the world.

When I left Jo's house it was as if a great weight had been lifted from my shoulders.

Jo was right about the Americans in Hanoi. Roughly eighty arrived in those first few weeks, and took up residence in the Hotel Metropole. In command was a Major Archimedes Patti of the OSS, the Office of Strategic Services, and he and his entourage soon proved to be openly anti-French. Refusing an audience with a delegation of high-ranking French administrators, Major Patti gave a similar frosty reception to a party of three French generals escorted from the Citadel by a Japanese patrol. The officers returned to imprisonment disappointed and humiliated.

Politically the French were out of the picture. A French government representative had parachuted in and been captured by the Vietminh, and Jean Sainteny and his delegation were under the equivalent of house arrest at the Governor's Palace. The Americans invited the Vietminh and even members of the Japanese High Command to some of their meetings. But not a single Frenchman was allowed to contribute.

Indochina was in a political vacuum. Since the coup in March the Japanese had installed a puppet regime under the Vietnamese Emperor, Bao Dai. This government, made up of politically inexperienced middle-class intellectuals, had been able to achieve little under the Japanese. They had broken the ties with France and changed the name of the country back to its original designation of Vietnam. They had also declared independence, but since the Japanese effectively remained in control, the declaration meant little.

The Japanese were now in no position to force the issue of to whom they would pass control. They would have much preferred to see power in Vietnam pass into the hands of a pro-Japanese nationalist group, but it was the Vietminh that was there on the spot. The French military remained incarcerated and the pro-Chinese Dong Minh Hoi was still in China. No other organised independent group was present in Hanoi to offer any opposition to the Vietminh. It was an exceptional opportunity, and already Ho Chi Minh had sent a delegation to Hue to receive the Emperor's abdication. The puppet government had collapsed.

In a small house in the old quarter, Ho Chi Minh had set up his headquarters. Pale and unwell, he had been hard at work on a dining-room table behind a portable Olivetti typewriter. At his side for inspiration were a copy of the American Declaration of Independence and the Atlantic Charter of 1941, and he had been poring over every word he had written. This would be the most important speech of his life, the speech he must have always dreamed of making. No longer would the people of Tonkin be known as Annamese. The country through to Cochinchina would be unified: once again Vietnam would be peopled by the Vietnamese, governed by the Vietnamese.

Ho Chi Minh had set 2 September 1945 to make his historic declaration. I was out on the streets on that sunny Sunday morning, and Hanoi was in a festive mood. Houses and trees were being festooned in red bunting and everywhere red flags fluttered. Great red banners streaked with nationalistic slogans were strung across the boulevards, with not a mention of Communist ideals. There was a little piece of history to be made today, and the Vietminh, still struggling to look bigger and more organised than they were, craved a huge audience. The youth propaganda squads had been out into the rural villages ushering the peasants into the city to witness the historic moment, and the ethnic residents of Hanoi were turning out in force to hear what Ho Chi Minh had to say.

I hurried back to the hospital to fetch Mother Superior's camera, returning in mid-afternoon. Never before had I witnessed such a crowd. Ba Dinh Square, the grassy esplanade in front of the Governor's Palace, was packed with perhaps 100 000 expectant people. The atmosphere was of Vietnamese unity, a gathering by the Vietnamese for the Vietnamese.

In front of the palace Ho Chi Minh climbed carefully onto the wooden podium. He looked thin and was dressed in what would become his trademark uniform, unassuming high-necked khaki tunic and pants, and rubber sandals. As he appeared the cheers erupting from the crowd seemed almost hysterical. I took a few snaps over a sea of heads and retreated a little to a vantage point further away. It was only when the man they would come to know as 'Uncle Ho' leaned forward to speak into the single microphone that the crowd began to settle. Much of it I did not understand, but his voice was quiet and articulate. He was reading a Declaration of Independence for his country and the words of a constitution for the new Democratic Republic of Vietnam, a goodly slice of which he had borrowed from the American Declaration of Independence. As fate would have it, a couple of American P-38 reconnaissance aircraft flew low over us and 100 000 faces looked up to see the aircraft bank, appearing to dip their wings to the occasion. Ho could not have hoped for an apparent US gesture of support for the Vietminh that was more impressive to the people watching that day. The reaction at the end of his speech was one of wild and unbridled enthusiasm.

Afterwards I watched with interest as the familiar figure of Vo Nguyen Giap took to the podium. Again I grasped only a fraction of what he said, but I recognised his resolute tone. In fact he was reinforcing the impression given by Ho of support from the United States, praising their 'intimate foreign relations' with China and the United States.

'France will land forces in Tonkin in an attempt to reconquer the north,' he warned, and 'the Vietnamese people will fight for independence, liberty and equality of status.'

It was strange to see him again, standing in front of such a vast crowd, inspiring the masses as he had once inspired me. Now, of course, his delivery was fiery and impassioned. The crowd was responding, and I left before it was over, unsure of what the mood of the people would be by the end of it.

As I made my way back to the hospital that afternoon I reflected upon the truth in what Jo had said. Nothing in Indochina would be the same again.

For the French in Hanoi the celebrations for the end of the war were well and truly over. With such disquieting historical events being played out around them, they were deeply concerned over their immediate future. Why was it that the Americans would not help them? Were they not France's allies? When would the French military be released? What would become of them all?

Under the tender care of the sisters my general health was rapidly improving. There were few enough beds in Hanoi for people in need and I knew it was time to move on. But where would I go? My father was still incarcerated and our apartment was wrecked. I could move in with Jo but much as I was fond of her the idea did not appeal. I had little money. At university I had worked for half-pay at GTEO, and the small amount I had saved at the Banque Franco-Chinoise would not go far in rent and expenses.

On the day of my summons before Mother Superior I still had no idea of my next move, but the nun's first words were comforting.

'Do not worry, Michel,' she said. 'I know you are still not fully recovered, and we don't want you getting into trouble again.' Her blue eyes twinkled and I wondered fleetingly if she knew of my visits to Jo. 'We shall be sorry to see you go,' she said, 'but we do need your room. I have done a little homework on the matter of your placement and have made an appointment for you to see a Madame Joli this afternoon, with a view to your moving into a room in her house. Madame Joli's husband is in the defence force, someone very high up I believe. He is, of course, in detention in the Citadel and she lives with a lady friend of hers in her comfortable villa close by. Your lodging will be rent free though you will make a contribution for food. The ladies have been very nervous without a man in the house, so you will be doing them quite a favour, as of course they will be for you.'

So I met Madame Joli, that afternoon, in the drawing room of her large French villa not far from the hospital. She was in her late fifties, small and neat, her soft greying hair swept up into a chignon. She struck me as warm, kind and generous of spirit. The turn of events in Hanoi had petrified her, and she had not been out of the house since the Japanese coup. She and her lady companion spent most of their time playing Solitaire or reading upstairs. The shopping was taken care of by Madame Joli's *thi hai*, an increasingly rare gem of an old-school colonial servant, and totally devoted to her mistress.

My room would be on the ground floor, from where I could observe anyone approaching.

My presence apparently brought the ladies great comfort. I was to spend the next six months living with Madame Joli and her friend, and during the entire time neither of the ladies ventured one step outside the locked and bolted front door.

It was a similar picture all over Tonkin. French nationals feared attack by the Vietminh, and remained holed up or moved about with caution. Tonkin was now Vietnamese territory. Hanoi, once the headquarters of the French administration in Indochina, had become the capital of the Democratic Republic of Vietnam. The streets were patrolled by Vietminh soldiers and the government administrators were now all Vietnamese. French teachers were thrown out of schools and the French doctors at the Pasteur Institute were forcefully ejected and much of their equipment destroyed or stolen. The once powerful French were made to feel like very unwelcome interlopers.

At least there was still peace above the 16th parallel. South of this line where the British zone began it was very different. The French military had been freed by the British, French officials sat in the government buildings in Saigon and the French High Commissioner was once again in office. The provisional Vietminh government had been ousted and, in the bitter battles for power that followed, violence begat violence. Around that city French soldiers and Vietnamese guerrillas, soon to be referred to as the Viet Cong, died every day. Many

Japanese soldiers had sold their arms to the highest bidder and headed for the bars in the Chinese section of Cholon, and religious sects such as the Cao Dai and the Hoa Hao and the secret society known as the Binh Xuyen were armed and fighting both the French and amongst themselves. Chaos reigned and civilians cowered in their homes as Saigon became a burning, treacherous enclave where atrocities from both sides escalated the bloodshed.

By contrast, in Hanoi I could not help but feel that despite the fear around me the revolution had been extraordinarily quiet. Though we were not aware of it, Ho had an official policy of nonviolence towards the French in Tonkin at this stage. In practice, however, Ho was not in control of all his supporters. In the early weeks after the end of the war sporadic violence in the countryside saw the Vietminh ruthlessly slay some influential Mandarins, Vietnamese landowners and certain people who had held high office under the French.

From the point of view of the people in the north, Vietnam was now independent and governed by the Vietminh. Ho Chi Minh, however, was a realist and well aware that the French would be massing forces to land at the earliest opportunity. He also realised the need for French capital to further develop the country, and he was willing to negotiate with the French. The Americans on the spot were reluctant to broker such negotiations and it was several weeks before a meeting was finally arranged between Jean Sainteny and Vo Nguyen Giap, now Minister for the Interior in the new government. Other meetings followed, but Sainteny did not have the authority he needed from Paris to guarantee independence to Vietnam within a five- to ten-year period. Sainteny could only assure Giap that, yes, France was willing to negotiate.

To the Vietnamese, gold was an important status symbol. Wealth was measured in how much gold you had. Anyone who could afford it had some, and the wealthy had a great deal which they kept in vaults at the banks. Gold was revered, though only in its purest form. When my family's *thi hai* had become a godmother of a new baby born into her Catholic family, she was very excited, and to celebrate we bought the baby a nine-carat gold bracelet from a French jeweller. Our *thi hai* was thrilled, I remember — until the next day, when she appeared with a long face and refused to speak to anyone. She had been to a jeweller, discovered that the bracelet was nine-carat gold and considered it a total insult. It would have been better not to have given her anything at all. It had to be eighteen carats or it was not gold. As Europeans we did not think the same way, but we learned our lesson.

Ho Chi Minh's first problem was lack of finance, and he had little alternative but to appeal to the public to donate their gold to the treasury of the Vietminh. The response was immediate and overwhelming.

There were many crucial problems to deal with, the most urgent being the famine. In the rural areas where there was no military presence, the daily struggle for survival had fallen to banditry and anarchy. Ho had all rice in Japanese-held granaries immediately seized and milled for distribution. He introduced new laws, increasing the land under rice cultivation for the next harvest, in the spring of 1946. And, with the help of Jean Sainteny, Vo Nguyen Giap arranged for the French administration in the south to send large quantities of rice to the north.[13]

In Tonkin the Vietminh organised food distribution centres in the rural regions, handing out food to the emaciated population. In many areas the Vietminh were hailed as the saviours of the people.

Throughout this early period the Vietminh shrewdly represented themselves as Nationalist, and Ho even brought a Catholic and a couple of moderate Nationalists into the provisional government. He was still playing to the conservatives and to United States support. There would soon be challenges from other political factions more likely to enjoy the support of Chiang Kai-shek's approaching troops.

All was not as it seemed, however. In the remoter areas where Communist cells had long been working, there were those who would not be fooled by the Vietminh's Nationalist propaganda. Shallow graves appeared, and grisly mounds of bone and ash, homes were burned out, and in some places entire villages were

---

[13] The south of Vietnam had had successive bumper harvests and, unlike the north, the US naval blockade of the South China Sea had prevented the Japanese from exporting any rice at all.

destroyed — penance for refusing to support the Vietminh. Leading ethnic opposition leaders who emerged in the early months after the war were murdered. All this was blamed on retreating Japanese or bands of nonexistent French extremists.

In the meantime most French waited fearfully in their houses, for what they could not tell. They lived in hope that a new contingent of French forces would arrive from the south, that those imprisoned in Hanoi would be freed, or that something would happen to bring stability back into their lives.

I ventured out often, visiting Mireille or Jo, running errands for Madame Joli. Since my prison experience, I yearned for the open air, and I wanted to keep in touch with the mood on the streets of Hanoi. The thin, goateed face of Ho Chi Minh hung everywhere, printed on posters or crudely depicted on home-made banners draped from windows or slung from street signs. Most street names had been slashed out, the French names replaced by the names of Vietnamese revolutionaries, and in the old quarter where streets bore the Vietnamese names of the traders who inhabited them, the French translations on the blue and white street signs were painted out.

The Vietminh patrolling the streets had changed radically since they had first appeared in Hanoi. The army I had seen entering the city in brown cotton pants and tunics had now donned neat khaki uniforms of medium-length tunics, something like the US Marine battle-dress. Simple red and gold insignias displayed rank and they wore khaki-covered cork helmets, slightly smaller than the old colonial version.

Two more US missions arrived in Hanoi. One was charged with looking after the needs and welfare of prisoners of war, the other was to prepare America's strategic design for the country. None of the new arrivals showed any sign of being more sympathetic to the cause of the French.

Frustration consumed me. France had fought hard for her own democracy and owed the same to Indochina. I felt that real democracy was only going to happen if independence came slowly, under the guidance and tutelage of a France now free of German occupation. I was disillusioned with my own country for not having moved sooner to give some measure of autonomy to the Vietnamese. Looking back, if the fair-minded negotiator Jean Sainteny had been given the authority to negotiate a workable, amenable agreement with Ho Chi Minh, how different things could have been.

It appeared the Americans who were in Tonkin knew little of the country, nor of the passion and politics of the Vietminh. Their apparent support of the Vietminh and their continued refusal to release the French military gave great prestige to the Vietminh, prestige that was vital to the success of the revolutionaries. Leaving the French military incarcerated had created a power vacuum in the north, allowed the Vietminh more time to gain popular support and build military strength, a transformation that would ultimately lead Indochina into tragedy.

Later the Americans would have a change of heart about the Vietminh, but too late. The scene was now set for war in Vietnam, war that would span three decades, war that was actually two wars and in which millions of people, Vietnamese, French and Americans, would die wretchedly. It was war, I think, that could have been avoided if events in Indochina had been allowed to take their course, if the United States had stayed out of Hanoi after the capitulation of the Japanese, allowed the release of the French forces and left France to make her own mistakes, to find her own reluctant, recalcitrant, begrudging way along a path that would certainly have led, eventually, to independence and democracy for Vietnam.

But it didn't happen like that. The result would be a catastrophe, long drawn out and of immense proportions.

Twelve

Warlords and Locusts

A thin veil of opium smoke wafted across my nostrils and I breathed in its sweetness, privately pleased that I could resist its allure in these troubled times. I had not touched opium since the difficult period after my mother died. During the many hours I had since spent in conversation with Jo in her den I had watched her carry out the seductive ritual time and time again.

The wad of opium bubbled in the bowl on the pipe and the many lines on Jo's upper lip puckered as she drew back deeply. I wondered how many pipes a day she was smoking now — surely thirty, perhaps forty — yet her mind was sharp and analytical. Her intelligent discourse was a welcome change from the twitter of dear Madame Joli and her friend. And with my father still interned in the Citadel, Jo's knowledge and network somehow lent me a sense of physical security.

Now she was pressing 2000 piastres upon me, far more money than I thought I needed.

'It's too much,' I protested, but Jo insisted. I was embarrassed at her generosity, and promised to repay it as soon as I could earn a salary.

She smiled gently, and murmured, 'Of course, Michel, but don't worry about it too much for the moment.'

Under the high ceilings of the Banque Franco-Chinoise that afternoon I regarded the fat balance in my passbook with awe. Never had I had so much money. I felt rich and secure, at least as secure as possible under the circumstances. For it was not only the Vietminh patrolling the streets who made the French uneasy. Less visible but very much a presence were the Japanese troops, who were still armed and under orders from the Americans to keep the peace until the Chinese arrived to disarm and repatriate them.

For a month now we had been living in a sort of limbo, waiting for something else to happen, knowing that the Chinese were on the way and, if nothing else, looking forward to the end of the Japanese occupation. The Vietnamese had suffered Chinese rule for a thousand years before finally defeating them in 939 AD. Between then and the time of French colonisation they had rarely been free of attempts by the Chinese to reconquer them. And during the recent war years the Chinese government had nurtured pro-Chinese Vietnamese Nationalist groups on their side of the border. It was hard not to be sceptical of their claims of neutrality.

On the 20th of September 1945, the first wave of Chinese soldiers arrived in Hanoi. They looked polished, well trained and disciplined. Equipped with American arms, they rode in American trucks. In a moment of optimism I imagined they might efficiently oversee the departure of the Japanese, but my relief was short-lived. These were the crack units, the elite of Chiang Kai-shek's army.

Within days some 100 000 regular soldiers flooded Hanoi and poured into the surrounding countryside. Ragged, dirty and disorderly, they barely looked like an army, let alone a victorious one. The faces of the men were sallow and drawn, their uniforms tattered and stained after years of fighting the Japanese.

For every Chinese soldier there was a porter who bore his load, usually in baskets on a shoulder pole. In theory their role was to carry food, arms and equipment. In practice they carried the loot pillaged by the soldiers from the population.

Nearly one year of Chinese occupation lay ahead for the north of Vietnam. Such a large number of Chinese troops were in Hanoi that there was almost one soldier for each resident. It would be a year in which unruly Chinese soldiers would systematically plunder the areas where they were stationed. It would be a year in which much of the wretched local population would see their meagre food stocks seized, their houses ransacked. It was a year in which any half-hearted efforts at peace-keeping would give way to anarchy and terrorism.

In Hanoi, General Lu Han, commander of the Chinese occupation army, took over the Governor's Palace from Jean Sainteny. Outside of Hanoi the provincial capitals and country areas were put under the control of two Chinese warlords who commanded a rabble of undisciplined mercenary divisions. From his splendid quarters, General Lu Han exercised little control of the warlords and their locust-like troops. Their provisions soon ran out and the soldiers lived off the land by looting what little livestock and grain there was to feed the starving rural population.

Ships to repatriate the Japanese were not available for what seemed an eternity. Lack of transport was a ready excuse for General Lu Han to use the more disciplined Japanese troops to his own advantage. The atmosphere on the streets was unpredictable, and it seemed everyone was permitted arms but the French. Lu Han refused to cooperate with the French in any respect.

The Japanese surrender ceremony should have been a joyous occasion, a day of relief and celebration. Instead it proved a direct insult to the French. As the ceremony began beneath the fluttering flags of the victorious Allied nations, one flag was conspicuous by its absence. The organisers had refused to fly the French tricolour. France's representative, General Alessandri, was highly offended and walked out in a fury.

Gone was the once tranquil ambience of Hanoi's wide French boulevards, as government propaganda blared incessantly from loudspeakers. The main streets now thronged with people, including the tens of thousands of Japanese troops who were yet to be moved out to the port of Haiphong. More French civilians now braved the open, and as I wove my way through the crowds of local Vietnamese, the Chinese and Japanese troops, the spattering of Americans, I exchanged greetings with friends I had not seen for many months. A few shops closed and barred for months opened their doors for the first time and the odd sidewalk café came back into business.

But trouble was quick to return. Inflation had risen dramatically during the Japanese occupation; in early November 1945 it began to soar. The Chinese administration decreed that the Chinese dollar, valued at about 33 cents or one-third of a piastre, was revalued at 3 piastres — an increase of 900 per cent. The two banks in Hanoi, the Banque de l'Indochine and the Banque Franco-Chinoise, refused to transact at the new rate, but shop owners and business people were forced at gunpoint to accept it. The already groaning economy was thrown into turmoil, and even the Chinese businesses in Tonkin were badly hurt.

The Chinese occupiers took possession of a huge number of 500-piastre notes, mostly issued by the Japanese before the end of the war. Under advice from the Banque de l'Indochine, the French High Commissioner in Saigon declared invalid all 500-piastre notes issued between the time of the Japanese coup and the surrender, and recalled them. The Chinese black marketeers and Chinese Army authorities were caught short and hit hard. As tension mounted they threatened the French with trouble, but there was no French authority in the north to deal with the problem. The Banque de l'Indochine, having stood as a bastion of French financial imperialism throughout the colonial period, became the scapegoat.

The day after my twenty-fourth birthday, the 15th of November, having perhaps drunk one too many paddy cassis sodas the previous night, I was out for a stroll, hoping that the fresh morning air would clear my head. Outside the Banque de l'Indochine an angry crowd of protesters was rallying. I had noticed the heavy, barred gates closed as I passed, the edgy Chinese troops guarding the bank, and the volatile mood of the crowd. They were demanding compensation for their 500-piastre notes. As the first shots rang out, I turned to look back — and saw the guards panic, and fire every which way into the crowd. Vietnamese and Chinese protesters hurtled in every direction, leaving eight or so bodies sprawled upon the sidewalk outside the bank.

The guards who killed them were Chinese, but it was the French who would wear the consequences.

The uneasy calm began to disintegrate. Within days the French Chief Executive of the Banque de l'Indochine lay slain on the steps of the bank. Violent skirmishes pockmarked the city and as order broke down the Chinese and Japanese troops roaming the streets became more unpredictable. Any semblance of normality rapidly evaporated. Hanoi was on a downward spiral into chaos.

By the new year of 1946, pro-Chinese Nationalist groups had launched a concentrated campaign of terror, randomly targeting French and Vietnamese alike. Once again the French population waited with trepidation behind locked and bolted doors. But in the prevailing lawlessness a number of disgruntled servants saw their opportunity, and there was a spate of poisonings. In some cases entire French families died, their food having been laced with datura, a strong narcotic plant extract. Their bodies were found days, even weeks later, their houses stripped and ransacked.

If Madame Joli had spoken of perhaps leaving the house for a promenade on the boulevard, she spoke of it no more. Rumours were rampant. A general uprising against the French was planned. It would be a massacre, French civilians, women and children. Nobody would be shown mercy.

I had chosen to spare the ladies these reports, but they found out from Madame Joli's son, a cold, distant sort of character with a superior attitude who visited weekly on Sundays. All the calming words I could muster later did nothing to dispel Madame Joli's fears. Her dread was palpable, my frustration burning. We French had celebrated the end of the Second World War along with our allies. Like them we had cried tears of elation and relief, and grieved for the souls that had been sacrificed to the cause. But the relief was over. The French civilians in Hanoi had felt deserted at first, then trapped, now hunted.

* * *

The word from Jo was that the Chinese in power would do nothing to stop the violence. Despite their promise of neutrality they wanted the French out, and it appeared too that the current trouble was all part of the Chinese plan to strengthen the position of the pro-Chinese Dong Minh Hoi. They had brought their own candidates for government when they crossed the border and this semi-anarchy was designed to undermine the chances of an agreement between the French and the Vietminh. Already the hostility had resulted in a compensation agreement for the Chinese over the 500-piastre notes, and had done much to destabilise the new Vietminh government.

One afternoon Jo begged me to stay with her.

'Please let me help you,' she said. 'You do not have your father to rely on for information any more, and at least here you will be forewarned. I can arrange an escape route out of Hanoi if necessary, and a place where you will be safe until the danger is over.'

But I had pledged to look after the ladies, to defend them if the need arose.

'Then go now and do not go out again,' she implored, 'not even to visit me. I will send word.'

I left Jo's house severely unnerved.

Like most of the French community I had no weapons and no idea how I could defend my ladies. I sharpened the *thi hai*'s kitchen knife, blunted it again fashioning a couple of lethal-looking stakes from bamboo, then sharpened it once more. Out in the streets fate alone determined the next victim of random attack. In political circles the attacks were more calculated.

As the opposition parties put pressure on the Vietminh to include them in the government, the most vocal on both sides became targets of kidnapping and assassination. The Chinese command sent demands or threats to Ho Chi Minh every day. Ho was forced to change his place of residence and travelling plans often, and several houses in which he stayed were blown up. We were all suspicious that the Chinese military was orchestrating both the violence and the scapegoats to bear the blame. So concerned was Commissioner Sainteny that he requested an appeal to the United Nations for an inquiry into the Chinese occupation. At the same time he was desperately negotiating with Ho Chi Minh, aware that failure to reach an agreement could lead to more bloody violence.

Ho in the meantime had been performing a tightrope act between negotiating with the French and placating the Chinese-backed Nationalists. His fledgling government balanced precariously as it also tried to solve the crisis in the rural regions. Amid the chaos, the Vietminh began a major campaign against both famine and illiteracy. At the same time it began to break down the old established order of the villages, arresting or executing the Mandarins and abolishing the Councils of Village Notables in favour of 'People's Committees', controlled by the Vietminh. Though Ho still played down the Communist element of his government, the propaganda machine was working hard, and all the while the military was recruiting and indoctrinating.

It was a confusing time. Some Vietnamese, like Madame Joli's *amah* and her family, regarded the Vietminh with great suspicion. They had been content enough under French rule, and though they wanted independence for Vietnam, they would have preferred to see it happen under French auspices. They were not in a great hurry and were frightened by the instability and violence around them.

Others were far more impatient. Young Vietnamese were more likely to be Nationalists or Vietminh who could not wait for change.

There was no curfew at night during this period but most French were keeping a low profile. George and I knew we should not have been out on the streets but it was late, well after midnight, and we hadn't expected to see anyone. We had been playing bridge and were returning home when we were surrounded by an armed group of six, apparently a Vietminh army patrol, or perhaps Vietminh partisans.

George began waving his arms about and surprised me by speaking in English (which I learned later he had studied at school). I couldn't understand a word of what he said, but gathered he was trying to pass himself off as American, so I just nodded mutely. But the Vietminh were not impressed.

We were taken into a house, separated and searched for weapons. The American ruse was obviously up.

George was in another room and I was invited to sit down with three of our captors. To my surprise, there began a mild-mannered interrogation in French. Who was I? What was I doing? What were my political views?

Soon we were exchanging ideas on the general situation, both political and economic, on their aspirations, on my aspirations, on facts and figures, on education, the public service, many other issues. If they were right I would agree with them, and if I felt they were wrong in their thinking I said so. It was strange in the middle of the night, in the midst of revolution and while being forcibly held, to be telling the Vietminh they were wrong. But somehow I no longer felt threatened, and they appeared interested in what I had to say. I made no move to leave, indeed thought it wise not to, and during the course of the discussions an urn of tea was brought to lubricate the throat. It was close to sunrise before the debate ended and George and I were released. We parted on good terms with the men, shaking hands all round.

All the same, it was the last time George and I ventured out late at night during that period.

Then, as if to appease everyone, in the midst of the violence of January 1946 Ho called a general election. He was keeping a promise he had made to the people, though by now the pressure from the opposition had forced him to agree to give them a percentage of seats no matter the outcome. The ballot was neither secret nor scrutinised, but Ho Chi Minh enjoyed a great deal of popular support and nobody in Hanoi queried his landslide victory.

Events however, began to conspire against Ho. In both Hanoi and Chungking, France had been negotiating hard with China to get the Chinese troops out of Tonkin. The Chinese Nationalists were fearful of Communism and France had some large carrots to dangle: the renouncement of her territorial concessions within China, and an exemption from duties for Chinese goods on the railway from Haiphong to Kunming.

Agreement was reached and a time frame for Chinese withdrawal put in place. Now Ho's negotiating position with the French was weakened.

His tone, already conciliatory, became appeasing. Around the city more rumours spread that French troops from the south were preparing to invade the northern part of Indochina. In the face of such a threat, Ho's militia was in no position to defend the new Republic.

In fact the French General Leclerc, in Saigon, was equally keen to avoid a battle with the Vietminh. He had only 20 000 troops to send to Tonkin, while along with an unknown number of Vietminh militia there were some 185 000 Chinese soldiers in Vietnam north of the 16th parallel. Incredibly, four months after the Chinese had arrived, around 30 000 Japanese soldiers were still in the area, most of whom were armed. My father and the rest of the French military remained locked up in the Citadel or in prison camps in the country, and there were around 25 000 French civilians in Tonkin, all at risk of a much-mooted massacre prior to the arrival of the Corps Expéditionnaire. Returning by force would be an ugly eventuality, so General Leclerc was eager to strike an accord that allowed French troops to return to Tonkin in peace.

The task of governing the country was presenting enormous difficulties to Ho Chi Minh. There had been starvation, chaos and violence to contend with, as well as the financial and general ransacking of Tonkin that resulted from the Chinese occupation. There had been the complications of the presence of so many different Nationalist factions, all with their own objectives and most, including the Vietminh, working behind the scenes to eliminate their opposition. Ho Chi Minh wanted an accord with France. Perhaps he, too, had high hopes that the present strong political left in France would result in a new France, a better France, and a sympathetic colonial policy that would guide Indochina firmly towards independence over a short period of time.

His negotiations with Jean Sainteny led to him reshaping his government to include more opposition members, who demanded that Vo Nguyen Giap should be expelled from government. Ho complied. A frustrated Giap rejoined the army of the Vietminh as Commander in Chief, and his illustrious career path was set.

On 6 March 1946 an accord with the French was signed. It was a positive start for Ho Chi Minh, though far less than he had hoped for. In return for his allowing French troops to come back to the northern half of

Indochina, France would recognise the Democratic Republic of Vietnam as 'a free state with its own government, parliament, army and finances, forming part of the Indochinese Federation and the French Union'. There would be a cap on French troops of 25 000 (15 000 French and 10 000 Vietnamese) and a guarantee — the crucial promise — that the troops would be withdrawn in annual instalments over a period of five years so that by 1952 no French troops would remain north of the 16th parallel.

When the accord was made public I was ecstatic and full of the optimism borne of youth and naivety. France *would* do the right thing for Indochina. Over the next five years we would continue the expansion of education for rural people, train the Vietnamese in industry, in finance, in government, nurture the country towards the democracy that France herself had fought so hard for. Suddenly I felt a glimmer of hope that I could be proud of my country, feel for the first time a true Frenchman. We would make up for past injustices and I could see my life rolled out in front of me, happy and peaceful, living in my beloved Indochina free of the discomfort I now felt about what had gone before.

The liberating French soldiers of the Corps Expéditionnaire arrived and surely the whole of the French civilian population of Tonkin was gathered in the streets to greet them. From open windows French flags kept under wraps for so long fluttered gaily. Flowers littered the boulevards where they had been tossed towards the troop trucks. Enraptured women threw kisses wildly, people sang and danced and all around me tears of joy and relief streamed down French faces. I found Mireille among the revellers and rushed, thrilled, to her side. Nearby her parents were smiling and laughing, happy as I had never seen them before, and I stole a kiss from their eldest daughter, then another. I felt as though I was walking on air.

Gone were the flags of the Vietminh, flown now only on the official government buildings. The huge red banners strung across every street still proclaimed freedom and independence in large gold letters — '*Viet Nam Doc Lap*' — but it didn't seem to matter, a fact that augured well for change. Having landed in Haiphong, over 20 000 French troops entered Hanoi that day, with them some 500 vehicles, tanks and half-tracked armour-plated units in a cavalcade that took over two hours to pass.

Yet at the back of the crowds there was no joy on the faces of the Vietnamese as they watched the arsenal roll through their city. They looked bemused, as though they could not understand how Ho Chi Minh had let this happen. My heart went out to them and for a moment dampened my euphoria. I found myself wanting to tell them, it will be all right, you will see.

When I was not talking at the top of my voice or being slapped on the back out of sheer bonhomie, my thoughts were of my father. The procession of troops was heading to the Citadel, that bastion of colonial power, so surely he would be released today. He had been imprisoned there for almost a year now, five months under the Japanese and then seven months since the Japanese surrender. It seemed a disgrace that he had been left locked up like a war criminal after the end of the war. I wondered where he would go when he was released and where I would find him.

That night I returned to Madame Joli's house. Almost everyone I knew had braved the streets today, but not my ladies. They were waiting for a detailed account of the day's celebrations. When would their husbands return, they asked. Very soon, I promised, maybe tonight, probably tomorrow.

In the morning I left them. I packed my pitifully few belongings into a small bag and bade them farewell, thanking them, promising to keep in touch.

Within an hour I had the information I wanted. A number of senior officers had been transferred from the Citadel to the Hotel Metropole, and I set out to look for my father there.

Walking up the marble stairs and through the huge revolving doors of the Metropole was like walking into another time and place, somewhere away from the chaos and uncertainty that reigned outside. The smiling, elaborately uniformed Vietnamese who greeted me that day looked as though nothing would ruffle him and, inside, the ambience was of cool elegance and order.

At the reception I was told that yes, Colonel L'Herpinière was indeed there. My relief was immense.

* * *

My father was much thinner than I remembered — but then we were all thinner. He looked a bit older. And there was something else . . . an obvious delight at seeing me, a warmth somewhat akin to the warmth in which my mother had encased me. It still wasn't the same, but it was a change in him.

We were all changed. War puts life into perspective. Papa had lost much, but he still had me. And I had him. I guess that was probably it.

Around us, the hotel swarmed with people. White-clad Vietnamese waiters carrying silver trays wove their way around potted palms and cane lounge chairs, and glided through noisy throngs of French officers — some just released from internment in the Citadel, others new arrivals to Indochina — and the richly tessellated lobby abounded with reunions. The whole place was alive and bustling and my father and I found refuge at a table in the open air of the back garden lounge. There was much to speak of, much to recount.

Inside, the high-pillared lounge bar resounded with the inevitable postmortems of World War II. Many of the new arrivals were Free French troops who had trained with de Gaulle in England, and as discussions ranged long and loud, we could not help but hear an undercurrent of resentment towards the officers who had been in Tonkin throughout the war. The local contingent, we heard, had simply not done enough against the Japanese. I looked at my father and wondered what they expected us to have done.

We had been 50 000 French and Vietnamese troops, including the *garde indigène*, half noncombatants, thinly disbursed over the whole of French Indochina taking in Cambodia, Laos, Cochinchina and Annam. In Tonkin we had faced an advancing army of ten divisions, close to 100 000 Japanese, in percentage terms far higher odds against us than the Allied troops later faced in the battle for Malaya and Singapore. We had also taken heavy casualties.

It was typical of the attitude that has since prevailed in many history books, recording that the French 'collaborated' with the Japanese. I could not see it myself.

Thirteen

Chinoiserie

My father arranged for me to take the room adjacent to his. Louis Blouet of the Metropole was a friend of his, and the extra hospitality he offered lent our new situation a homely air. It seemed ideal and once again I wondered at my good fortune. It all seemed too good. And, of course, it was.

Two weeks later I was recalled into the army, and back with my platoon.

The handsome triple arches of the railway station's entrance stood in solitary dignity, devoid of the lively scrum of rickshaws and porters and bustling passengers in pre-war days. At the height of the famine the station platforms had provided shelter to many starving families, but now the squatters had moved on and there were few people around. The line to the south remained closed from the bombing, and although the line to Haiphong had been repaired, trains were still few and far between. Across the road from the station, we were on guard duty inside the heavy iron gates of the Shell depot, where Hanoi's only bulk fuel supply was stored.

All was peaceable on the Boulevard Gambetta. With so little activity outside, the day had been quiet and long and languid.

I was not happy to be back in the army. The war was over as far as I was concerned. I had done my bit against the Japanese, for what it was worth, and had thought I'd finished with the military. The recall of the five or six thousand reservists had come as a surprise.

It was a temporary measure, we were told. We had been deployed to keep order until Tonkin was rid of the Chinese, who showed no sign of honouring their agreement to leave the country. We had been briefed to expect unpredictable and capricious behaviour from the Chinese patrols and their factions.

Today the afternoon sun was lazily overhead, the men were relaxed and at ease, counting down the hours to the end of their shift. Then the sound of gunning engines brought everyone to attention.

Four GMC transports groaning with Chinese soldiers skidded to a halt right outside the Shell depot. The troops swarmed off the trucks — and we watched incredulously as they scurried like nesting rats to sandbag a semicircular covering wall on the road outside.

Within minutes a menacing arsenal of machine guns had been deployed over the top of the sandbags, aimed directly at us.

My orders were clear. 'Hold your fire. Remain quiet. Do not, repeat, do not shoot.'

For a minute or so there was a standoff, and we faced each other expectantly. Nothing happened, until suddenly the Chinese soldiers began darting back and forth in front of the gates, taking cover behind the high depot fence, taking aim at us with their weapons, then disappearing behind the sandbags again. Piercing whistles and shouts gave the impression we were under attack. But minutes passed and nobody fired a shot.

It was all a game. The Chinese were doing their utmost to entice us into shooting first, inviting us into another bloody little skirmish.

My men held fast, resisting temptation, watching these histrionics with the aversion, perhaps loathing, that had crept into all our beings since the beginning of the Chinese occupation.

They kept it up for almost an hour and I had to give them credit for their efforts. It was a fine performance. Finally the order was given and as abruptly as they had arrived, they piled everything back into their trucks and departed.

The only positive thing about being back in the army was meeting with my old friends again, particularly the quiet, reserved Maurice L'Huillier from Cambodia days and, of course, the reliable and ever-cheerful

Claude Mary. Our first reunion in the Officers' Mess had been a long night, for I had seen neither of them since the Japanese attacked the Citadel. Indeed Claude, like my father, had been released from incarceration only recently. The discourse had slewed wildly that night. Hilarity at Claude regaling us with his efforts to keep himself amused while imprisoned veered abruptly every so often to sombre reflection. There had been so many deaths. The names of old acquaintances kept cropping up and Claude's face would darken. I thought I had heard it all from my father. The banter continued, while inwardly we mourned.

The killing, however, was far from over. Street clashes between the Chinese and French patrols were commonplace and each day brought more dead — five, ten, fifteen a day passed through the hands of the morgue attendants at the General Hospital. Most were French. Young soldiers, many of them reservists expecting to return home to France with their families within weeks of being demobbed, died at the hands of the marauding Chinese.

Guard duty and day patrol had not sounded like dangerous work. But the Chinese had their own stratagem: to create havoc, to provoke skirmishes and blame the opposite side, to cause dissension between the French and the indigenous people, and to bring disrepute to the French. Their commanders had no wish to leave Tonkin, and saw the disorder they created as an excuse to stay.

One day Maurice did not return from a street patrol he had been leading in central Hanoi. The next morning his bunk was still empty. I thought at first that he may have been posted to a different duty roster, but when I returned from patrol the next evening and he had still not appeared, I became concerned. If anything had happened to him I prayed he had spent the night at the hospital, in a bed of crisp sheets and plumped pillows, attended by pretty Vietnamese nurses and dreaming of the repatriation that would soon be his. With foreboding I went to the administration centre to check the casualty list. There was his name. Maurice L'Huillier. Killed on patrol. Second from the top, in black print as though it was a name on a list of people rostered for breakfast fatigues.

A wave of shock swept over me. Why gentle Maurice? I had been at school with him. Only a few days ago he had read out a letter from his grandmother, saying how she was looking forward to seeing him again. His family had just moved from Hanoi to Saigon, and they were planning to return to France together within months. They were so close to going home.

We were living a tragedy. Surely it should not have been like this. The war with the Japanese was over. There was an accord in place with the Vietminh. Why should this be happening?

General Leclerc had arrived in Hanoi. One of de Gaulle's most trusted officers, he had led the division that entered and liberated Paris. My father was impressed with him and assured me that he was of like mind to Sainteny in dealing with the Vietminh in Tonkin.

'You may rest assured,' he said, 'that Leclerc will pursue a policy of negotiation until a solution is found.' The implications of his words hit me. I had thought a solution was already in place, that we already had an accord with the Vietminh. 'It is only an accord in principle,' my father said then, 'nothing more than an agreement on what should be done. There is opposition to it in some sections of the French military and administration, and the hardliners within the Vietminh government. There is still much to be worked through.'

With growing unease I realised that the agreement might not be adhered to, that France might not back her word.

'It is only Sainteny's word,' my father explained. 'He does not have the authority. Admiral d'Argenlieu is expected back in Indochina from France soon, and he is yet to be convinced.' I was stunned, disappointed, but my father was reassuring. 'Leclerc is a good man,' he said. 'I am confident he will do what he can to continue Sainteny's excellent work, convince d'Argenlieu and the colonial administration to negotiate a compromise everyone will be happy with.'

General Leclerc began talking with French planters, including the Reynauds and the Guillaumes. The *colons* were outraged at the outcome. They wanted to reclaim their properties immediately, by force if necessary, and they expected the French military to help them. Leclerc would have none of it. Most of the country outside a few major towns was now under some sort of political and military control by the Vietminh, and Leclerc had neither the resources nor the inclination to challenge the situation.

At Mireille's house, Monsieur Reynaud was furious.

'What sort of society will this be if the French have no right even to their own land?' he said in disgust. 'That land is our life! What is there left for us here in Indochina now?'

I made the appropriate sympathetic noises, secretly agreeing with Leclerc's nonconfrontational approach. Later I realised the implications for me. The Reynauds would return to France, claim their war-damage reparation and start a new life. I had been seeing a lot of Mireille in the last few weeks. We had become closer, but my relationship with her parents had not changed. They were still cold and distant. Now they would be taking my girl to France, out of my life perhaps for ever.

There were few enough single European women in Indochina. Of those there were, many would be preparing to leave with their parents now that the war was over, and my father had done his best to steer me towards the daughters of some of his friends. There had been dinner parties at the home of Monsieur Picard, the big jeweller in Hanoi, whose daughter Monique was pleasantly good-humoured. There had been drinks at the Bellots, after which my father would extol the virtues of the dark and beautiful Maddy. She was a *métisse*, her father French, her mother Vietnamese. Unlike the British colonies, there were few prejudices about mixed-blood marriages in Indochina and such unions were commonplace. *Métisse* girls were often stunning, the Vietnamese attractive and graceful, and either were popular as wives. Many mixed-blood families promenaded with other French families in the cool of the evenings, finely dressed *métis* children gambolling around with their fairer-skinned friends.

No, that was not an issue. Both Monique and Maddy were very nice girls. I did have, however, a natural resentment towards my father choosing a wife for me.

Unhappily, Mireille and Papa did not see eye to eye, perhaps because she sensed he did not like her family.

'She is a third-generation *colon*,' he reminded me. 'Her family think they are Indochina's aristocracy, and look down upon us because we are military, transitory people, not one of them.'

I did not see myself as transitory. I wasn't going anywhere. As far as I could see, it was they who were leaving, and we who were staying. If only I could convince Mireille to remain behind I would have her to myself, her closest family a comforting five-week sea journey away.

I would have to ask her to marry me, and sooner rather than later.

It did not seem like a big decision, for I was convinced my future lay in Indochina. The woman who shared that future would have to have an equal passion for the land and its people, be resolute in the face of the difficulties that might lie ahead for the country, have no desire to flee to France at the first sign of trouble. Mireille was all of those things.

I was eager to confide to Jo my plans to propose, but her reaction was disappointingly lukewarm.

'Think about it a little longer, Michel,' she said. 'The political situation here is still anything but certain. You might find that you too will have to leave Indochina and you will have gained nothing by rushing into marriage in this way. There is blood in the streets, no certainty in anything and right now it is no place for a family.'

I appreciated her concern, but in my enthusiasm and vanity wondered if perhaps she was a little jealous at the idea of another woman in my life. In any case I dismissed her counsel. I knew Mireille's love for Indochina ran as deep, if not deeper, than my own. She would know that once she left for France there was a real chance she would never return. She was born here. This was her country. I would be her reason to stay.

While my days were filled with the duties of a soldier and my nights with romantic notions, up in the beautiful, mountain resort of Dalat, in southern Indochina, a conference was in session. The French High Commissioner, Admiral d'Argenlieu, was holding fast to his principles. Since his return from France he had made his position clear, declaring publicly and bluntly, 'I am amazed — yes, that is the word, *amazed* — that France's fine expeditionary corps in Indochina is commanded by officers who would rather negotiate than fight.'

It was April by now, 1946, and he was parrying all the important issues with a Vietminh delegation led by Vo Nguyen Giap. Among many other matters, there was Vietnam's ultimate sovereignty to consider, French cultural and economic interests to agree upon, and the status of Cochinchina to settle. But as French and Vietnamese ideology clashed, deadlock after deadlock ensued, and the optimism felt at first by both sides waned dramatically. D'Argenlieu eventually suspended negotiations, insisting the issues could be dealt with only at a higher-level meeting in Paris, which would be in early June of 1946.

The mild and humid April days passed and the tension on the streets of Hanoi began to ease. May of 1946 dawned to the beginning of the long-awaited withdrawal of the Chinese Army. The process was prolonged, slow and agonising to watch, for the Chinese left as they had arrived, looting anything they could carry along the way. They were on their way home and their material aspirations had grown. Crammed among the troops on the trucks was an incredible assortment of plunder, everything from personal effects and furniture to bathroom fittings, handbasins, taps, baths and even bidets. It was a particularly abhorrent sight. Had not the people of Tonkin suffered enough during the war years? It seemed to me the ultimate affront, the final insult.

The Chinese threat had begun to abate, but it was far from over.

In the convivial milieu of the mess, a young French NCO took a short, sharp draw on the dying butt of his

Gauloise Troupe. He did not linger to savour the taste of the harsh black tobacco, for the atmosphere was charged with excitement and he began to speak quickly, eagerly, his face full of longing and expectation. He was one of eight NCOs present, all of whom had just received news that they were to be repatriated to France within weeks. Their spirits were soaring. These men had been in Indochina throughout the long war years and could not wait to leave the country.

In the pale blue haze that hung over the room I listened to their lively banter. It was little wonder these soldiers didn't feel for Indochina as I did, for they and their families had endured mostly turmoil since they arrived six years before. I was glad for them. They had homes and extended families back in France and were itching to return. Indochina had been a sentence for them, and they had done their time.

France was where their hearts lay, they knew their place in the world, and for a moment I envied them. I regretted not being able to feel my roots in the same way. Why was it that France held so little attraction for me? It was my place of birth, it was my parents' place of birth, it was my ancestry. Yet the reality was that I had very little family there. Papa had given no indication that he wished to return to Europe, and besides a few distant cousins I had barely met, there was no one there for me. Except for Claude, who was also going, these men were married and lived half a kilometre west of the Citadel, in married quarters. As they made moves to leave, I imagined what it would be like to have a wife and family to go home to in the evenings. I knew it was something I needed.

We finished our drinks and they left as a group, all seven of them, just after dusk. I shook aside my melancholia and thought no more of them.

But that night none of them arrived home. In the morning their wives appeared to make frantic inquiries, but the High Command was not overly concerned. The street brawling had calmed and the immediate crisis was over, they said. The men were full of high spirits so surely they had gone out on a spree for the night. They would turn up soon when they had sobered up. Claude and I did not agree. We knew the men and their families, and it seemed unlikely. Besides, if there was any spree to be had Claude would most certainly have been in on it. No, the men had been on their way home.

By early afternoon there was still no news. Claude had been fidgeting all day and we decided to retrace their steps from the Citadel to their homes. The north gate was close to the mess where we had last seen them and from there we turned west, four of us walking the grassed apron parallel to the heavy walls. Alongside lay the trench dug by the Japanese during their attack the previous year, and I searched its length for signs of a struggle, personal effects, anything that might give us a clue. At the northwestern corner the trench ended, and we turned south as the NCOs would have done. Then the hair on the back of my neck began to rise.

This was strange, too strange. There were seven men, and nothing along this stretch but one house, besides

Jo's the only other to be built on the apron of the Citadel. A little more than a hundred metres and the men would have left the apron to walk the couple of blocks through a well-populated European area to their houses.

Piercing whistles interrupted my chain of thought, and a flurry of activity and shouting outside the house on the apron stopped us in our tracks. A dozen Vietnamese in pale blue-grey uniforms similar to those of the Chinese Army were running towards us brandishing rifles and handguns. We were quickly encircled and hustled, protesting, towards the house. A small flag, red with a blue square crossed with three white bands, floated above the apex of the roof. I recognised it, for it had appeared all over Hanoi during the last few months. We were in the hands of the pro-Chinese Nationalist group, the Dong Minh Hoi.

The front room of the house was spartan, furnished with a bare desk and a chair. A man in civilian clothes appeared and sat down behind the desk. He looked us over slowly, his face aloof and cold. The unease in the room was palpable.

With excellent French and an icy manner he asked what we were doing outside, and Claude launched into a voluble, nebulous explanation. I interjected, summoning an authoritative air I did not feel. We were an official delegation, I said, under instructions from the French High Command to investigate the disappearance of seven NCOs the previous evening. Our orders were to inspect the trenches around the apron of the Citadel and immediately report our findings.

The official's face relaxed a little and we waited as he considered his reply.

'Yes,' he said finally. 'This is a good idea. The Vietminh occupying the Number Two Police Station across the road have been conducting a campaign of kidnapping and torture of the French. I believe you need look no further than there to find your answer. I will make some inquiries of my own and report to your authorities.'

He waved us away and we were herded out of the building, through the small garden and back onto the apron. The uniforms disappeared and we were left standing, laughing in nervous relief and feeling a little foolish at the discomfort we had felt.

Glad to be out of the house, we continued with our search, finding nothing.

Then the Sûreté became involved. But with all its resources over the next three months nothing was uncovered. The disappearance of the men remained a mystery until the end of August.

By then, Claude had returned to France and all the Chinese troops and their satellite groups had left Hanoi. The French military reoccupied the house on the apron to which we had been taken by the Dong Minh Hoi. And there they found the cellar transformed to a grim prison.

Chains and shackles were fixed high up in the concrete walls and there were bloodstains on the walls and the floor. There was evidence of disturbed earth in the back garden, beneath which the bodies of the seven NCOs were found. They had been buried close together in a standing position, hands and feet bound, tight gags through their mouths. Postmortems disclosed soil in their lungs. They had been shackled and gagged in the cellar, and put into the grave alive, with time to think of family and what could have been, as shovel by shovel, inch by inch, death crept inexorably upon them.

Perhaps I was in search of some small vengeance against the Chinese for the misery and death they had wrought upon a country already miserable and in many places ravaged by war. That and some spur-of-the-moment thing that struck me and my old cell mate, George, as we strolled the centre of the city. It was a quiet evening and we had left the Café de la Paix to walk the Rue Paul Bert. As we turned the corner of the Boulevard Henri Rivière, the imposing entrance of the Hotel Metropole shone like a beacon in the humid night air and the white-gloved doorman stood statuesque before the revolving door at the top of the steps. An open jeep roared past and pulled up outside the hotel, and we watched languidly as one, two, three Chinese military types alighted and entered the hotel, accompanied by the doorman.

A Chinese flag stood sentinel on the bonnet of the jeep, and there was a four-star insignia on the left mud-guard. It was General Lu Han's jeep. I shot a furtive sideways look at George that said, 'What do you think?'

He winked in acquiescence and we slowed to an amble to pass the revolving door. A few people milled about in the lobby, none of them Chinese, and the doorman had not yet reappeared. Without a word we doubled back. An emphatic gesture from George indicated that I was to do the driving, and as I slid rapidly into the driver's seat George leaped in as passenger. I pushed the starter button gently but the engine exploded into life like a fifty-pounder let loose on Hanoi. Sure that the city was alerted for miles around, I slammed it into gear, U-turned with a screech and hit the pedal for a fast getaway.

Twenty metres on the engine coughed, spluttered and suddenly died.

'*Merde!*' exclaimed George. I concurred volubly.

We were still in full view of the Metropole, right under a glaring street light. It seemed like a fuel problem. Desperately I fumbled under the dashboard looking for a fuel line while George, still swearing — '*Merde,* oh *merde*' — checked his side.

The urge to flee was primeval — but my fingers, finding a quarter-turn tap, wrenched it on as I frantically pumped the accelerator. I hit the starter button again and the engine kicked, the tyres squealed and George, half out of the jeep and not to be left behind, clutched his way back into his seat.

Up the Rue Paul Bert, not daring to look back, past the police station where we had been interned, into a small square leading to a quiet unlit street behind the cathedral and we halted, breathing heavily and shocked at what we had so unthinkingly done.

While we regained our composure and our nerve, George removed the flag and insignia and said, 'Now what? Do we dump the blasted thing in the Red River?'

Flushed with success now that it was over, I had a better idea. The chief mechanic at the workshop of the Second D.B. always worked late. Taking a circuitous route through the back streets we reached the Citadel, where, sure enough, half a dozen mechanics were still at work. The fact that this was Lu Han's jeep seemed to energise the tired mechanics and, congratulations and back-slappings over, we were given an assurance that by morning the jeep would be unrecognisable. That night I slept soundly and righteously.

It would be almost a year after the end of the war before the last of the Chinese troops left Tonkin, and the resident population, French, Vietnamese and local Chinese alike, could breathe a heartfelt sigh of relief. There was talk of the occupation by the marauders from the north having been 'worse than the atomic bomb', and it was not until the last truckload left the city that any real feeling of normality began to permeate back into our lives. There was still much to do to find a resolution for Vietnam, but once again a sense of calm settled upon us all.

Fourteen

The Ecstasy and the Agony

Outside the Catholic church in the French quarter a small group of onlookers gathered to watch an event that had become an unusual spectacle in Hanoi. An old woman from upcountry shuffled over for a closer look at the pale silk gowns of the bride and her seven bridesmaids. She pushed back her wide straw hat to stare openly, smiling and displaying her once fashionable black enamelled teeth.

As we waited for the congregation to emerge behind us, several young boys abandoned their reed ball to inspect our wedding coach. The magnificent Mercedes Benz roadster, once in Hitler's personal fleet, had been acquired at the end of the war by a friend of my father's, a colonel who had arrived in March with the Corps Expéditionnaire.

Great effort had been put into preparing for this day. More than ever, a European wedding in Hanoi was a real occasion.

That night, through a champagne-induced haze, warmth and bonhomie infused the reception room at the Metropole. Our guests did not waste the opportunity for revelry and George was exuberant as master of ceremonies. I was proud and happy to be married to Mireille at last. I had tried not to notice the tears that left tracks through the make-up of Madame Reynaud at the church ceremony, the dullness in her eyes at the reception, like candles snuffed out among those shining about her. Soon she would be leaving Indochina, without her eldest daughter. My only regret was that Jo could not be with us to share the celebration. Her presence was impossible, for she was well known among the top military echelons and it would have been the last straw for the staunchly Catholic Reynaud family.

Much had happened in the last two months. After my demobilisation from the army at the end of May I had been looking forward to resuming work for GTEO. The news that Les Grand Travaux d'Extrême Orient was pulling out of Tonkin had left me stunned. They said there was no more work for me, and I was released from all obligation. It was the last thing I had expected. GTEO was the biggest civil engineering firm in the north of Indochina, and many other French enterprises were back in business. With so much restoration work to be done the decision to pull out seemed difficult to understand. But the board of GTEO had no faith in the future, they said. The political situation seemed stable for the moment, but they distrusted the Communist roots of the Vietminh, and had no confidence in the French government to find a solution. By pulling out now they could claim war reparation and walk away with something. Later, when the trouble began again they would risk losing all: 'The Vietminh is not weak. Every day their army is growing. When the time comes, it will be ready.'

But the words of Ho Chi Minh's pledge remained fixed in my mind: '. . . we admire France and have no desire to sever the bonds that unite our two peoples'. I felt that bond, and still imagined my countrymen to be as dedicated to peace and accord.

In any case there was work to be done, reconstruction, repairs and maintenance, new construction. I was committed to helping build a future for Indochina and now for my future family. Here was an opportunity not to be missed.

A new business, Société Tonkinoise de Travaux et Entreprises, began. It was an equal three-way partnership between my father as Managing Director, myself as Technical Director and an industrious Italian builder, Gino Simonetti, as Field Manager.

Gino came with a useful stock of equipment. Anything else required we had picked up at GTEO's liquidation sale. Recently retired from the army, my father had quickly secured a contract with the military

Corps of Engineers, restoring buildings in and around Hanoi damaged by the Japanese and Chinese armies. Then we won accreditation with the Paris-based War Damage Commission and our workload expanded exponentially. Many large industrial and commercial companies in Tonkin had suffered huge material losses. To assist with reparation dossiers for compensation claims alone, I employed a team of four Vietnamese draftsmen and two estimators. Now it was a struggle to keep up.

So in the busy weeks leading up to our wedding I had been supremely optimistic.

Then, honeymooning in the best suite at the Metropole, relaxing in the cool ambience of the hotel, the problems of Indochina faded into oblivion or did not exist at all. Here it was easy to believe that Hanoi was back on the road to security and prosperity, that Société Tonkinoise de Travaux et Entreprises would continue with its meteoric growth, might eventually assume the place of GTEO as the leading engineering and construction firm in Tonkin.

I even imagined that perhaps the potential of our new business had earned me more respect with my future in-laws, that they had softened a little towards me. By the time of our marriage in late July 1946, it seemed everything was falling into place. The war years were well behind us, the Japanese, the Chinese troops gone at last. Vietnam had its own government, and France, I thought, was working through the issues with Ho Chi Minh. I was now respectably married to a daughter of one of Indochina's oldest French families. At twenty-four I was a partner in what was proving to be a profitable and successful enterprise. After years of personal insecurity and lack of confidence, I suddenly felt I had arrived. I could see my future laid out in front of me, rolling like the ripening paddies of the Red River Delta, golden into the distance.

From mid-1946 many French families were preparing to leave Tonkin for France. The Reynauds were among the first to go, and a week after our marriage, Mireille and I were there at the airport to say goodbye. Their departure was a tearful affair — the heartbreak of leaving and the realisation of broken dreams had, in the mayhem of preparing to leave, been put off until this moment. Though they still spoke of returning, I could not imagine either the French or Vietminh governments encouraging it. I found myself sorry for them: their fall from grace had been swift and hard. Ahead was a long sea voyage from Saigon to France, a country that was to them rather new and strange. I imagined them trying to begin life anew in the suburban environs of Aix en Provence, their privileged life as plantation owners in Indochina with them for ever as memories, distant and bittersweet.

As the Junkers lifted slowly from the steaming runway so too did a weight lift from my shoulders. I was not sorry to see them go, but I put my arm around Mireille's shoulders as I sensed her inner turmoil. She was quiet and a little distant. She would need time to come to terms with the fact that now she was alone but for me, that the life she had known and the security of her family were already a world away.

Still, I was confident that the transition to married life would be smooth. Mireille had lived an existence where everything was done for her, and I had made sure to employ the services of her parents' own *thi hai* and *thi ba*. We were living in the rented three-storey house in which she had lived with her parents since leaving Son Cot, so there had been few changes on the domestic front. But I was often away for days or weeks. Many of my clients were large industrial firms based in the provincial capitals of the Delta region, within a radius of 100 kilometres of Hanoi.

One of the biggest cloth producers in the country had been Société des Filatures de Nam Dinh. Nam Dinh was once known as the spinning mill of Indochina, but along with much of the town the factory had been badly damaged, first during the Japanese coup of 1945, and then later during its occupation by Chinese troops. Much of the facility had been built decades ago by GTEO and I had collected all the blueprints I could find. Even so, it took me a fortnight to rebuild the town and industrial complex on paper, and the job had barely begun.

Once in Nam Dinh I was offered hospitality in a plush compound, surprisingly untouched by war. My hosts, the only three executives still remaining, were an unusual group, married without children and all highly extrovert. Most of the women I had known were of sober character — my mother, Madame Joli, Madame Reynaud, indeed Mireille — but here the evenings were full of fun and laughter, occasionally risqué.

In the garden there was a tree, old and unusual and laden with exotic fruit, three pieces of which took pride of place on the dining table. Their erotic appearance having passed unnoticed by me, I inquired as to their nature, and the answer left such an impression that it has always remained with me. The smallest one, I was told, was *Mon petit mignon* (My little darling), the next one up, *Oh doux Jesus* (Oh sweet Jesus), and the oversized one, *Tant pis si j'en creve* (Don't care if I die, or, in today's parlance, To die for).

I enjoyed these sojourns in Nam Dinh and other towns. And looked forward, too, to slipping home for a few days to my new wife, so impatiently awaiting me in Hanoi. My work was interesting and challenging, and I was more than happy with my situation.

News that there had been a bloody little fracas from Vietminh extremists in Bac Ninh washed over me. Reports indicated that it had been calmed by a diplomatic effort from both sides and I thought little of it. Yes, travelling by road in the countryside carried the risk of ambush by political bandits, but where possible I used the trains, with the Vietnamese, and felt secure enough. In Hanoi the situation seemed well settled, relations amiable, and I continued in my buoyant frame of mind.

But our enterprise had been launched into politically calm but cool waters, beneath which lay an undercurrent of revolution. Buried as I had been in myriad work schedules and blueprints and site visits, in the wedding and its preparations, the fact that negotiations with Ho Chi Minh in France did not go well escaped me. All through the summer months of June and July 1946, Ho and his delegation had haggled with the French, determined to find common ground. France herself was still politically unsettled with only a provisional government in place, but the French delegates had their own designs.[14] The Vietnamese camp, already frustrated by French violations of previous agreements, had become frustrated and angry. The meetings ended in an impasse with the Vietnamese delegates leaving for home in disgust. Only Ho Chi Minh had remained behind, doggedly refusing to leave France without at least something to take with him back to Hanoi.

Still I remained unaware of the change of mood within the Vietminh since the return of Ho's delegation from France; that General Giap, in authority in Ho's absence, had had difficulty controlling the hard-liners. Through July and August 1946 I went about my business more than content with the direction of my life, blissfully ignorant of a major push from within the Vietminh for an all-out revolt against the French.

---

[14] The French government intended Indochina to be part of the 'French Union', their new name for France and its colonial empire, in which a closely linked group of states would be governed by common institutions. Ho wanted an arrangement more in line with the British Commonwealth, with independent countries linked by specific treaties having respect to their right to self-determination. The difference in concept was critical.

At the same time I tried to ignore the great exodus of the French from north Vietnam. The first to go had been the roughly 7000 military personnel who had been in Vietnam prior to 1939. That was all right. We all expected them to leave. I had said my goodbyes and they had been amply replaced by fresh troops. Then in late August and September of 1946 came a mass departure that I had not envisaged. Thousands of public servants, administration personnel, employees of large firms and disheartened business people, planters and the like, packed their bags and left. Indochina would never be the same again, they said. It was over, they said. Even if the French government worked out a solution, it was the end of the golden years of Empire. They had seen the good times, but they could not forget the pain. There had been too much pain. It was time to pick up the pieces, go back to France and start anew.

I just did not see it that way. I was still young. I saw a new Indochina, a better Indochina. During the war years I had seen many changes for the good. Since salary differentials had been abolished, Vietnamese nationals had risen to increasingly higher positions in the administration, and well-educated, well-trained professionals now abounded to replace the departing French.

Despite the political problems I truly believed there was a cultural affinity between our two peoples. I could feel it, the way the Vietnamese melted so easily into French ways, our café habits, our romanticism, our music, our wine and food snobbery, among intellectuals even our philosophical tastes. The very elegance and grace of the Vietnamese was at one with the French notion of aestheticism. That the beauty in both cultures seemed to meld together so easily was the thing I loved most about this country. I desperately wanted it to remain for ever that way.

Yet old friends and acquaintances became scarcer by the day. Soon General and Madame Joli left, then Papa and Mama Heissler left with George's sister, Nicole. All of Mireille's friends from school departed with their families, and suddenly most of the people we knew were gone. Mireille became quite distressed about it and I could not help but feel her sorrow. I consoled myself that at least I still had George. What would I do without old George, my cell mate, my best man, my hilarious and profitable bridge partner. A confirmed bachelor, he changed girlfriends nearly as often as his socks, and I counted on him to be around in Tonkin for many years to come.

Then George met Isabel. It was a whirlwind romance that wrought havoc upon my friend over a fortnight I was out of town. Isabel was a freelance journalist based in Saigon, in Hanoi briefly to report on the situation for a French weekly magazine. She was intelligent. She was stunning. She swept George off his feet.

In early October they married, with me as best man and witness, at a small civil ceremony. Drinks at the private bar of the Café de la Paix with half a dozen guests and it was over. George left for Saigon the following day.

* * *

About the time George left in October 1946, Ho Chi Minh returned from France. All he had to show for two months of negotiations with George Bidault's government was a draft accord, the '*Modus Vivendi*'. It contained so many concessions to the French that the hard-core militants in the Vietminh were incensed. The problem areas of the status of Vietnam within the French Union had been skirted, along with the vital matter of Cochinchina.[15] The only issues to receive further attention in the accord were cultural and economic matters, and even these had seen further concessions from the Vietminh. Ho was disillusioned and exhausted. Before he signed he had said, 'Don't let me leave this way. Give me some weapon against the extremists. You will not regret it.' His words had fallen on deaf ears.

The draft accord contained a pact that there should be no hostilities between the French and the Vietnamese before a final meeting to be held no later than January 1947. By that time, Ho believed, France would have an elected, stable government and be in a better position to finally settle the affairs of Indochina.

The extremists rallied. Ho had sold out to the enemy, they cried. The French must be punished. In the halls of the Vietminh parliament the hardliners labelled Ho as *Viet Gian*, traitor to the nation, and even Giap attacked

[15] High Commissioner Admiral d'Argenlieu had proclaimed Cochinchina a colony in the name of France, in breach of the March 6th agreement, and Ho was desperate to have this revoked, for the unification of Vietnam was close to his heart.

Ho's policies. Again Ho called for calm and moderation, and again his popularity with the masses silenced the opposition. Ho's tolerance ran deep, but he must have known that peace could not last much longer. All that fateful year of 1946 Vo Nguyen Giap had been building his army, recruiting largely from the upper Delta regions, training and arming his forces out of the Chinese arms trade. The number of hard-core Communists in the cabinet of the Vietnamese government doubled and in twelve months the size of the Vietminh army increased tenfold. Including the partisan and youth paramilitary groups known as *bo dois*, Giap had around 100 000 men at his disposal by the end of 1946.

I continued with my head buried in the sand. I could not even conceive of the hostility that was building, of what lay ahead. One day my rucksack was stolen by a rickshaw coolie, a large and strapping fellow more like a Korean than a Vietnamese, who had taken off at a great rate after I'd paid him, ignoring my shouts. When I saw him next I was so furious I hopped into his rickshaw, produced a pistol (which I didn't normally carry) and ordered him to the police station. There were twenty or so armed Vietminh guards standing around as I marched the fellow in at the point of a gun, insisting on seeing the superintendent.

The superintendent appeared and, still with the pistol in the fellow's back, I demanded he be locked up and that they investigate what had happened to my bag. Stunned, I presume, he said he would do it. I left the station, and never did get back my bag, which had a camera and important personal papers in it, and not long after that, all hell broke loose.

It would only occur to me later what a fool I had been to try such a stunt.

General Leclerc had now finished his tour of duty and had been replaced in Saigon by the uncompromising General Etienne Valluy. When my father heard of a memorandum proposing a showdown to remove Ho Chi Minh and Vo Nguyen Giap from power, he was incensed. Who did these people think they were? They came to Indochina with a belligerent attitude and little understanding of the complexity of the problems the country faced. We both knew that the time was long past when Indochina could be ruled by force. Our local commander in Hanoi, General Morliere, was a man of diplomatic and moderate character, and we could only hope that his superior officer, Valluy, could be similarly persuaded.

It was not to be. In the most unstable region of Tonkin, the port city of Haiphong, tensions were high. The right to collect customs duty from shippers was claimed by both the Vietminh and the French and skirmishes took place almost daily. In mid-November a French patrol boat detained a Chinese junk loaded with contraband goods, and the Vietminh intercepted both vessels, taking the smugglers and the French crew prisoner. The local French garrison commander reacted violently and for a short time the fighting got out of hand. Negotiators from both parties quickly put an end to the incident, but d'Argenlieu and Valluy had seen their opportunity. The Vietminh forces around Haiphong were creating problems, they said, and would be cleared from the area once and for all.

Much as one would like to believe it was the actions of one or two overzealous local commanders, approval for what happened next came from the very top. Valluy bypassed General Morliere in Tonkin and went to French Prime Minister Georges Bidault himself. General Giap was given forty-eight hours to pull all Vietminh forces out of Haiphong. And though the instruction met with protest and requests for a joint-discussion commission, communication reached a stalemate.

The force subsequently unleashed by the French military on the little port city was staggering. A full regiment of infantry was sent in behind armoured units, and it swept through the indigenous district seeking out Vietminh regulars and guerrilla squads, house to house. French aircraft strafed Resistance posts, a French cruiser shelled the flimsy outskirts of town, and the frightened population fled to the countryside. The operation took four days and who knows how many lives. The French Army collected and buried a thousand Vietnamese bodies, but the Vietminh would have taken many of their dead with them. Though the figure could have been as many as 6000, the 20 000 dead claimed by the Vietminh was nothing like reality. The French lost fifty men, mostly from sniper fire. I was glad to be out of the army, for I wanted no part in this business.

I was not politically inclined, but there seemed little doubt that the pro-independence sentiments I'd had as a university student had remained with me. The recent performance of the French government had done nothing to change my bent. The news that the election in France had produced a new socialist prime minister, Leon Blum, was a great relief. Prime Minister Blum was an old comrade of Ho Chi Minh and my spirit of optimism, crushed by recent events, made a fleeting return. But as fate would have it, it was all too late.

Perhaps as planned, the French assault on Haiphong sparked bitter clashes in Hanoi and all over Tonkin. Ho worked frantically to stem the tide of hostility on both sides, appealing to the parliament in France to honour the accord he had signed on 6 March and respect the agreement he had signed later in Fontainebleau. When Blum was elected as the new French Prime Minister on the 16th of December, Ho sent an urgent telegram to Paris pledging reconciliation based on independence for Vietnam. While the telegram sat in Saigon, delayed by censors for a week, the French military hit the Vietminh with the supreme affront, an ultimatum to disarm and return the security of Hanoi to the French Army. Ho appealed to the French to withdraw their demand, while Giap, now highly sceptical of any good intentions from the French, deployed 30 000 troops in the outer suburbs of Hanoi.

For me, 19 December 1946 was just another hectic day in the office, and I didn't notice the shops being closed and boarded up, the tension in the Vietnamese population, their rapid exodus to the countryside. I went home late with a pile of work. So removed was I that when our house was plunged into darkness at 9 p.m. I had a fleeting thought that there had been a technical failure at the plant. But then came the gunfire.

I called for Thi Ba to bring candles, but nobody answered. Mireille went downstairs to find the two servants, but there was no sign of them. Along with most of the Vietnamese population, they had disappeared.

I could not believe it had come to this. Thrashing around in the dark, barricading doors, I was enraged that the French government, whose actions could only have nourished the seeds of revolution, had brought this upon us. The mood in the Vietminh camp would be venomous. Instinct told me the main offensive would be house-to-house fighting, to terrorise the community and inflict maximum hurt on French society. This would also be most difficult for the French Army to contain quickly.

There was no doubt now that Hanoi was in for a rough time.

We would need provisions. The water in the municipal pipes would not last, for the pumps were electrically driven. Mireille moved quickly to fill as many receptacles as possible and collect what food she could find in the kitchen, while I prepared our defensive position on the flat, terraced roof of the house. I had an arsenal left with me by departing friends, and hauled everything we needed up through a trapdoor on the top floor.

With food, water, a few rugs, pillows, blankets and personal items, I pulled up the ladder and bolted the door. Our fortress was ready.

The December night was cold and clear, and under a pallid moon I did a stocktake of our armoury. There was a 7.65 Russian-issue sniper rifle, an automatic US carbine, a double-barrelled twelve-gauge shotgun, over 1000 rounds of ammunition and, for good measure, a case of twenty-four offensive hand grenades. I gave Mireille some belated instructions on how to use the sniper rifle and tucked the carbine under my arm, confident that with this little lot we could hold out for a while.

Small-arms fire sounded close, over the more distant artillery. Ours was a short street and the activity appeared to be in the wider streets at either end where, in the gloom, dark and fleeting figures dashed across at the junctions. I guessed no French, *métis* or Vietnamese French sympathiser would be out of doors now. Anyone not in the uniform of the French military could then be assumed to be an enemy, and I told Mireille to shoot in the direction of anyone else entering our street.

Soon after midnight there was a furtive incursion from the closest intersection, quickly cleared by the staccato blast of my carbine. Nothing happened for an hour or so, and then a larger group appeared. Adrenaline coursing, I let loose another long volley from the automatic — until they too were scuttling in retreat. Holed up in our rooftop bastion we worked in shifts, keeping vigil in two directions. We had no communication, no telephone, no radio receiver, nothing to tell us what was happening in the more populated areas of the city. The hours passed unbearably slowly.

More information would have brought us little comfort. The sabotage of the power station had been the signal for the Vietminh *bo dois*, backed by the Vietnamese Army, to begin a massacre. As Ho Chi Minh headed for the safety of the mountains, General Giap was left in charge. His war-cry was loud: 'I order all soldiers and militia in the centre, south and north to stand together, go into battle, destroy the invaders and save our nation.'

To the west of us now where the action was concentrated, Giap's troops were smashing their way into French homes and abducting or slaughtering the occupants. There was blood not only in the streets, but in the kitchens, the hallways, the bedrooms.

I ruminated that a murderous campaign against innocent civilians would do nothing for the cause of the Vietminh. If the objective was to terrorise the remaining French into leaving Vietnam, politically it was a move that would only incite repression. Street by street, house by house, the soldiers of the French military would be fighting back. Their frame of mind, I knew, would be ugly.

Dawn broke and sunshine flooded Hanoi, somehow dulling the sharp edges of the sounds of battle. With the daylight I unbolted the trapdoor and Mireille made a rapid foray into the house for more supplies for our stronghold.

The respite from the strain of keeping watch at night was too brief though, the day too short. The sun set, and darkness fell about us again in a damp, suffocating shroud. Gunfire splintered the night, piercing and intense and seeming to come from every direction. Then a few hours later everything was quiet.

Midnight approached and sudden terrified screams aroused Mireille from a fitful doze. Wrapped in a blanket, she stood close to me, peering fearfully into the blackness towards the east. Women and children shrieking and crying, men shouting and yelling, gunshots.

'Where is it coming from?' Mireille asked, eyes wide with fright.

'It's close to the Pasteur Institute,' I said, guessing that the nearby medical research centre was under siege.

Later I would learn that the screams had come from a large group of Vietnamese women and children being used as cover by a formation of *bo dois*. As they forced the frightened civilians before them they shouted '*Tien len, tien len, tien len*' (forward to assault), and the French troops wavered, letting off volleys of shots over their heads until panic saw the formation break up.

That night the Institute was retaken by the French, but it was an empty victory. The building where so much brilliant work had been done during the isolation of the war years was wrecked. Nobody even bothered to guard it.

The sound of the screams remained with us for the rest of the night. Mireille settled again, leaving me alone with my thoughts and a backdrop of cracking gunfire, with the occasional distant mortar trace arcing through the night sky. Surely the French military could deal with the situation — and for our sakes I hoped it was sooner rather than later, for every French or *métis* man, woman or child was now in very real danger.

In the immediate vicinity all was quiet and again I reflected upon what a disaster, what a blind, stupid tragedy it was. Reprisals by the French would set the reconciliation and negotiation process back many years. Few Vietnamese people, whether pro- or anti-French, could fail to feel disillusioned and cheated. So much had been promised by Ho Chi Minh, so many hopes had been raised, and I felt the people would never again accept another era of French rule by force. I looked for blame in the French camp, for the broken promises and intransigence, for the government in Paris having allowed High Commissioner d'Argenlieu such exorbitant powers. And I failed to see the point in reconquering a land where the social climate was ill to the point of being dangerous.

I felt in my heart that Ho was a good and reasonable man, pushed to extremes by the hardliners within the Vietminh. Many of the Nationalists within the Vietnamese government had appeared happy enough to go along with the French notion of independence over a period of time, but the militants in the Vietminh wanted control immediately.

* * *

A second day, a third night crawled by, as the strain of watching and waiting, the tension of seeing off random incursions into our street, began to tell. Mireille had coped well with our circumstances, remaining calm and focused throughout her watches, following my instructions to the letter. I could not help but be proud of her. She was worried, though, about a *métis* family living further up the street, and in particular about some friends of ours a few blocks away in the Vietnamese district. I too was concerned for them. Neither all French nor all Vietnamese, they were in an unenviable position and would not be trusted by either side.

There were times when the fighting seemed very close and I expected French troops would soon be marching through the district and it would all be over. A few hours later it sounded miles away and I wondered what the hell was going on.

By the dawn of the fourth day I was becoming agitated, for I had not expected the battle to take this long. The longer it dragged on the bigger the death toll, the more tragic the outcome. Our food was running short despite our rationing. A few more days of this and we would be living off water alone. Even our water could not last for ever, for Hanoi's water supply had been cut off days ago.

On the morning on the fifth day I was dozing after another long night when the unmistakable clatter of an approaching tank woke me. I had barely gathered my senses before it spun around the corner at the intersection, charged down our street and stopped right outside our house.

The turret popped open and a leather-helmeted soldier emerged.

I called down to him from the roof, and he asked me my name. He had been sent by my father at the Metropole, he said, to check on us and confirm we were alive and well. I briefed him on our circumstances, that we were fine but for a shortage of food.

Ducking back through the turret he reappeared with a small ration parcel which I thankfully collected at the front door.

The battle was nearly won, he said. French units would soon be mopping up in our district, probably tomorrow.

Then he was gone.

On the sixth day regular armoured vehicles were traversing the larger streets in our district. I ventured down to the T-junction and looked along the road. The only activity was a company of French infantry, patrolling a hollow victory.

Hanoi lay barren, traumatised, a shell empty of amity and goodwill, hopes and expectations. The battle was over, for now.

Fifteen

The Eye of the Storm

The streetscape was eerily desolate. The lifelessness of Hanoi hit me with a sense of *déjà vu*. I had seen it before, not so long ago, after the French defeat by the Japanese in March 1945. Slipping out to Bernard's in search of intelligence that morning, there had been this same uncharacteristic, unimaginable quiet about the place. I had been agitated, anxious, worried about what would happen next, about what would happen to my father. It was the French who had been defeated then, but even so it had been better than this. Then there had been no moral turmoil, nothing like the wretchedness I felt now. Apparently there had been a French victory. But for me there was no victory, only relief that the killing had stopped.

Two doors from our house I called in on a neighbour. Paul Meunier was a real *colon*, and had been in Indochina since the mid-1920s. A scholar, he was now over sixty and had settled in Hanoi for life. As chief editor of the French daily newspaper in the north, *L'Avenir du Tonkin*, he was normally a wealth of knowledge and information.

I found him fine and in reasonable spirits. He thanked me for my efforts in defending our street, but for once he knew little more than I did about the general situation.

A stone's throw from there I called in upon the Lemaires, one of the families for whom we were concerned. Jean Lemaire greeted me at the door and I climbed inside through a mountain of barricades pushed askew. He and Simone, both *métis*, were okay, though shaken and very concerned for relatives who lived deeper into the Vietnamese district. I was heading that way, I told them, and promised to check on their welfare.

On the main boulevard I found a French military patrol and requested support on my venture into the Vietnamese quarter, the site of one of the main battlegrounds. Three men were released to accompany me, and we walked, reaching the outskirts where the houses were all shop fronts at ground level and where the streets normally teemed with people. Now there was no one, not even a skulking dog, just a chilling, terrible emptiness.

Further on we stopped outside a small terraced house. The paint was peeling and the shutters were closed.

There was a home-made rocking-horse near the front door but no sign of life. I motioned to the soldiers to wait while I knocked. There was no response and I knocked again, louder this time. My heart sinking, I pushed the door firmly and it swung open — revealing a forced lock.

The entrance hall looked undisturbed. On the floor was a large, almost black stain. Another step and I found my friend Xuong, just inside the front room.

He lay face down, a vicious gash in his throat extending around to his ear. His body was slashed again and again, suggesting a frenzied, malicious attack. In one corner his wife lay slumped in an *ao dai*, covered in congealed blood from a single slit to her throat. I sprinted for the stairs, too afraid to think of what I might find.

The children were there in their bedroom, two of them in their bloodied nightclothes, one still tucked up under the covers, his pillow a dark stained mess. A violent wave of nausea hit me and I sat down on one of the beds, my head in my hands. Who could have done such a thing to these innocent souls? What sort of hatred could drive anyone to this? I saw the little faces as I had last seen them, brimming with childhood *joie de vivre*, full of fun and laughter — then in bed, eyes wide in terror at the sounds of their mother's screams. I saw them on their father's knee, smiling, sleepy in the evening — then suddenly grotesque with blood and rigor mortis and the smell of death. It was a vile nightmare and I longed to awaken from it.

Boot steps on the stairs roused me and I looked up at the soldier, staring grimly at the little corpses on the beds.

'I am sorry,' he said. 'We'll deal with this. There is nothing you can do.'

Through this distress I remembered my promise to check on Jean and Simone's relatives. They lived a block away and I left the house, hurrying along the street. Anger once more welled up within me, anger at the Vietminh, anger at the French authorities, anger that there was nobody in this country who seemed to have the will and the authority to stop the tragedy of it all. Enraged, I wanted to lash out at someone or something. Instead I strode out ahead, leaving one of the soldiers who had followed jogging to catch up. In front of the house my anger evaporated. The front door was wide open. The soldier pushed past me and I was left standing for a moment, throat tight, muscles locked. He was already bending over the bodies when I entered.

It was less messy this time. The young couple had been shot once through the heart at close range. I turned away and continued through to the back of the small house in search of the infant. One door was still closed and I opened it.

It was a tiny room, barely bigger than a cupboard and obviously used as a nursery. Inside lay a basket and in it a three-month-old baby, their first child.

Her eyes were closed, and there was no sign of life, nor of injury. I put my hand to her head and marvelled at her warmth on this morning of bleak, hideous, cold. I picked her up and she did not open her eyes. Her little body was limp with dehydration.

I found some water and put it to her lips. There was no response. I wrapped her in a blanket.

The Lanessan Hospital was not far away and I stumbled out of the house in that direction.

Away from the soldiers and holding the baby close against me, I wept. How many more children had died, how many innocent civilians?

Later I would hear figures. Around a hundred French or French sympathisers were massacred in their houses. Half of that number again were abducted, most presumably killed. The Lagiers were among them, the family of the chief engineer with whom I had worked during my years at GTEO. They had chosen not to leave when the company closed down, and the four of them, including two teenage children, had disappeared. None was ever seen again. And there was Belinda, the Swiss girl who had owned the little haberdashery shop beneath Papa's old apartment. She had been kidnapped on the first night of the attack, her husband shot dead in their house in the French quarter.

Belinda was lucky. For two years she was imprisoned in a rugged guerrilla camp between Son La and the north Laotian border. Only after strong representations from the Swiss government was she finally released by the Vietminh. She returned to Hanoi on her way to Switzerland. I saw her briefly, thin and pale, her once lively spirit crushed.

Many innocent Vietnamese had died in the city's heavily populated old artisans' quarter. In the battle for Hanoi the Vietminh had put up a stoic defence from a labyrinth of passageways linking the houses, and the hapless civilians were killed in the crossfire. The wrong place at the wrong time.

During our rooftop vigil my concerns for Jo had remained unspoken, though I was confident of her ability to look after herself. The next day I found her middle-class Vietnamese enclave apparently deserted, but Jo was still there, safely at home with her faithful Hong. She laughed at my concern.

'It was I who was worried about you!' she said, embracing me. 'Come and sit. Hong will prepare tea for us, and we have other visitors.'

In Jo's sitting room two elderly Vietnamese ladies, two of the few in the district who had remained behind and who had taken refuge with her, sat perched on the couch listening to the conversation. There was much of which to speak. Jo was full of questions, quickly becoming incensed about what could only be described as the current state of war. What had happened to the March 6th agreement? Why couldn't the French government and negotiators compromise and reach an accord? And why did not the French government in Paris have a stricter rein on d'Argenlieu? I could not tell. I made no excuses.

As the conversation turned to Ho Chi Minh, the old ladies leaned forward in concentration to keep abreast of what was being said. They were of the Vietnamese middle class and their families had done well under the French. They distrusted the Communist roots of the Vietminh and were afraid that the party would succumb to its own political extremists. They were frightened of what might happen under a Vietminh regime, and of how their lives would suffer as a result. While Jo spoke of her respect for the efforts of Ho Chi Minh in trying to negotiate a solution with the French, one or other interrupted often for a translation, or to probe her with a question for me. We were all in it together, Vietnamese, *métis*, French. None of us was happy with the way it was going.

Days passed, a week or so, and a trickle of people began to return to the city. Still the streets were lifeless, the markets empty, the hawkers nowhere to be seen. Then one day I saw a cyclo rider waiting under his usual tamarind near Le Petit Lac.

He was one of the enterprising fellows who had seen the potential of these new machines, made by a Swiss company in Hanoi. Like a tricycle with a large and comfortable passenger seat at the front, they had been giving the old rickshaw coolies a bit of competition. I wanted to rush up to him, shake his hand, tell him I was glad to see him. Instead I asked for a ride, and took a jaunt once around the lake for no other reason than to give him some business and tip him handsomely. That afternoon I saw a hawker and found myself standing up in the street consuming a bowl of steaming *pho* with relish. I wasn't even hungry. I just wanted everything back to normal.

To our great relief, within two weeks Thi Hai and Thi Ba returned to our house. They said they had run away because of the fighting, though they had obviously gone before it began. Through the Vietnamese language press the indigenous population had known something was about to happen well before the first shot was fired. The girls said they were frightened of the Vietminh, that they had heard they were ruffians from the country, wild and unclean. Like many Vietnamese people who were happy with their lot, the politics of the situation did not come into it. Like me, they just wanted to be left in peace to get on with their lives.

Meanwhile, in their ‘mopping up’ exercises French troops were ferreting out all the Vietminh from Hanoi, and pockets of sporadic fighting continued on the outskirts for many weeks. Over those same weeks we worked hard to regain some semblance of normality. The French authorities reinstated the government departments and public services as they could, but since the mass exodus of former Vietnamese public servants there were few experienced hands about for a time. The sombre quiet in the city, punctuated occasionally by short bursts of small-arms fire, again made it barely recognisable.

It was almost time for Tet, late January 1947. For the biggest celebration in the Vietnamese festival calendar, Hanoi was usually a frenzy of preparation. The city should have been festooned in red and gold decorations, the markets filled with branches of pink peach blossoms and kumquat trees, tanks of carp for release into the rivers and lakes, festive masks and great heaps of square-shaped *banh chung*, a Tet favourite of pork, rice and bean paste wrapped in *dong* leaf parcels tied with bamboo twine. This year was a pale reflection of others, and it brought home to me that without the indigenous population Hanoi was a vacant, soulless place, devoid of heart and spirit and character.

Still, the trickle of returning people was at last turning to a steady flow, and the capital was slowly metamorphosing back into life. The French had by now set up a new government in the city, including many influential Vietnamese opposed to the Vietminh. Outside of Hanoi and the surrounding Delta region however, the government of the Democratic Republic of Vietnam continued in authority. The veterans of the battle for Hanoi may have been licking their wounds, but their comrades in the propaganda units were working the villages efficiently, sometimes ruthlessly efficiently. Ho Chi Minh worked to maintain support from rival factions, while also trying to rally support for his cause on the international stage. For the moment however, the attention of the major powers was focused on other post-war hot spots in Asia. There was little interest in Indochina.

On the other side of the world the wheel of French politics ground inexorably on. There were times when hope for a solution lifted my worn spirits, but nothing ever quite fell into place. Despite his alleged friendship with Ho, the socialist prime minister, Leon Blum, did little towards reconciliation. He had denounced the old colonial system and pledged independence for Vietnam 'within the French Union', but only when the army of the Vietminh laid down its arms. The time for disarmament had passed, however. Respect for General Giap's hardline authority was too great, extremist elements too strong and sentiments too deep.

Security in the Delta region began to improve and I was able to work outside of Hanoi once more. My problem now was a shortage of labour and the only way through it was to make use of a new government scheme allowing the employment of skilled or semi-skilled political prisoners. I was sceptical at first, imagining that the unguarded prisoners would escape at the earliest opportunity, but with no other avenues open I signed up, to find the system worked incredibly well.

Hanoi Prison was rank and overcrowded and the largely Vietminh candidates proved glad of the opportunity to get out of it. Each morning I collected the inmates from the prison gates, returning them at 5 p.m. During that time they were my responsibility and I treated them no differently to any other labourers. They were given a midday meal and tea and water during the day. They were paid half the normal rate, as prescribed, which was put into a special fund in their names, to be available to them on their rehabilitation and release. Their production was about commensurate with their level of pay, and I judged the system fair enough. I was on good terms with them and eventually employed thirty prisoners, who worked in groups of five or six on different jobs and mixed freely with other workers. Perhaps they were performing useful service to their party by indoctrinating the other workers, but even so I was astonished that in the ensuing eighteen months we had not one single defection.

Through 1947, with every passing month, the tension in the city gradually evaporated. On the surface at least, time once more began to heal the wounds. Those Europeans who had remained in Hanoi were looking to the future, while coming to terms with the fact that life in the city was now very different. Gone was the society whirl that was pre-war Hanoi. People socialised at home mostly, among a dwindling number of friends. I still played bridge a couple of times a week, and very occasionally there might be a special function, a celebration in a dance hall for some reason or other, but they were fewer and much further between.

There was no more racing. Not since the Japanese coup had there been a race meeting, for the horses had simply disappeared. Many would have been stolen during the prevailing chaos or taken by the Japanese. Sadly most had been destined to be slaughtered for food during the desperate months of the famine. The once manicured Bagatelle Racecourse, a place that evoked so many cherished memories for me, now lay abandoned and overgrown. It was still my great hope that eventually, when the political situation was sorted out and confidence restored, everything would return to the way it was.

In France there was a succession of changes in government. Then Jean Sainteny, the French negotiator who had tried so hard, came to the end of his mission. A week before he left Hanoi he received a letter from Ho Chi Minh. To preserve Ho's trust he did not make it public for a long time, and when I read it many years later I was once more overcome with profound sadness and anger about what happened and what could have been. The letter read (my own translation):

To Monsieur Sainteny, Commissaire de la Republique.

Dear Friend,

I have just learned that you are going to return to France. I send to you and to Mrs Sainteny my best wishes for a good trip and good health. I am certain that, like myself, you deeply regret that our joint endeavour for peace was ruined by this fratricidal war. I know you well enough to say to you that you are not responsible for this politic of strength and conquest. That is why I want to tell you again that, despite what has happened, you and I remain friends. And I can affirm to you that our two peoples also remain friends. There is already enough death and ruin!

What must we do now, you and I? It only needs France to recognise the independence and the unity of Vietnam, and immediately hostilities will cease, peace and trust will return and we will be able to start working for the common good of our two countries. For my part, I am ready to work for peace, a peace just and honourable for our two countries. I hope that, on your side, you will work in the same way.

Let us hope that God will grant us success!

Yours faithfully,

Ho Chi Minh

24 February 1947

* * *

It was not every day that I went deer hunting with a Prince, and I thoroughly enjoyed the experience. T'ai chieftain Deo Van Long was known in these parts as the Prince of Lai Chau Province, and his federated mountain kingdom stretched far and wide. The Prince's residence lay in the small town of Lai Chau, nestled in a range of mountains close to the border of Laos. The high country of the mountains was inhabited largely by Tonkin's ethnic minorities, essentially tribal people who were racially different, and kept themselves separate from the lowlanders.

I quickly learned that there was no love lost between the Vietnamese and the people we knew of generally as *montagnards*. The Vietnamese, I was told, regarded the T'ais as second-class citizens and wanted nothing to do with them. The T'ais, in turn, had no wish to assimilate with the Vietnamese. Though Vietminh guerrillas had gained control of much of the rural area that surrounded them, here in this remote outpost there was a real enclave of French support.

There was no road and my father and I had been invited by Deo Van Long to fly to Lai Chau and discuss the possibility of providing the town with electricity. The Prince was a delightful fellow, all of about twenty years old, who had been to France and studied at the Sorbonne. He had great loyalty to the French, and I could understand why, for through his French connections he did very well indeed. The T'ai people did well enough already out of marketing the opium grown on the higher slopes, but as well as this I got the impression that anything the Prince asked for the Prince got.

Our deer hunting expedition was a social affair, and along with the T'ai chieftain we were accompanied by Lai Chau's portly and cheerful French Administrator, his deputy and, to provide assistance, a small entourage from the royal household. The forests around Lai Chau were steep and thickly wooded, and despite my military training, when my big opportunity came I missed. Then, as if to further impress, I managed to trip on a tree root and sprain my ankle, rendering me something of a handicap to the party.

The Prince was most courteous about my mishap and graciously suggested we adjourn to his residence for refreshments and an evening meal. What the Administrator referred to as 'the Palace' was a complex of many buildings, the main one sumptuously furnished with a mixture of Chinese, Vietnamese and European furniture. In the corner of the large reception room was a beautiful Steinway grand piano that had been flown in specially, and it looked a bit incongruous in this remote and isolated place.

It was a pleasant evening, during the course of which the Prince impressed us with a talented performance on the grand piano. At the end of it the applause was long and loud, and I could not help but notice the warmth in the relationship between Deo Van Long and the French Administrator. It was obvious that each of them knew just how important it was in these difficult times.

Years later I heard or read about a French pilot flying near the Laotian border and seeing, unbelievably to him at the time, what he was sure was a grand piano sitting beside an old air strip at the edge of a forest. I felt I had known that piano, and it brought back to me that evening I had spent, sitting and listening to the T'ai Prince playing Mozart so beautifully. I hoped that this charming young man had made his way to safety.

Back in the lowlands the prospects for peace came, then seemed to disappear just as quickly. When, in early March 1947, Admiral d'Argenlieu was at last dismissed as High Commissioner to Indochina, a crack of light appeared at the door leading to reconciliation. The ever-hopeful Ho Chi Minh responded by suggesting a cease-fire to prevent the escalation of the war.

But in France the new government now refused to negotiate at all with Ho Chi Minh or the Vietminh. Instead it turned to the former Emperor, Bao Dai. The man known since his abdication as Citizen Vinh Thuy was still held in high regard by much of the local populace. If the Emperor was reinstated and a stable government formed, it was hoped he could win back the support now enjoyed by Ho Chi Minh.

Negotiations began, and the fuss made of it in the French media produced new hope in many of us. Bao Dai insisted, though, that before he would once more wear the crown, France must pledge independence and unity for Vietnam. The dialogue continued but by the end of the year Bao Dai, still unsatisfied, had returned to self-imposed exile in his château on the French Riviera.

For the moment the Vietminh had disappeared completely from our lives in Hanoi, and French control of the strategic Delta region remained unchallenged. But up in his hideaway near the Chinese border, General Giap, incensed by the snubbing from the French, was regrouping and replanning his strategy. The Vietminh's recruitment and indoctrination arms were hard at work and the regular army and auxiliary guerrillas, the *bo dois*, were still growing at a formidable pace.

Around us the Vietnamese population appeared to bustle contentedly about their daily lives, though it must have been that behind some of the polite smiles in the streets lay mindsets firmly under the grip of Ho Chi Minh. Still it was easy to believe that despite the reduced French population things were back to something akin to normal, and as we entered 1948 there was still no question in my mind that I had made the right decision to stay.

Our business partner, Gino, was not as content. During the trouble in late 1946 he had been severely shaken by the death of two of his closest friends. The Italian builders had been killed in a violent ambush by the Vietminh on the Haiphong–Hanoi road, and since then Gino had spoken often of returning home to Italy. When the decision came it was a severe financial blow for my father and me. We paid market value for Gino's contribution, the plant and the equipment, but by then business was slowing and there was far more hardware than we wanted or needed. Gino's departure left us with a severe cash shortfall, and with nothing to be done but swallow the pill, we tightened our belts and worked even harder to ride out our crisis.

Then, in September 1948, we had a new addition to the family. In Dr Patterson's clinic — the clinic where my mother died, the clinic where I met Mireille — our first son, Guy, was born.

It was an unexpectedly intense experience, holding for the first time our perfect newborn baby, yet so close again to those final, sad hours with my beloved mother. I was suddenly awed at the miracle of conception and birth, at the fragility of life, at the grief and finality of death. And then there was the realisation that the birth of this child added another layer of complexity to our lives: the responsibility for an innocent. For the moment the security situation did not mute the joys of fatherhood. Later it would come to haunt me.

The rooftop terrace of our house was awash with the last rays of the setting sun, and the terracotta tiles of the surrounding villas took on a vivid, burnt-orange hue. Although we could not help but be reminded of the time we had spent up here during the siege of Hanoi, it remained an agreeable place for an evening aperitif. I had brought Mireille a cocktail and she sipped it contentedly while the baby, Guy, lay sleepy in her arms. She had taken well to motherhood, and our son was a strong and very contented infant. Still I knew it was not easy for Mireille with me being away, and I never liked telling her about these out-of-town jobs.

It was late in 1948; the French administration was coming to the end of its repair and maintenance program and I had been working hard to keep my men busy with small jobs in the nongovernment area. Several months ago my father had suddenly returned to France to settle some affairs and I had been left alone with the business at a time of rapidly declining job opportunities. In one way it was a relief, since our situation at home had become complicated by the increasingly obvious fact that Mireille and my father disliked each other. Papa and I were in business together, yet their cold demeanour one to the other made the situation difficult. Just as Mireille perceived my father as arrogant, my father saw Mireille as spoiled and selfish. Try as I might, there was nothing I could do or say to heal the rift.

The Lai Chau job had come through, and I waited for a while, choosing the moment carefully to tell her how long I would be away. She put down her drink and her face tightened as she looked at me with that sad, rather disapproving expression I had come to know too well. I wished I could do something to make her feel better. I had tried, but it was always the same. There was nothing I could say. I must go to Lai Chau the next day to negotiate the contract.

'Lai Chau again!' she exclaimed indignantly. 'Are you mad, working so deep into Vietminh territory? Are you sure of the loyalty of the *montagnards?*'

I reassured her. Neither the T'ais nor the Meos had any allegiance to the Vietnamese and were fiercely anti-Vietminh. Everything I had seen in my earlier trip indicated they were friendly, steadfast and loyal. There was no more than a small platoon of *garde indigène* patrolling the area, but I did not expect any trouble.

The electrification project had been fast-tracked by the military. Lai Chau was strategically important since it lay directly on the shortest route from Communist China through to Laos. It was believed inevitable that Lai Chau would be attacked by the Vietminh; and if it was taken, a corridor would be opened for the Vietminh through to Laos. Lai Chau also controlled the meeting point of the Black and Nam No rivers and was destined to become an important supply base for French commandos operating far behind Vietminh lines.

So the plan was to make Lai Chau the main base of defence against an invasion of the T'ai country and northern Laos, and electrification was a first step. I had been to see the manager at the Metropole, and had first option to buy the 400 KVH generator they had ordered during the crisis in 1946. It had taken so long to be delivered by sea from the United States that the troubles were over when it arrived and it had been sitting in their back shed ever since, never used.

Lai Chau was cut off by Vietminh-controlled territory, and I flew in and out with one of two ex-fighter pilots who operated the small local air-freight company. Their fleet consisted of a couple of ex-US Air Force DC3s purchased on a remote Philippines island at the end of the war. I did not mention to Mireille the fact that the generator weighed more than the recommended carrying capacity of a DC3. The suntanned Jacques had confidently predicted he could get the thing to Lai Chau when the time came. That would have to be enough.

I looked at my pretty wife, at the loneliness in her eyes. It was not just that I was going away again. Her family and so many friends had left Hanoi, and though she was passionate about what she saw as her country, her helplessness to improve her situation was plain to see. She didn't say much, just pulled the baby in close to her chest and stared blankly out across the street.

Sixteen

Behind the Lines

High on the mountainside, animated voices floated out from the large cobbled terrace of the French Residency, which sat imperiously overlooking the narrow valley of Lai Chau. It was an isolated and spectacular setting, with a commanding view over the small town of perhaps 200 timber and bamboo houses on stilts. At one end of the valley a wisp of mist hung above the junction of the Black and Nam No rivers, but it was otherwise clear across a valley of great beauty and serenity.

My host, the Administrator, had gone to great lengths to make me very welcome. The jovial bachelor was obviously delighted at the prospect of electrifying the town, and had accommodated my every wish. The supply and labour contract had been drafted within days and everything was now in place to begin work. To celebrate the occasion the local dignitaries were out in force, and besides the Administrator there were a handful of French officials and the officers commanding the small garrison of about thirty *garde indigène*.

Prince Deo Van Long joined me in admiring the view of the valley and pointed out the wide road that bore straight west through the centre of Lai Chau village to sweep up to the gates of his T'ai Federation Residency. The road, one of only two in the valley and dubbed 'the Boulevard', had been constructed principally for the use of his brand new Ford sedan, a gift from the French administration. The chief could now proceed unimpeded from his residence, past the airstrip and along the narrower, meandering road that climbed in lazy zigzags up the dripping mountainside to the seat of the local French administration, a return distance of less than 5 kilometres.

This was the heart of the opium country. Opium was the lifeblood of the region, both for the T'ais who dwelled here in the valleys and acted as middlemen in the export trade to China, and for the Meo tribespeople who grew the opium poppies on the higher slopes of the mountains. Tonight there were perhaps a dozen Meos[16] mingling happily among the guests, and though few people seemed to speak their dialect and communication was largely by gestures, the smiles of the people were profuse and charming. In stunning costumes of waxed

---

[16] Known more commonly now as Hmong.

indigo, red and pale blue cotton with heavy matching turbans and a mass of silver jewellery, the women were eye-catching indeed.

'Yes, they are a lovely people,' a young French official confided in me, 'and in case you are wondering, the women are very promiscuous. But a word of advice. If you want to take them to bed you had better give them a good bath and a scrub first.'

I laughed, noticing their bare feet and less than spotless leggings. I had no such desire and was simply intrigued by these small, rather flat-faced and immensely cheerful-looking people who were yet another fragment of the diverse cultures that made up the population of Tonkin.

The Administrator was keen for work to begin and we discussed again his plans to site the generator at the Residency. My greatest concern was still the flying of such a heavy piece of equipment into Lai Chau, but I saw now that getting it from the airport 500 metres up the mountain to this eagle's nest would be another challenge. I planned to build and transport a trailer strong enough to carry its three tons — but there were no vehicles in Lai Chau capable of pulling it. The Administrator had met my troubles with soothing words, and once more he reassured me.

'Don't worry, Michel,' he said. 'Here in the mountains we do things differently, but we do them just the same. I promise you I'll take care of getting the generator up the mountain. You just organise the trailer and get the generator to Lai Chau.'

* * *

The local mist we called *'le crachin tonkinois'* was conspicuous by its absence the morning the overloaded DC3 roared along the runway of Hanoi's Gia Lam airport at full power. In the cargo bay, especially strengthened for the job, the generator lay securely tied to brand new anchoring shackles with chains and wire ropes. I held my breath as the end of the runway drew rapidly closer, and then the aircraft lifted sluggishly off the tarmac into a clear, bright day.

I had done this flight to Lai Chau several times now and everything was running to schedule. The heavy-duty trailer I had built from old GMC truck parts was ready and waiting at Lai Chau airstrip. The electrical equipment and wiring had been transported and the locally cut power poles were almost all emplaced.

Jacques looked at me and winked, no doubt amused at my relief, and I sat back in my harness to enjoy once more the spectacle of the Red River Delta unrolling ahead. From here in the cockpit the view was magnificent, the countless villages and green rice paddies of the Delta, their irrigation canals unfolding in softly patterned grids and spotted by the huge, shady hats of the peasants. Here and there the spire of a Catholic church or the decorous tiers of a pagoda loomed out of the otherwise flat landscape. The plain gave way gradually to low, wooded hills, mottled by forests of deciduous trees and immense groves of bamboo, reminding me of the country around Lang Son, where I had spent so much time. Then the hills turned to high, irregular peaks, and the villages of the populated areas were left far behind.

Approaching Lai Chau by air over the mountains, it was hard to imagine civilisation existing among the jagged peaks swathed in a tangled mantle of dark green jungle, let alone envisage a place to land an aeroplane. Only after Jacques had put the aircraft into a nosedive and sent it plunging to earth could we expect to spot, as usual, the small gap between two almost vertical limestone mountains marking the access to Lai Chau airstrip. Even Jacques, the ever-confident ex-fighter pilot, had admitted it was one of the more difficult landings around. 'Get a lot of downdrafts,' he'd remarked. 'And updrafts.' I had noticed.

For a reason I could not fathom, meteorological reports were never available until mid-afternoon and all we had to go on that morning was the standard weather pattern of the district: cloudy with occasional fog until mid-morning, with a possible storm and rain in the late afternoon. As we passed over the small village of Quinh Nhai, I was happily calculating we were only 50 kilometres from Lai Chau when Jacques tapped me on the shoulder.

'Dirty weather ahead,' he remarked, casually pointing to the west.

I eyed the mass of dark, nearly black clouds rumbling, I reckoned, just about over Lai Chau, and swore under my breath. Already the turbulence had begun and as Jacques headed for more altitude to try to calm the ride,

I glanced behind at the chains securing the generator, stressing and slackening with every bump.

The altitude didn't help. There was no skirting this squall. We had to begin the approach.

Descending into the heart of the storm the aircraft began to plummet up and down tens, then hundreds of sickening feet at a time. Jacques was unusually quiet and as I gripped the seat in fright I tried not to notice the sweat beading his face, his brow knitted in deep concentration. With each unnerving lurch the chains behind me uttered a plaintive cry, like the shrouds of an old sailing ship caught in a tempest. At every moment I expected to hear them give.

Jacques began to veer in a 180-degree turn, following what he could see of the Nam No River, for our final approach. We both peered intently out through the driving rain in search of the high steep hills that overhung the runway, trying to find the opening on the north side through which we would drop.

'There it is,' Jacques shouted. 'Here we go.'

The aircraft plummeted like a stone. Halfway down we hit a lull, like entering the eye of a cyclone, and then the aircraft suddenly levelled a little before abruptly flattening, to skim alongside the Nam No River to the airstrip. We hit the ground hard. As we leapfrogged down the runway the chains screeched in protest — then settled at last, and gave their final moan as we rolled to a stop at the southern end.

Jacques sat strapped in his seat, looking straight ahead, breathing slowly and deeply.

For a few long moments neither of us spoke, then he said, 'Well, we made it.'

I opened my mouth but it seemed an eternity before I heard my half-choked reply, 'Yes, you made it.' It was a pretty ordinary response, but the best I could muster under the circumstances. Then suddenly we both exploded into the unrestrained laughter of the intensely relieved.

On the landing strip near the simple bamboo and thatch shelter that was Lai Chau Airport, the trailer was ready and waiting, alongside the jeep and driver who would deliver us to the Residency for luncheon. We found the Administrator in exceptionally good humour that morning. And later, as he tucked into a large plateful of roast duck, he promised us 'a sight to behold' in the afternoon.

He was true to his word. On the airstrip, over 100 tribesmen, bare-chested and dressed in loose-fitting black trousers, waited excitedly, ready to attach themselves to two long ropes fastened each side of the front of the trailer.

Having roll-loaded the generator out of the aircraft and onto the trailer, the hauling party hitched themselves up and the journey began. The trailer moved slowly forward as a dozen other men hovered around, helping the wheels over the rough patches. Yet another two acted as lead singers in chanting the tugging cadence, and around all of this the women hovered, gaily dressed and high spirited, offering plentiful words of encouragement. It was a fabulous spectacle, evoking images of centuries long past, of the epic days of the Egyptians building the pyramids or the Incas at Machu Picchu.

I left them to their work, and from the terrace of the Residency the chanting of 100 men carried up to us on the cool, afternoon air. When the tempo changed suddenly I knew the ascent had begun and, keen to see how they would manage the haul up the steep and tortuous track, I hurried down the mountain. The tugging cadence was now very different — a three-second prelude for tension, followed by six seconds of straining, then a pause. The enthusiasm on their faces had dampened as the men realised the immensity of the task ahead. Progress became painstakingly slow and the cheer squad of women began to filter away back to their houses. At the first sharp bend I saw the difficulty of negotiating the corners, and remained to supervise the rest of the journey. It was arduous and gruelling work but the men stuck to their task doggedly, no doubt inspired by the novel idea of electricity in the town and the simple expedient of flicking a switch. All that long afternoon the trailer inched its way across the mountain face and back again until, just before nightfall, the generator was safely in position at the small powerhouse built for it in the previous weeks. It was a job well done.

In this remote haven from the troubles of Indochina the *montagnards* did indeed appear loyal to the French. They had been better treated by the French, they said, than they ever had been by the Vietnamese, who regarded them with distaste or did not regard them at all. The relationship between the French and the tribal mountain people no doubt went back to the early days of the opium trade, the lawful foundation for the fortunes of many wealthy families, French and otherwise. In Lai Chau the Administrator and his French officials had an easy and amiable relationship with the locals, one that I had the honour of observing at close quarters when I was invited to accompany the official party to one of their customary feasts in a local Meo village.

The village to which we were bidden, I was told, lay at a distance of some three cigarettes. Most men in the T'ai district were chain smokers, and the customary way to measure time and distance was by counting the number of cigarettes it took to achieve things. A cigarette took about ten minutes to consume, walking pace in the mountains was around 5 kilometres an hour, so the village could be estimated at being 2.5 kilometres away.

In the fading light of the late afternoon the sum total of the district's vehicle resources ferried our small party carefully up the mountain tracks to the hosting village. In a jungle clearing was a small group of rustic wooden huts, home to perhaps fifty inhabitants. The smiles of the Meo people were wide and genial as they gathered around to welcome us, and then the men brought us to settle with them, cross-legged on the ground in a large circle. The French officials were obviously relaxed and with everyone nodding and smiling happily the celebration got under way.

I had learned a little of the Meo during my visits, and was aware that, unlike the T'ai, they had no system of chiefs with princely powers, and that they valued liberty above all else. Each small village was more of an extended family unit, which lived independently and apart from others, and they appeared happy and carefree. Wifely fidelity was not regarded as a matter of great import, although I had heard tell that the reason the men bestowed so much noisy silver jewellery on their two or three wives was that it helped to keep track of them. They enjoyed parties, and festive gatherings such as this were often held for no particular reason.

For this occasion a small wild pig had been roasted, along with some birds rather like pheasants, succulent and delicious, but messy to tear with one's fingers. Our hosts flung the bones with gay abandon in the direction of their many dogs, small white animals with thick, silky coats, and I followed their example. The evening jollied along with those who could converse doing so and those who couldn't doing their best in sign language. Bamboo pipes were passed around and the discourse was interrupted liberally with rice wine toasts to everyone else, as well as short intermissions in which the whole party burst into song.

It was an experience I never wanted to forget and I sat back to take it in, imprint it indelibly upon my memory. The sheer merriment of the occasion and the bonhomie between the Administrator and the tribespeople was a joy to behold, such a change from the way it was now in Hanoi. There was another toast and through my contented rice wine haze I watched the craggy face of the head man crinkle with happiness as he surveyed the scene.

Perhaps we enjoyed one toast too many, for someone decided to accept the offer from our host that the party spend the night in the village rather than take the short but treacherous journey back to the Residency. The decision set the Meo menfolk abuzz, and an elder disappeared to his hut, reappearing to my horror with some of the bottles I had seen in Mr Chan's herbological shop in the centre of Lai Chau. Of particular popularity, judging by the amount of stock kept by Mr Chan, were one-litre bottles of a browny liquid in which floated lizards, large black tarantulas or red centipedes. The potion, I had been told, was 50 per cent proof paddy alcohol, and each creature had to be alive when inserted into the bottle. Each of those containing a red centipede was also a powerful aphrodisiac. The bottle now heading my way housed an enormous red centipede. I watched with rising apprehension as my Meo neighbour gleefully filled my goblet, then with my throat contracting in anticipated revulsion and with all eyes cheerfully fixed upon me I forced a smile, toasted our hosts and swallowed the wretched brew in one gulp.

Though the Meo men showed no sign of intoxication I could not say the same for myself, and was inclined to distrust my impression that the songs being chanted had a distinctly erotic theme. A little later the festivities began to draw to a close and I was led by a female elder into one of the huts. Inside, the large communal room had as its centrepiece a small but welcoming fire burning between two stones. After my own heart, the Meo were obviously fond of animals, for I noticed not only a pair of monkeys residing within the walls but also a shaggy little pony. My hostess took me by the arm and showed me to a bamboo mat made all the more inviting by a nubile young girl who appeared from nowhere to rest close beside me. It was a homely touch, however the promoted properties of the acclaimed aphrodisiac centipede proved far less potent than the properties of the alcohol. Though I had no wish to offend, in an ambience cosy with warmth and sweet nothings, I fell rapidly and blissfully into a deep, dreamless sleep.

Dawn reached long, luminous fingers through the tangle of treetops and the two monkeys screeched in defiance as they tussled over a banana they had stolen. There was a smell of wood smoke on damp air and I could hear people already milling around. Beside me my companion lay curled up asleep, her lashes long and dark against her skin. I roused myself and arose, and she opened her eyes and smiled. I thanked her for her company, and once again reflected on my experience that the poorer the people and the simpler their lives, the more generous, warm and hospitable they were.

It was a quiet return trip, crammed into the jeep, everyone somewhat the worse for wear as we jolted over the rough mountain tracks. Perhaps the sudden melancholia I felt was triggered by a certain discomfort of the stomach, but as I relived the evening in my mind I could not help but wonder about what the future held for these people. Their lives in this remote and isolated part of the world had not yet been touched by war. Later, when the inevitable happened, the Meos would become an important part of the GMI, the Groupement Mixte d'Intervention[17] made up of small units of partisan *montagnards* working as guerrillas in enemy territory. Led from a central core by French commando officers or NCOs, they would act as eyes and ears of the French, cut communications and supply routes and generally harass and disrupt Vietminh operations. Of all the loyal ethnic minorities from the mountains to take part in the struggle against the Vietminh, it would be the Meos who would hold out the longest and be recognised as the most hardy and dependable of allies. They would also be among those to suffer most tragically in the aftermath of war.

The last of the twilight was touching the valley of Lai Chau as the speeches neared an end. Everything had gone according to plan, the Administrator said. Every house in the town had one fixed light and one power point, and there was still generating provision for the defence base as planned by the military. It was a job well done, nothing to be rectified, nothing to be modified.

---

[17] Initially the designation of the group was Groupement de Commandos Mixtes Aeroportes (GCMA) but it was changed later after it received control of all operations behind enemy lines, whether airborne or not.

I had said my piece, congratulated my team, particularly my leading hand who had put in a first-class effort. Darkness was falling quickly over the gathering and the speeches were winding up right on schedule.

The moment came and with maximum ceremony the Administrator threw the switch at last. A collective gasp escaped the congregation as the residency compound was illuminated like the Palace of Versailles. Down in the valley the windows of the houses glowed with a gentle warmth, and I imagined the smiles on the faces of the villagers.

Tomorrow morning I would be leaving Lai Chau for the last time. The final testing of the power supply was complete and I had tidied up the last of the business around town. I had paid Mr Tang, who had supplied me with the 200 or so wooden poles used to carry the power lines. And then there had been the matter of Mr Chan, of centipede and tarantula brew repute.

I had first met Mr Chan at the Residency, introduced as 'an influential businessman, with Yunan connections'. And some weeks ago now I had visited his premises, a crowded little shop in the centre of town emblazoned with the title 'Pharmacist and Herbologist'. His qualifications in the former were difficult to assess, but he more than impressed in the latter. However, it occurred to me that his title might aptly have also included 'Carnivologist'. Inside, his shop was crammed to the ceiling with dusty shelves of bottles and glass jars housing small, dried-up and mostly unrecognisable corpses and anonymous pickled organs, while the floor space was crammed with woven baskets containing an impressive assortment of horns and animals' teeth.

It had been during this visit that Mr Chan had lamented his shortage of conventional drugs such as penicillin, sulfanilamide, quinine and others. The population was suffering terribly with the scarcity, he'd said, and whipping a long list from his pocket he had asked if I could possibly resupply him. I'd had no idea, but had taken the list and said I would look into it. His terms were payment plus a 10 per cent commission on delivery, and in that part of the world a verbal agreement and handshake was as binding as any written contract.

Later in Hanoi I had called upon a friend of mine, the director of the Mental Health Hospital, and explained the situation in Lai Chau. He had readily provided me with the prescriptions and since Hanoi had no shortage of drugs, obtaining my order from the main pharmacy in town had been easy. The pharmacist had been a bit stunned at the magnitude of the order, and I in turn had been a bit stunned by the bill, some 100 000 piastres, or 5000 pounds sterling. I'd had to arrange a short-term loan from the bank to cover it, and that had been it.

It took the Administrator's jeep to deliver the massive cabin trunk stuffed with medicines in fancy packages. As I entered, Mr Chan was bent over a table at the back of the shop prodding some shrivelled and dubious-looking anatomical parts. At the sight of me struggling with the trunk his face lit up, and as I presented him with the enormous invoice from the pharmacy he raised not so much as an eyebrow. Still smiling, Mr Chan insisted my 10 per cent be covered with 'a little extra', and by way of payment he produced bundles and bundles of used notes in small denominations.

As he was counting them into a suitcase I idly inquired as to the nature of the packages on the counter, wrapped in banana leaves and tied with raffia. They were kilogram-packs of raw opium, I was told, grown locally and exported mostly to China by specialist traders.

'How much are they?' I asked.

'Oh very cheap here,' Mr Chan replied, beaming widely. 'Only 250 piastres each. Would you like to buy?'

Immediately I thought of Jo, imagining her delight as I presented her with a gift of several kilos of opium. Of course I would like to buy. I did not give the opium trading laws a thought.

Opting for 4 kilograms, I re-opened the suitcase Mr Chan had given me. It was now stuffed to the brim with bank notes and I peeled off 1000 piastres. Our business was concluded. I left Mr Chan delightedly shuffling through his packets of pills, and walked out into the street carrying my suitcase full of loot, feeling a little as though I should have had a driver for the getaway car.

I retired to my room late that night, a little saddened that I would be leaving Lai Chau for the last time. This little retreat in the mountains was like a refuge from the troubles of Indochina, and I knew that if I ever returned it would be to a different Lai Chau.

* * *

The aircraft was departing early in the morning and I packed my bags. In my suitcase I put my clothes and personal belongings, tossing the four parcels of opium in on top. The other suitcase was full of bank notes and, the cabin trunk now being empty, I put into it my stout Hermes typewriter.

Shortly after eleven in the morning the DC3 touched down at Gia Lam, Hanoi's airport. Just as I always did, I picked up my Lincoln Continental from the car park and drove it to the aircraft on the tarmac. I opened the spacious boot and loaded the two smaller suitcases into the rear. As I was lifting the cabin trunk in I felt a tap on my right shoulder and turned to see a French official in a khaki uniform. The embroidered word *Douane* leapt out at me as I tried to conceal my disbelief. I had done this trip to and from Lai Chau I don't know how many times before, and had never even seen a Customs officer before. Of all times, why now?

There were no formalities.

'What do you have in those suitcases?' the officer asked.

I gathered my senses and cheerfully as I could answered, 'Personal clothing and paperwork in the two suitcases, and a portable typewriter in the cabin trunk.'

'Open the trunk,' he demanded.

I did, and there was my faithful typewriter, sitting dutifully, innocently and alone.

'All right,' he said and, without bothering with the suitcases, he waved me on.

Closing the boot gently, I breathed a sigh of relief and drove carefully away. It was the first time it had even crossed my mind that I might have done something wrong in bringing home a little surprise for Jo, a souvenir from my travels, a bit of the local produce so freely and cheaply available in that remote part of Tonkin.

When I visited Jo to unveil my parcels of opium, her black eyes shot wide open in surprise. Happily I related my encounter with the Customs officer and for a brief moment she laughed, before her face turned serious. Suddenly she was furious with me. 'Don't you realise that opium has to be bought through official government channels, tax paid?' she thundered. 'Don't you know it is illegal to buy it direct from local traders? Don't you understand the risk you have taken, the consequences had you been caught? Fines — even prison — the shame of your family and friends. Never do such a thing again — promise me!'

I promised. It was the first and last time, I said. Her eyes softened and she calmed a little. The admonishment over, she patted the couch beside her in a gesture to show that I had been forgiven, and called Hong to prepare her a few soothing pipes.

Seventeen

Trial by Terrorism

The road between the border forts was rough and narrow and winding. A deep ditch overgrown with long elephant grass ran along its length, providing perfect cover for an enemy ambush. Marching the frontier route in French-held territory in the north of Tonkin, the platoon of North African soldiers of the French Corps Expéditionnaire formed a tight and edgy column. They were alert, the whites of their eyes startling against the blackness of their faces, ever vigilant, watching and listening for the smallest sign of movement in the undergrowth, for the dark arc of a grenade or a molotov cocktail, for the burst of machine-gun fire that would mark the first moments of an ambush by Vietminh guerrillas.

The soldiers had arrived in Tonkin to find themselves in the midst of a new and frightening bout of terrorism.

It had begun early in 1949 when General Giap ordered his guerrillas into the first phase of his campaign strategy. Using the element of surprise against road-bound French columns, the terrorists would appear as if from nowhere to strike quickly before vanishing into the surrounding hills, anonymous in their brown peasant-like clothes. The heavy weapons of the French were of no use if they could not be transported by wheeled vehicle to the battlefield, and the Vietminh had become adept at sabotage, making this already difficult task almost impossible. In the jungles and rural areas outside the Red River Delta, the Vietminh guerrillas had control of large areas of Tonkin. Quietly and proficiently, they had established themselves as masters of the peasant masses. Many of the guerrillas lived and breathed the art of jungle warfare, and were burdened by little other than their weapon, ammunition and a sock of rice. The attacks upon the French became more numerous and more successful.

My father had returned from France during the Lai Chau job with an unsettling announcement. He was leaving Hanoi for a permanent move to the French Riviera, and he wanted me to buy his half-share in the business, to be paid in cash. This set me reeling. It was not long since we had paid Gino out and this would mean taking out another bank loan. The future was bleak for government work and in the current political climate it was hardly a good time to be contemplating sole ownership of an engineering and construction enterprise.

For the first time I considered closing the business, abandoning our lives in Indochina as so many had done before us. But Tonkin was all Mireille knew and it was all I wanted. Hanoi was our home, for all its troubles, and we had made a commitment to the country. Recently there had been much hope generated in the French community by talk of the 'Bao Dai solution'. We would not give up yet. For us there was too much at stake, our hearts, our happiness, our lives together.

In Hong Kong and in his château on the French Riviera, in Geneva and on a warship in the spectacular Halong Bay — the courtship between the exiled Emperor Bao Dai and the French government had taken place in the most exotic of settings. In March 1949 the consummation came in the form of the 'Elysée Agreement'. The Emperor had at last been enticed back to Indochina.

A new provisional Vietnamese government sat in Saigon, and in Hanoi the developments were debated with great eagerness among the French. There was much brouhaha about the Emperor being once again in his place as figurehead for the people. The truth was that this new arrangement was little more than a thin disguise: the real power remained with France, and the agreement was yet another flourish of mostly meaningless words.

So the 'Bao Dai solution' was just another French solution. For all the hope it had instilled in us, it would be a disaster.

With the Emperor once more on the throne the French authorities had no reason to cultivate relations with the Vietminh, and every reason to eliminate them by force. Ho Chi Minh now had no prospect of resuming negotiations with the French, and no one but the Communist-bloc countries to turn to for help. Any hope there was that the Vietminh might be influenced away from their Communist ideologies was gone. It would be a fight to the finish, and the soldiers of the Vietminh were now formidable opponents. Their training was expert, their weaponry modern, their mindset passionate.

As I contemplated what all this meant for our future, I found myself struggling to come to terms with the present. The proceeds of the Lai Chau job had barely paid the bank loan covering my father's share of the business. Papa returned to France and I was left on my own with an empty bank account, very little work and a useless and practically worthless surplus of equipment. The temptation to travel outside Hanoi to find work was ever present, but the danger was increasing by the day.

In the rural areas around the city and the small provincial towns, the guerrilla war was escalating. It was a war with no front and in which the enemy could be neither seen nor recognised. To the French every humble peasant was a potential killer in disguise, every mother potentially acting as the ears and eyes of the Vietminh. It was warfare all the more hazardous because the enemy lurked everywhere, in the reeds of the rice paddies, waiting in ambush behind the dykes, in disguise in the markets of the villages.

Previously I had found the safest means of travel to be unobtrusively among the Vietnamese rail passengers. Now the railway was open only to freight. Several locomotives had been destroyed by mines and as insurance the engines pushed ahead of them two flat-top wagons ballasted with sand. But it was only a matter of time before the Vietminh would devise mines equipped with delayed charges, and the railway authorities would be back to square one.

Driving myself was out of the question, for Vietminh guerrilla cells were particularly active along the lines of transport and communication, especially the Hanoi–Haiphong route, a vital link to the port city and the outside world. The alternative was to use the local 'specialist' taxi service. The intrepid Chinese entrepreneur who ran the business had a fleet of a dozen Ford Customline ranch wagons. For an exorbitant fee the vehicles could be chartered for what was necessarily a hair-raising journey. The much-promoted safety record of the drivers was based on the principle that the faster they drove the best chance there was that the car would either fly over a mine before it exploded or at worst have it explode under the rear of the vehicle. With this in mind I always sat in the front.

The terrorism in the countryside turned out to be only a prelude to General Giap's main performance. Shunned by French negotiators and isolated in his mountain stronghold, he had been following closely the bitter civil war in China. With satisfaction, he watched as China's

Nationalist defense began to crumble under the relentless pressure from Mao Tse-tung's Communist forces. From what he learned he planned his own war.

The outcome of the Chinese conflict was important to Giap's success, and as he prepared his regular army for the second phase of his campaign, time was on his side. Ho Chi Minh was confident that the voters in France would not watch their sons die in a long and bloody struggle for Vietnam. And Giap believed that the morale and determination of the Vietminh would long outlast that of the French troops.

For now the terrorist guerrillas were doing their work. The real offensive was yet to begin.

It was October 1949 and the headlines screamed from the front page of *L'Avenir du Tonkin*. The civil war in China had ended in victory for the Communists. The French community in Hanoi was appalled.

China, under Mao Tse-tung's Communist regime, was now a safe haven for Vietminh soldiers and guerrillas. The face of the war in Vietnam was about to change, along with the course of world history.

The Chinese Communists stepped up training of the Vietminh, arming them with the modern American artillery weapons they had recovered from the defeated Nationalist forces. In a matter of months the Vietminh army was transformed into full field formations. Rumours abounded that the situation in Tonkin would soon degenerate into full-scale war, that Giap was preparing to launch a massive offensive.

Suddenly the optimism I had always clung to began to evaporate.

On every front my situation was deteriorating. Société Tonkinoise de Travaux et Entreprises was in desperate straits. The few jobs around were small and I had to compete with a crop of fly-by-night indigenous builders who, unmindful of the quality or endurance of their work, tendered at ridiculous prices. I became depressed. I had stopped seeing Jo for moral support, for I was so low I wasn't sure I could withstand the temptation to find some artificial release from my problems. I found solace in my regular stroll alone around Le Petit Lac. There I could submerge myself in the languid atmosphere, the sameness of the walk, past the old couples and the lovers, the girls in their colourful *ao dais*, then north to the little peninsula to cross the graceful red Rising Sun Bridge to the small eighteenth-century Confucian temple. Resting there in the shade of the trees, just as I had always done, it was as though the Vietminh and the French authorities between them were now slowly but surely eating away at my every chance of happiness.

Then one day the unthinkable happened. I don't know how or why or exactly what the catalyst was, but from the moment I decided to visit Jo again I knew I would succumb. Just once, I thought, I needed to feel a real peace and contentment.

The ebony opium bench felt hard and unfamiliar in repose. It had been six or seven years since I had smoked opium, and for the occasion Jo prepared my pipe herself.

She had welcomed me like a missing son after my absence of months, but disapproved of the reason for my visit. I'd laughed, telling her I had no intention of resuming the habit. She had scolded me gently.

The pipe was an unusual piece, one I had not seen before, longer than normal, exquisite with jade inlay and a jade mouthpiece. I fitted my lips around its smoothness, feeling it with my tongue, then as she gently inserted the tiny, magic liquid ball of opium, I inhaled deeply, drawing the vapour into my mouth, my throat, my lungs. A few more draws and the anguish within me began to evaporate into the cloud of blue smoke that hung heavily upon the close, sultry air. As I sank into blissfulness there was a lingering notion at the back of my mind that I was a fool to have resisted opium's sweet temptation for so long, that I should have sought release before. In another deep recess alarm bells rang at how good this felt, and there was a twinge of guilt that I had succumbed so readily. But then another pipe, another deep draw and all unsettling thoughts were banished into a delicious fog of calm and euphoria.

In January 1950 our second son, Philippe, was born. As I was handed another tiny, white-swathed bundle I felt the weight of the world on my shoulders. What was the future for my sons here in Tonkin? Was I a bad father to allow them to be born here in Hanoi, in a place that would in all probability soon become a battlefield? Had I made the wrong decision to stay? Could I ever forgive myself if my boys became victims of my stupid, selfish love for a country that did not even belong to me? The images of those *métis* children, dead in their beds, returned to haunt me as never before.

A wiry cyclo coolie brought his contraption to a stop outside the barber, Chez Pierre, on the corner of Rue Paul Bert opposite the lake. As I paid for my haircut, I looked up and saw the Vietnamese man breathless from the exertion of pedalling his cyclo with two large and heavy Legionnaires as passengers. The soldiers got out and stood towering over the coolie, and there seemed to be an argument over the fare. One of them became angry and as he hurled abuse the footpath miraculously cleared of locals. For a short while the little man stood his ground, but when I next looked up the Legionnaire was chasing the coolie down the street. I walked out of the barber's in time to witness the soldiers heaving the poor fellow's cyclo into the shallow water of the lake.

It was a miserable, ignoble spectacle that could have happened anywhere, but to the Vietnamese who saw it, it was just another example of the arrogance and contempt of the ruling *colons*. I walked away unhappily, suddenly overwhelmed with a strong perception that, whatever happened, we were never going to win the war.

Tonkin was a tragedy unfolding by the day. In the Delta region outside of Hanoi the situation deteriorated rapidly, with terrorists causing the deaths of people I knew or knew of, several times each week.

Early in 1950 General Giap moved into the offensive phase of his campaign and through the censored reports of the battles to the north we tried to glean what was happening. With every defeat of Vietminh troops, with every Vietminh victory that seemed to follow, the hopes of the population rose and fell in opposing crescendos. Then for a time there seemed to be a military stalemate until, with the support of Communist China and the sheer weight of numbers at Giap's disposal, the tide slowly began to turn against the French in Tonkin.

We were now well into our second war in a decade, only this time we were engaged in a struggle against the very people we wanted to be our countrymen. Even if the French were to regain the initiative, the problems would be far from solved.

The sentiment consumed me, but I was helpless to change anything. I found myself going back to Jo's again and again, and as the weeks passed I slipped inexorably into apathy and, once again, the formidable grip of opium addiction.

I entered a period of denial, depending upon opium to help me turn a blind eye to what was happening. Knowing liberation awaited me in the afternoons I carried on as normal, ignoring hard decisions I would soon have to make about the future. Despite her disapproval, Jo could not refuse me, for I had supplied her with enough opium from Lai Chau for many thousands of pipes.

Mireille could not understand why I was suddenly 'working' so late, and confronted me with jealous suspicions about another woman. That I had an addiction to opium would never have crossed her mind. Mireille had never associated with anyone who smoked opium in front of her, and just had no idea. But that addiction, I realised, was beginning to affect our marriage.

In many ways my relationship with my wife was reserved. The colonial world as I knew it was a highly structured, ordered society with a strict code of behaviour. It was a time of extreme manners, where a mannered person would do nothing to attract attention. One did not drink to excess in public or engage in unruly conduct without being ostracised. This was a world of privacy and discretion. Opium smoking was acceptable, though not in public. A woman's world revolved around the household — the children and servants — and social occasions. Wives were not included in a man's world. It was expected that they be well treated and kept in comfort both financially and otherwise, but they were kept apart from the everyday cares of life. My mother did not know what my father earned. Mireille did not know what I earned. Matters of business and finance, even those that might directly affect her, were simply not discussed until absolutely necessary. Mireille was astute enough to stay abreast of the political situation through the newspaper reports, but knew little of what I was going through. I carried the burden of my problems without my wife.

All these years I had tried to remain positive, to have faith in the ability and desire of France to find a peaceable solution. Now in my heart I knew for certain that it was never going to happen. I was at the lowest ebb of my life, knowing that if I remained in the country I loved I would probably lose everything I had built up and worked for. If I left now, there was no doubt I would lose everything. There seemed no solution.

Vietnam had become a nation torn between East and West. Now, with the sponsorship of China, the threat of Communism was casting a shadow over the whole of Southeast Asia. In American eyes the 'colonial war' in Vietnam had at last become a matter of world interest, a war in defence of the free world against Communism. A week after Russia and her allies endorsed Ho Chi Minh's government, the United States and Britain formally recognised the Emperor Bao Dai as the ruler of Vietnam.

In France the war in Vietnam was an increasingly unpopular cause and it had become politically impossible to obtain conscripts from home to bolster the French forces. Vietnamese soldiers for Bao Dai's army were recruited from among Catholic and other politico-religious sects within the country. Others came from within the impoverished groups who had sought refuge from war in the towns still held by the French.

Even as French civilians became fewer and fewer in Hanoi, they were replaced by newly arrived soldiers from far-flung French colonies, many of them Africans from Algeria. A new flavour was infused into the streets of Hanoi, a Middle Eastern tang brought by the troops and the little groups of African women in brightly coloured flowing robes who could occasionally be seen making visits to the military hospital for their health checks. Well paid by the French military, they had come to earn the large dowries that would see them marry well on their return home. It was an arrangement seen by the military as a practical way to keep the troops happy, at the same time protecting the Vietnamese girls from unwanted advances from the towering Africans.

Despite the big military build-up, out on the battlefields the Corps Expéditionnaire lurched from debacle to fiasco, as the numerical strength of the Vietnamese Army continued to astound. In May 1950 three French companies at Dong Khe were battered and the outpost taken by four full battalions of Vietminh, Chinese trained and armed. The French government became desperate. Once again it appealed to the United States for military equipment and the United States, with its interest in Vietnam renewed, began to send equipment to bolster the French Expeditionary Corps.

But then, in June 1950, Communist North Korea invaded the southern part of that divided nation, and the United States launched a major military effort in defence of South Korea. Once again Vietnam dropped out of the foreign affairs limelight, and as America threw her military might and resources into Korea, every French effort in Tonkin was frustrated by the ever-strengthening army of the Vietminh.

In the late afternoons I would sit companionably with Jo for a couple of hours before she left me to prepare for the arrival of her evening clientele. She seemed to have eyes everywhere and was always keen to speak of the latest developments. Patiently I would listen for a while, but I had come here to escape talk of the war. This was my haven from the real world. This was where I was at peace. I would settle upon her couch and put my hand up to signal Jo to change the subject. She'd look at me disapprovingly, but indulge me in my wish. There would be no more talk of trouble for now. Hong would be at her work, her bony fingers skilfully rolling the opium paste into a ball. I would wait expectantly. Soon the troubles of Indochina would vanish from the smoky passages of my mind.

Then one afternoon I found something had changed in this woman to whom I was so close. Despite her efforts at levity there was a sadness in Jo's normally lively eyes. I had noticed it only rarely before, and said nothing for a while, hoping it would go away. But finally I asked her what was grieving her. And then she jolted me out of my reverie, brought me crashing back into the real world. Jo was planning to leave for Saigon.

I was stunned.

She spoke quickly, spilling it out, all the things she had been wanting to discuss with me over the past few months. Tonkin would fall to the Communists. She was sure of it. It might be this year, next year, perhaps two years. Who knew how long the French could hold out. But that was all they were doing. Holding out.

She did not want to be here at the end.

Eighteen

Adieu Hanoi

In the late afternoon the shadows cast by the line of flame trees down the boulevard were long and languid. I drove slowly, the engine of the Lincoln Continental purring gently. I rested my arm on the windowsill and the fresh air washing over me was cooling after the unusually long and unsettling afternoon at Jo's. Suddenly I felt tired. Very tired. I knew the time had come, that I could no longer ignore the facts. Yes, there were still many Vietnamese who remained steadfastly behind the French presence in Tonkin, others who supported the French because they were anti-Communist and could see no other way. But Jo was right. The masses had been won over by Ho Chi Minh. General Giap had the might of Red China behind him and time was rapidly running out for the French in Tonkin.

A wave of despair swept over me. My business was teetering on the edge of bankruptcy with only the odd, small, ongoing contract barely covering day-to-day expenditure. There was nothing on the horizon. While I had been struggling on, almost all major companies and multinational organisations had permanently left the country. It was ignominious, a sign of pending defeat. The future of my wife and two sons was under a cloud of uncertainty and peril. I had to be ready to evacuate them from Hanoi quickly, should the need arise. My problems were vast and I would have to work through them one at a time, starting with my addiction. I could not take it with me from Indochina.

Jo, once again, was there to help me.

It would not be as easy this time, she told me. I had gone too far. It would be a long and painful process, requiring a great deal of willpower over a period of months.

The litre bottle she produced for me contained 900 millilitres of French cognac and 100 grams of pure opium. The written instructions were clear: drink a small liqueur glass of the mixture in the morning and refill the bottle with an equal quantity of pure cognac. Repeat the same procedure in the evening.

The concoction tasted appalling, something like a quinine tablet, but I tossed it down twice a day, keeping rigidly to the program. Days, then a week passed, and the drug content in the bottle dwindled with each glass. Withdrawal symptoms began to consume me and my every fibre craved opium. The pain increased by the day.

It took every ounce of mental strength to keep going without succumbing to a yearning that never let up. I felt wretched, that my life was a mess. At the worst of times I drew strength from Jo's words: 'You have only yourself to blame!' How right she was. I did not trust myself to visit her often, and did so only on the better days. Of those there seemed fewer and fewer. Then I stopped going completely.

French troops manning the flimsy forts to the north were about to meet with a disaster the likes of which had not been seen in a French colony for almost two centuries. Surging across the Chinese border came a massive force of new Vietminh battalions that rapidly crushed the line of French defence. The French command ordered an evacuation and sent a relief column to meet the retreating troops, unaware that there were five Vietminh regiments in the area to the south. Troops from both columns were strung out along the isolated mountain passes when the Vietminh attacked, and around 6000 French were either annihilated or taken prisoner.

In Hanoi the French Command panicked, and ordered the withdrawal of all forces from the region, from Lao Kay as far as Lang Son. Hastening in retreat, the troops had to leave behind huge amounts of equipment, which fell to the already well-supplied Vietminh army. The north of Tonkin was now wide open.

A wave of alarm swept through the French civilian community. There was talk of broadcasts from Ho Chi

Minh on the clandestine radio of That Nguyen, that he intended to lead his victorious army into Hanoi on the 19th of December, the fourth anniversary of the Vietminh's attack on Hanoi in 1946. Suddenly people who had never talked about leaving began making plans.

One evening our neighbour, newspaper editor Paul Meunier, called in for an aperitif. He was bearing a map of Tonkin showing the regions still in the hands of the French and the dispersion of the relative forces. I had not realised the extent of Vietminh-held territory. In Tonkin only the Red River Delta, a small coastal strip and the T'ai region in the mountains remained French territory.

'It's time you got your family out,' Paul said bluntly.

I had already closed my technical and accounting office, unable to afford the rent and wages. Reduced to a dozen permanent workers, it had taken all of my resources to keep them employed each day. Jo had offered to help financially, but I had refused. She had helped me more than enough.

I thought about going to Saigon. But the south of Vietnam seemed a very different place to the north, with a different history since the Japanese surrender. In Cochinchina it had been the British who presided over the end of the war, and the old colonial order had been restored for now. But compared with our beautiful, slow-paced city, the southern capital teemed with people and hassle and bustle.

Mireille and I, like most northerners, did not care for Saigon at all. We had visited it once, and that had been enough. Saigon had no leisurely air like Hanoi. In Saigon the street vendors were pushier, the cyclo drivers harder bargainers, the cafés fuller and louder. It was over a thousand kilometres away and I knew Mireille did not consider it her country. The devotion she had for Tonkin was not there for Cochinchina. For myself, making a new start in the engineering or building field in Saigon would, from what I had heard, be difficult, if not impossible. Besides, it seemed probable that when the Communists took over in Tonkin the problems of the north would filter through to the south. I did not want to go through another revolution. I just wanted a normal life.

France was an obvious solution but held little appeal for either of us. There we would have the added complications of disapproving parents, and the European situation seemed precarious, with tension and the Cold War making the spectre of a third world war appear ever closer. Mireille knew nothing of France and it was almost a strange country to me. Besides, the way the French authorities had dealt with Indochina had left a bitter taste in my mouth. I felt no attachment to France, no allegiance. My loyalty lay here, in Tonkin, but I was being rejected for the simple reason that I was French. It did not seem something to be proud of.

Of the country way to the south called Australia I knew little. In our desperation it was enough to know that it was a long way from Europe and it was keen to accept foreigners. Others had fled Tonkin for Australia, and an enthusiastic letter from a friend of Mireille's clinched our decision. We would apply at the British Consulate in Hanoi.

It had all happened exactly the way Jo said it would. The months of my rehabilitation had passed slowly, until at last the pain began to ease. Now I began to feel well enough to start replacing the twice-daily refills of cognac with water.

I became more confident and visited Jo again. Her worn, heavily made-up features lit up as she realised the success of her cure.

'I knew you could do it,' she said quietly, squeezing my hands with her long, red-lacquered fingers. I'd been surprised that she had not moved faster to make the shift to Saigon, after her dramatic announcement three months ago. I wondered, had it been her way of shaking me out of my bleak and futile mindset, making me accept that my life here was over — for the sake of my family.

I thought so. Intelligence reports were indicating that General Giap was planning a large-scale attack on the Delta and Hanoi in the near future. Apprehension among the French civilian community began to turn to fear. Suddenly there was a scramble to get families out of Tonkin. Then news came for us at last from the British Consul: the Australian government had granted us an assisted passage.

It should have been a relief. At least we had somewhere to go. Instead I felt flat, defeated.

* * *

We made plans to fly south, to join the 20 000-ton cargo ship *Polynesian*, sailing from Saigon for Melbourne via the New Hebrides and New Caledonia. The final weeks flew by, and in the last few days of November and early December we carefully packed some possessions into a few cabin trunks to be sent ahead to Saigon. Among the clothing and photographs, I carefully tucked my most treasured items: four small ivory figurines, a couple of unusual opium pipes and two rare and exquisite poetry books. They were all presents from Jo, and were destined to become the most cherished keepsakes of my life in Indochina.

There was much that we could not take. In Hanoi nothing was saleable except solid gold objects, of which we had none. Thi Hai and Thi Ba would be the happy recipients of the entire furnishings of the house.

A week before the departure date I finished the last of the small building jobs and regrettably said goodbye to my crew. They had been an excellent team and despite the fact that the majority were Nationalist or pro-Vietminh ex-political prisoners, they had served me loyally. Putting them off was one of my worst moments. My leading hand, Loc, had been with me since the beginning and as a parting gift I gave my old faithful a huge box of tools and a large trailer-mounted concrete mixer I knew he coveted. Even at this stage I still hoped to find a buyer for some of the equipment, but the spectre of Communism was looming and no one was buying anything.

The day before we left was confused and busy. I was on my way down to the agency to pick up the air tickets for Saigon, when I saw one of my trucks driving along the boulevard with the concrete mixer trundling along behind. Loc was in the driver's seat and he waved cheerfully as he passed. Well, good luck to him, I thought. It wasn't any good to me. I had come to terms with the fact that the only item of any monetary value was my Lincoln Continental, my pride and joy that I had bought in the early days of the business, when we were doing well. It was the only one in Hanoi, and I had managed to sell it to a wealthy Chinese gentleman for a tenth of its worth, to be picked up from the airport on our departure. The rest — the trucks, the cranes, the compressors and a vast array of building equipment — I just left where it stood, in the depot next to our old office. No doubt it would not be there for long.

The only money I had in the world besides the few piastres in my wallet was still owed to me from a government job. It had been promised daily for weeks now and, for the last time, I went to the bank to see if it had been deposited. There should have been 30 000 piastres, nearly 1500 pounds sterling, but still nothing was there. Again I tried to convince the bank to advance me some money. Again I was refused. We were leaving the country, I was told, and nothing could be done.

Suddenly I felt desperate, like a refugee, a displaced person, and it occurred to me that this was exactly what I was. I would have to hope for the best aboard the ship, and when we arrived in our new country — well, I had no idea.

There were two more calls to make that day. One was to say *au revoir* to my old friend, Claude Guinet. His horse training days over, he now managed the second-biggest hotel in Hanoi, Le Splendide. Claude was a top-class bridge player and since George left he and I had spent many an evening together as partners, winning a large East Asian Bridge Tournament in Hanoi in 1948. As I entered his ground-floor office he rose to greet me, almost simultaneously reaching into his desk cabinet for a bottle of Pernod and two glasses.

'How's the packing?' he asked as he poured a couple of solid shots and added a touch of water from a jug on the side table. 'You look as though you could do with a drink. Did you manage to get rid of any of your trucks?'

I admitted I had sold nothing, which didn't surprise him.

'They all know there will be free pickings when the rest of we French move out,' he said. 'I guess I am lucky because about the only things I own in Hanoi are my striped trousers. Did you finalise the business of your government contract?'

Again I admitted that nothing had come through.

'Heaven preserve us from government departments,' he said and, rising, he walked the few steps to the wall safe behind his desk, opened it and came back with a wad of notes. 'There you are,' he said, pushing the bundle across the desk. 'That's all the cash I have here — 20 000 piastres. You can repay me when you can.'

I sat bemused for a moment, then he urged the cash towards me again and I accepted it with relief. Thanking him, I wrote an undated cheque for the amount and asked him to cash it in the near future when the guarantee money was paid into the bank.

'That's no concern,' he laughed. 'My major worry now that you're leaving is, where do I find another bridge partner like you. My out-of-hours income is going to take a hell of a beating.'

We laughed, downed our drinks, and I stood up to leave. Claude walked around his desk and we clasped each other at the shoulders.

'*Bonne chance*,' he said. 'Good luck.'

'And to you,' I replied, and turned quickly to leave.

I left Jo until last. It was a moment I had dreaded ever since I knew fate would see us go our separate ways. She was waiting for me in her little private room, where we had spent so many happy hours.

'Tomorrow then?' she said, drawing me down beside her.

'Yes, and you? When are you leaving for Saigon?'

She laughed. 'My dear, you forget I am *métisse*, a half-breed. Like a chameleon, I can change. Do not worry about me. I will go to Saigon, but not yet. I love Hanoi as you do, and have only myself to consider, myself and Hong and perhaps one or two of the girls who want to come with me. There will be no problem. I have money enough for all of us.'

For a little longer we talked, but already the emotion welling within us made light conversation impossible. I made a move to leave and we rose together, she standing small and straight before me, her black eyes looking up into mine. I took her hands, kissed the palms, the backs, the palms again. She reached up and stroked my hair with her fingers, and suddenly I had my arms around her, holding her tightly to me. She stayed there for a few moments, resting quietly. Then, pushing me away, she looked up as her eyes flooded with tears.

'*Dieu tu bénisse*, Michel,' she said softly. 'God bless you and go with you.' Then she turned and I watched her walk away, quickly, through the door, her high heels tap-tapping.

Hong came out to the pavement, tears streaming down her kind, ugly face.

'She will miss you so much, and so will I. Come back to us soon.'

But she knew and I knew that would never happen. I kissed the top of her head, which made her laugh, and as I turned to leave I struggled to hold back my own tears.

The parting with Jo had been more difficult than I had imagined. I felt that for a second time I had lost my beloved mother, and my distress twisted at my heart.

I drove in the quiet dusk down the main street, past the apartment my father and I had shared, past the police prison that had housed me for nearly six months, turned left at the post office and past the Chamber of Commerce building which had been one of my first building jobs, and stopped along the side of Le Petit Lac. The lights along the far shore had just turned on, reflecting upon the still water, and I thought to walk along the banks one last time. I had strolled around the lake so often at this time of day, when the heat had gone off the streets, or in that late afternoon cessation of rain in the monsoon season — with my mother; with Mireille; with George as he told me of his latest escapade; with Claude who, despite his down-to-earth approach to life, had an eye for beauty; once with Marie Claire when, on a Sunday afternoon, I had borrowed Papa's car to drive her from Bagatelle into the heart of the city on some errand of hers. I was only sixteen and I remember how she had teased me as we walked, her arm tucked firmly into mine, telling me that some day I would walk there with *une petite amie* of my own. She had seemed then so much older than I, so much more sophisticated. Strange that only a few more years would bridge the gap.

I had not yet come to terms with having to leave Hanoi. I reflected that loving this city was like loving a beautiful woman. It had charmed me, captivated me, yet held in its bosom secrets that were dark and dangerous. My love for Hanoi was unrequited. I had been spurned. Not far from the edge of the lake two people were standing beneath a favourite old tamarind tree, a young man and, I suppose, his *petite amie*. They had opened one of the long, brown beans and were biting tiny pieces to get the bittersweet taste of the tamarind on their tongues. I remembered doing the same thing, under the same tree in my youth. It seemed a long time ago. Watching them sent a pang of hurt through me, and I envied their being Vietnamese, being a part of this enchanting land. I was French, and though everything in my being wanted to stay, here where I felt I belonged, for the sake of my family I would have to go.

I had wondered in those last few days what it would be like when the last of the French had left and the Communists took over. Would the easy charm of the place remain when the country was taken over under a state-run collective economy? What was going to happen to the small business people and the Vietnamese who had remained faithful to the French, to the Catholics and the professionals who had trained under the French and worked in French institutions?

Suddenly I was consumed by grief for the disenchanted affection between the French and the Vietnamese, for the hopes dashed, the chances missed, for the conceit of my countrymen and the political marionettes that had danced to the tune of arrogant high commissioners and generals, men who had no understanding of Indochina and its people. I could have wept for the fact that the one thing the Vietnamese people wanted, *doc lap*, true independence, was never given to them, and for what could have been if it had.

The call of a cyclo coolie scouting for business along the shore interrupted my thoughts. It was getting late. Darkness was closing in and I had to get home. Home. What home? I turned, and for the last time walked across the grassy apron and back to my car.

No one was there to bid farewell at the airport in the morning. We had said our goodbyes. The plane was an old Junkers bound for Saigon, still with the seats from its commando days running lengthwise along its corrugated sides. It took off slowly, almost reluctantly, its three engines drowning out the yells of fright from my elder boy, Guy, sitting on my lap. By the time I had quietened him and turned to look through the small window behind my shoulder, Hanoi was way below us. The plane circled to the south and the green fertile plains of the Delta were suddenly hidden by cloud, blocking my last sight of Tonkin. My heart tightened, a confusion of memories flooding my head. Memories of my mother and of the friends who had given their lives for this country; memories of the happy times, and of the way it was, when I thought it would never end. Too many memories. Too many.

I closed my eyes.

Adieu my love, Hanoi.

The Final Curtain

General Giap pressed ahead with his plan to storm the Delta region and take Hanoi by the spring. Within weeks of Michel's departure, in mid-January 1951, two Vietminh divisions came storming down from the mountains into the Delta around Vinh Yen, 50 kilometres from Hanoi. They were met however, with a new and tough adversary. General Jean de Lattre de Tassigny, one of France's most distinguished and successful soldiers, had arrived in Hanoi on the 19th of December 1950. De Lattre had been given total military and political responsibility, and as a morale booster for the pro-French Vietnamese and the armed forces, he put an embargo on any more civilians leaving Hanoi. Michel and his family had reached Saigon only two days before.

De Lattre immediately initiated a change of tactics. To defend Hanoi and Haiphong, he ordered the construction of a series of concrete blockhouse fortifications from the sea to Vinh Yen and then southeast back to the coast. When Giap attacked, the charismatic general took personal command of his troops and the once tranquil Red River Delta became a war zone. De Lattre used greater air support and a more offensive strategy, including napalm, a new and deadly fire that scorched and decimated the land. The assault was repelled and, after so many defeats, there was a victory for the French.

There was a short lull and the morale of the French troops lifted. Maybe they could win this war. Then Giap attacked, again and again, and the fighting was fierce, with casualties heavy on both sides. Once again the French deterred the assaults, and de Lattre was convinced. The French forces were superior, he felt, both psychologically and militarily. The coup de grâce *to end the war, however, was just out of his reach. For this he needed more aid from America, particularly air support. But there was no more. The United States was heavily committed in Korea and an unstable Europe, and for now Vietnam must wait. De Lattre was disappointed and racked with pain. He returned to Paris, terminally ill with cancer of the hip. By February 1952 he was dead. His loss was a great blow to the French campaign.*

From then on, despite massive counterattacks from the French and enormous casualties to the Vietminh, French success was limited. The prophetic words of Ho

Chi Minh to the French in Fontainebleau were proving all too accurate: 'If we kill one of you for every ten of us who die — we win.'

The large, green valley the Vietnamese traders called Dien Bien Phu nestled between the razorback mountains of the great Tonkinese limestone massif, and formed a strategically crucial hub between the routes to Laos and China. Into this patchwork of rice paddies dotted with small villages and surrounding low hills, General Giap deployed three infantry divisions in April 1953, and from there he made incursions into the newly independent Laos, still promised French protection.

In July 1953 an armistice was signed in Korea and aid from Communist China and the United States began to flow more freely to both sides. By the end of the year, however, public opinion in France was turning against continuing the war. The nineteenth government to have been in power in nine turbulent years in Paris was keen for a decisive confrontation that would at worst allow ceasefire negotiations to begin on an equal footing, and in an effort to extract itself respectably from the conflict it approved the plan by military leaders to close the gate at Dien Bien Phu.

Lai Chau was no longer to be the centre of French operations behind Vietminh lines. The new blueprint required the retaking of Dien Bien Phu, from where General Giap had invitingly withdrawn the bulk of his deployment, and the establishment of a powerful air–land base from which to launch offensive operations in the region. The base was to be maintained by air from Hanoi, 350 kilometres away,

The strategy was based on the belief that, at 500 kilometres from their base and with no aircraft, the Vietminh could maintain a maximum of two divisions at Dien Bien Phu. The theory was that French air and weapons superiority could overpower an enemy with no air support operating in steep and difficult terrain. It had been done before, behind Vietminh lines in the valley of Na San, when Giap had attacked ill-prepared, and lost a battalion among the barbed wire and mines of the fortifications. Giap however, had learned from the experience.

The operation, known as 'Castor', began on 20 November 1953, when a carousel of French Dakotas operating day and night began to disgorge battalions of paratroopers into the sky over Dien Bien Phu. By day three, over 4000 men had been dropped into the valley, and the Vietminh forces had been dislodged. An airstrip was prepared and within weeks Dien Bien Phu had become a gigantic building site.

The French built a defensive perimeter around the valley's 17-kilometre length, heavily fortifying the few rounded hillocks that provided some small elevation from the valley floor. Infrastructure for 13 000 troops was constructed, along with blockhouses and underground bunkers and tunnels, with every position defended and linked by trenches and reinforced with barbed wire. Over the first three months, as each side prepared for an all-out battle, engagements with the enemy were few. They were enough, however, for the French command to begin to realise that they had underestimated the Vietminh's capacity to transport weapons up the treacherous mountainside, and overestimated their own capacity to locate and destroy them.

The evidence of massive Chinese assistance to the Vietminh was also of concern, as 75 000 Chinese coolies built a road linking China with a large new logistics base for the Vietminh forces 55 kilometres northeast of Dien Bien Phu. French air sorties sent to bomb the route were only mildly successful, for the damage inflicted was quickly repaired by the swarms of labourers recruited to the task. At the same time, tens of thousands of Vietnamese porters were carrying food, weapons and ammunition up the mountains sharply overlooking Dien Bien Phu. From Vietminh positions an intricate system of trenches and tunnels were dug, while heavy artillery and anti-aircraft guns were dragged manually, impossibly, inch by inch, to emplacements high above the French position in the valley.

By the 13th of March 1954, Giap was ready to launch his offensive. The battle of Dien Bien Phu began with a barrage of unimagined firepower from Vietminh artillery, eagle-nested over Dien Bien Phu. Within the first minutes of battle, four officers commanding one French position were killed by a direct hit, while fierce fighting on the ground led to severe casualties on both sides. Several French positions were quickly overrun, and by day three the French artillery commander, realising how badly he had underestimated the enemy's ability to position heavy artillery above them, had committed suicide with a hand grenade.

A fortnight into the 46-day battle all flights into Dien Bien Phu ceased because it was too dangerous to land the lumbering French transport planes. The wounded could no longer be evacuated and the French had to rely on air drops for reinforcements and supplies. The siege of Dien Bien Phu had begun.

Giap's strategy on the ground was to surround French strong points and infiltrate the positions using a network of trenches that were being dug continuously. Despite fierce fighting and counterattacks by the French, the tactic of asphyxiation and constant harassment forced the French command to draw their defenses in tighter and tighter.

The bombardment from above was constant. As the weeks passed conditions within Dien Bien Phu became increasingly difficult, with thousands of wounded overflowing into the fetid tunnels leading to the underground hospital. Towards the end of April a severe monsoon arrived. The almost continuous bad weather combined with heavy artillery and anti-aircraft fire made even overflights hazardous. As the French lost more ground and the drop-zone target contracted, more and more parachute drops ended up in the hands of the Vietminh. Dien Bien Phu became a quagmire and food and ammunition were in short supply. The exhausted French were fighting hungry and wet, in the slime and mud of the trenches. In the heat of the battles they were slipping and tripping on the bodies of their dead.

The last of the French reserve paratroopers dropped out of a leaden sky in early May, just in time to encounter General Giap's renewed offensive drive. Six Russian tube rocket-launchers that had been manhandled up the tortuous mountainside were let loose on the bedraggled French position. A new and hideous howl heralded great explosions as clods of sodden earth and infrastructure were blasted to new heights over the scene of chaos and destruction. For days heavy, constant rain hampered any aerial assistance until at last, on 6 May, the sky cleared and a huge armada of French bombers appeared over Dien Bien Phu. In response the Vietminh silenced their guns. Hidden as they were, entangled in jungle and secreted in limestone caves and tunnels, they sat out the attack quietly.

When it was over the Vietminh answered with everything they had, including a ton of TNT exploded in a tunnel beneath the last major stronghold in the valley. The garrison had been reduced to a third of its strength, and ground assaults kept coming from nowhere via the trenches that laced the few remaining defences. Dien Bien Phu was littered with the wreckage of blown-up fortifications and barbed-wire entanglements, collapsed trenches and bunkers filled with mud and corpses and wounded from both sides.

By the afternoon of the next day the French command had neither the ammunition nor the reserves to mount a counterattack. There was no surrender, no white flag. The final message from the French command to Hanoi was, 'We're blowing up everything. Adieu.*' An order to cease firing was given and at around 1700 hours on the 7th of May 1954, Vietminh forces overran the French command post. A red flag with gold stars appeared over the top of the bunker. The battle for Dien Bien Phu, one of the most momentous ever between East and West, was over.*

It marked the end for the French in Vietnam.

For the Americans, who in the final year had funded almost 80 per cent of the French war effort, it was just the beginning.

An elderly Frenchman sits on the steps to one side of the state-owned department store on Trang Tien Street. He has caught a chill and his wife, my mother, has gone in search of something to relieve his fever.

It is forty years later and Vietnam, having been closed to the West for so long, has recently opened its doors again. Michel has returned to Hanoi at the first opportunity and found little in the city centre has changed. Most of the places once so much a part of his life are still there. There are a few signs that the flood of foreign capital that will flow into the country in the years ahead is about to begin. But Hanoi is dirtier, less colourful and the buildings are crumbling.

On the streets there is an impression of drab olive green, and he misses the graceful girls who once floated down the street in their gossamer *ao dais*. The population has swollen and many of the neat little gardens in front of the French villas have been filled in with ramshackle buildings. Loudspeakers blare government propaganda into the streets and officious men in uniform seem to appear from nowhere each time he unpacks the camera.

Beneath the surface, however, the beauty of Hanoi remains. Not the obvious, orderly beauty of his youth. More like a gorgeous woman fallen on difficult times. Proud, defiant, a bit hard.

It has been strange for Michel to see Ho Chi Minh again, pale and peaceful, lying embalmed in state. He has been laid to rest, if rest it is, in a huge mausoleum built after his death near the old Governor's Palace, from where Michel watched him declare independence for Vietnam on that fateful day in 1945. He wonders what Ho, who had been a determined yet modest man, would have thought of it all: the pomp and ceremony, the white-gloved guards goose-stepping in his honour, the long queues of people waiting to view his body. And the people in the queue: the four Americans in front of him, dressed as civilians but obviously military with their huge shoulders, immaculate dress, their close-cropped haircuts. What were they thinking? They had not said a word the whole time they waited and only afterwards, filing out of the other side of the mausoleum, did one of them finally speak. 'Gee. That was weird.' And the veterans sprinkled through the line, khaki-clad men about his own age who had put on their crumpled old Vietminh Army uniforms and dusted off their medals for the occasion. They had stood waiting, proud and solemn, and looked so small against the Americans. How brave they had been, how determined, to fight as they did.

It has been a nostalgic visit for Michel, and he cannot help but reflect again on the unimaginable suffering that has gone before. What was it all about? Thirty years of war. Millions of people dead, most of them civilians. Who won? Not the French. Not at all. The Americans? Certainly not. The North Vietnamese? He looks around at the dilapidated city, the bicycles and the few smoke-belching old Russian-made vehicles in the streets. No. He does not think so.

He sighs. How different it could have been.

It is late, he is tired and can feel his fever worsening. He had been looking for his mother's grave, and could not understand why he could not find it. But today he was introduced to a Vietnamese man, a respected surgeon at the time of the French who, after Communism, was reduced to carrying bricks for a living. He had worked on a government building site over the top of the old French cemetery where Michel's mother lay. He mops his brow. It has been a long day.

An old woman is shuffling past, her loose brown tunic and trousers faded from wear. She glances at him, and notices that he is unwell. She turns, and comes to sit down on the steps beside him.

'*Monsieur?*' she says, queryingly. It is about the only French she can remember.

He smiles at her. She smiles back. There is nothing more to be said. She briefly touches his hand in a sympathetic gesture, and takes off her large, straw, limpet-shaped hat.

Gently, she begins to fan him with it.

Acknowledgments

This book could not have been written without the full support and dedication of its subject, my stepfather, Michel. I have immense gratitude for the work he put in, and in particular for allowing me access to those experiences that I know he would rather not have relived after so many years. I have been privileged, and I hope I have done them justice.

My sincere thanks must also go to my mother, Barbara, for her love, encouragement and invaluable suggestions, and to my husband and those friends who provided a helpful critique in the early stages of the manuscript. Thank you also to my agent, Margaret Kennedy; editors Judith Lukin-Amundsen and Sophie Hamley, for their wise counsel; and publisher Linda Funnell of HarperCollins, for seeing it through the publishing process.

Sadly, Michel died in April 2005, shortly before this book first went to print.